BETWEEN HEAVEN AND EARTH

DIVINE PRESENCE AND ABSENCE
IN THE BOOK OF EZEKIEL

BIBLICAL AND JUDAIC STUDIES FROM THE UNIVERSITY OF CALIFORNIA, SAN DIEGO

Volume 7

edited by
William Henry Propp

Previously published in the series:

1. *The Hebrew Bible and Its Interpreters*, edited by William Henry Propp, Baruch Halpern, and David Noel Freedman (1990).

2. *Studies in Hebrew and Aramaic Orthography*, by David Noel Freedman, A. Dean Forbes, and Francis I. Andersen (1992).

3. *Isaiah 46, 47, and 48: A New Literary-Critical Reading*, by Chris Franke (1994).

4. *The Book around Immanuel: Style and Structure in Isaiah 2–12*, by Andrew H. Bartelt (1996).

5. *The Structure of Psalms 93–100*, by David M. Howard Jr. (1997).

6. *Psalm 119: The Exaltation of Torah*, by David Noel Freedman (1999).

BETWEEN HEAVEN AND EARTH

DIVINE PRESENCE AND ABSENCE IN THE BOOK OF EZEKIEL

by

John F. Kutsko

EISENBRAUNS
Winona Lake, Indiana
2000

Published for Biblical and Judaic Studies
The University of California, San Diego
by
Eisenbrauns
Winona Lake, Indiana

Cataloging in Publication Data

Kutsko, John F., 1963–
Between Heaven and Earth : divine presence and absence in the Book of
  Ezekiel / by John F. Kutsko.
      p.   cm. — (Biblical and Judaic studies ; v. 7)
  Includes bibliographical references and index.
  ISBN 1-57506-041-8 (cloth : alk. paper)
  1. Presence of God—Biblical teaching. 2. Hidden God—Biblical
teaching. 3. Bible. O.T. Ezekiel—Criticism, interpretation, etc.
I. Title. II. Series.

BS1545.6.P695 K88 1999
224'.406—dc21
                                                            99-046778
                                                            CIP

For Carolyn

Hearts and Bones

Contents

Preface and Acknowledgments

This book is a revision of my doctoral thesis, *The Presence and Absence of God in the Book of Ezekiel* (Harvard University, 1997). Anyone even remotely familiar with the members of my dissertation committee will understand how I have benefited from their scholarly breadth and depth. Many of my ideas gained focus from the engaging inquiry of Jon Levenson and James Kugel. And my adviser Peter Machinist was a veritable *deus ex machina*. It goes without saying, however, that while I availed myself of their input, the persuasiveness of this argument remains mine to demonstrate, and any errors of judgment or fact contained herein remain mine to bear.

I would surely omit someone accidentally if I tried to list all those who aided and abetted me along the way. I take this opportunity, however, to thank Patrick Alexander, who helped me move from thinking about a dissertation to thinking about a publication. That was no small task during that time when, I confess, I was still under the spell of "dissertationese."

Finally, I wish to thank William Propp, David Noel Freedman, and all of those connected with the series Biblical and Judaic Studies from the University of California, San Diego, for their patience and support.

Abbreviations

The abbreviations for biblical, deuterocanonical, pseudepigraphical, Qumran, and rabbinic texts follow the conventions published in the *The SBL Handbook of Style* (Peabody, Mass.: Hendrickson, 1999).

General

AsBb	*Ashur-Babylon* text, recension A. Pp. 78–91, §53, in R. Borger, *Die Inschriften Asarhaddons, Königs von Assyrien.* Archiv für Orientforschung Beiheft 9. Graz: Weidner, 1956
Assur	*Assur* text, recension A. Pp. 1–6, §2, in Borger
Bab	*Babylon* text, recensions A–G. Pp. 11–29, §11, eps. 1–41, in Borger
ep(s).	episode(s); section of an inscription or section of a common narrated event extant in more than one inscription
BM	Tablets in the collections of the British Museum
H	Holiness Code
J	Yahwist Source
K	Tablets in the Kouyunjik collection of the British Museum
LXX	Septuagint
Mnm	*Monument* text in Borger
MT	Masoretic Text
Nin	*Nineveh* text, recensions A–R. Pp. 36–69, §§26–38, in Borger
no.	number
obv.	obverse (front) of a tablet
P	Priestly Source
pl.	plural
ptc.	participle
rec(s).	recension(s)
rev.	reverse (back) of a tablet
sg.	singular
Tg.	Targum

Reference Works

AB	Anchor Bible Commentary Series
ABC	Albert Kirk Grayson. *Assyrian and Babylonian Chronicles.* Texts from Cuneiform Sources 5. Locust Valley, New York: Augustin, 1975
ABD	David Noel Freedman (ed.). *The Anchor Bible Dictionary.* 6 vols. New York: Doubleday, 1992
ABL	R. F. Harper (ed.). *Assyrian and Babylonian Letters.* 14 vols. Chicago: University of Chicago Press, 1892–1914

ABRL   Anchor Bible Reference Library
AfO   *Archiv für Orientforschung*
AfO Beiheft   Archiv für Orientforschung Beiheft
AHw   W. von Soden (ed.). *Akkadisches Handwörterbuch.* 3 vols. Wiesbaden: Harrassowitz, 1959–81
AKA   L. W. King and E. A. W. Budge. *Annals of the Kings of Assyria,* vol. 1. London: British Museum, 1902
AnBib   Analecta Biblica
ANET   J. B. Pritchard (ed.). *Ancient Near Eastern Texts Relating to the Old Testament.* 3d ed. with supplement. Princeton: Princeton University Press, 1969
ANETS   Ancient Near Eastern Texts and Studies
AOAT   Alter Orient und Altes Testament
AOS   American Oriental Series
ARAB 1   Daniel David Luckenbill. *Historical Records of Assyria: From the Earliest Times to Sargon.* Vol. 1 in *Ancient Records of Assyria and Babylonia.* Chicago: University of Chicago Press, 1926
ARAB 2   Daniel David Luckenbill. *Historical Records of Assyria: From Sargon to the End.* Vol. 2 in *Ancient Records of Assyria and Babylonia.* New York: Greenwood, 1927
ARI 1   Hans Goedicke (ed.). *From the Beginning to Ashur-resha-ishi I: Records of the Ancient Near East.* Vol. 1 in *Assyrian Royal Inscriptions,* ed. Albert Kirk Grayson. Wiesbaden: Harrassowitz, 1972
ARI 2   Hans Goedicke (ed.). *From Tiglath-pileser I to Ashur-nasir-apli II: Records of the Ancient Near East.* Vol. 2 in *Assyrian Royal Inscriptions,* ed. Albert Kirk Grayson. Wiesbaden: Harrassowitz, 1976
ASTI   *Annual of the Swedish Theological Institute*
BA   *Biblical Archaeologist*
BASOR   *Bulletin of the American Schools of Oriental Research*
BBET   Beiträge zur biblischen Exegese und Theologie
BDB   F. Brown, S. R. Driver, and C. A. Briggs. *A Hebrew and English Lexicon of the Old Testament.* Oxford: Clarendon, 1907
BETL   Bibliotheca ephemeridum theologicarum lovaniensium
BHS   K. Elliger and W. Rudolph (eds.). *Biblia hebraica stuttgartensia.* Stuttgart: Deutsche Bibelgesellschaft, 1983
Bib   *Biblica*
BibB   Biblische Beiträge
BibOr   Biblica et Orientalia
BiOr   *Bibliotheca Orientalis*
BJRL   *Bulletin of the John Rylands Library*
BKAT   Biblischer Kommentar: Altes Testament
BWANT   Beiträge zur Wissenschaft vom Alten und Neuen Testament
BZAW   Beihefte zur Zeitschrift für die Alttestamentliche Wissenschaft
CAD   A. Leo Oppenheim et al. (eds.). *The Assyrian Dictionary of the Oriental Institute of the University of Chicago.* Chicago: The Oriental Institute of the University of Chicago, 1956–
CBQ   *Catholic Biblical Quarterly*

ConBOT   Coniectanea Biblica, Old Testament
COS 1   William W. Hallo (ed.). *Canonical Compositions from the Biblical World.*
      Vol. 1 in *The Context of Scripture.* Leiden: Brill, 1997
CT   Cuneiform Texts from the British Museum
CTA   A. Herdner. *Corpus des tablettes en cunéiformes alphabétiques découvertes à*
      Ras Shamra-Ugarit de 1929 à 1939. Mission de Ras Shamra 10. Paris:
      Imprimerie, 1963
EvT   *Evangelische Theologie*
FRLANT   Forschungen zur Religion und Literatur des Alten und Neuen
      Testaments
HAT   Handbuch zum Alten Testament
HKAT   Handkommentar zum Alten Testament
HSM   Harvard Semitic Monograph
HSS   Harvard Semitic Studies
HTR   *Harvard Theological Review*
HUCA   *Hebrew Union College Annual*
ICC   International Critical Commentary
Int   *Interpretation*
JAOS   *Journal of the American Oriental Society*
Jastrow   M. Jastrow. *Dictionary of the Targumim, Talmud Babli, Yerushalmi, and*
      the Midrashic Literature. Reprinted, New York: Judaica, 1971.
JBL   *Journal of Biblical Literature*
JCS   *Journal of Cuneiform Studies*
JEA   *Journal of Egyptian Archaeology*
JHNES   Johns Hopkins Near Eastern Studies
JNES   *Journal of Near Eastern Studies*
JNSL   *Journal of Northwest Semitic Languages*
JQR   *Jewish Quarterly Review*
JR   *Journal of Religion*
JRAS   *Journal of the Royal Asiatic Society*
JSOT   *Journal for the Study of the Old Testament*
JSOTSup   Journal for the Study of the Old Testament Supplement Series
JTS   *Journal of Theological Studies*
KAH 1   L. Messerschmidt. *Keilschrifttexte aus Assur historischen Inhalts,* vol. 1.
      Wissenschaftliche Veröffentlichung der Deutschen Orient-Gesellschaft
      16. Leipzig: Hinrichs, 1911
KAH 2   O. Schroeder. *Keilschrifttexte aus Assur historischen Inhalts,* vol. 2.
      Wissenschaftliche Veröffentlichung der Deutschen Orient-Gesellschaft
      37. Leipzig: Hinrichs, 1922
KAI   H. Donner and W. Röllig. *Texte.* Vol. 1 in *Kanaanäische und aramäische*
      Inschriften. Wiesbaden: Harrassowitz, 1962
LAS   Simo Parpola. *Letters from Assyrian Scholars to the Kings Esarhaddon and*
      Assurbanipal. Part I: Texts. Part II: Commentary and Appendices.
      Neukirchen-Vluyn: Neukirchener Verlag / Kevelaer: Butzon & Bercker,
      1970–83
LCL   Loeb Classical Library
NCB   New Century Bible

OBO	Orbis Biblicus et Orientalis
OIP 2	Daniel David Luckenbill. *The Annals of Sennacherib.* Oriental Institute Publications 2. Chicago: University of Chicago Press, 1924
Or	*Orientalia*
OTL	Old Testament Library
OTP	J. H. Charlesworth (ed.). *The Old Testament Pseudepigrapha.* 2 vols. Garden City, New York: Doubleday, 1985
RB	*Revue biblique*
RIMA 1	Albert Kirk Grayson. *Assyrian Rulers of the Third and Second Millennia BC (to 1115 BC).* Royal Inscriptions of Mesopotamian, Assyrian Periods 1. Toronto: University of Toronto Press, 1987
RIMA 2	Albert Kirk Grayson. *Assyrian Rulers of the Early First Millennium BC I (1114–859 BC).* Royal Inscriptions of Mesopotamian, Assyrian Periods 2. Toronto: University of Toronto Press, 1991
RIMA 3	Albert Kirk Grayson. *Assyrian Rulers of the Early First Millennium BC II (858–745 BC).* Royal Inscriptions of Mesopotamian, Assyrian Periods 3. Toronto: University of Toronto Press, 1996
SAA	State Archives of Assyria
SAAB	*State Archives of Assyria Bulletin*
SBLDS	Society of Biblical Literature Dissertation Series
SBS	Stuttgarter Bibelstudien
SBT	Studies in Biblical Theology
SWBA	Social World of Biblical Antiquity
TDOT	G. J. Botterweck, H. Ringgren, and H. J. Fabry (eds.). *Theological Dictionary of the Old Testament.* Translated by J. T. Willis, G. W. Bromiley, and D. E. Green. Grand Rapids: Eerdmans, 1974–
THAT	Ernst Jenni and Claus Westermann (eds.). *Theologisches Handwörterbuch zum Alten Testament.* 2 vols. Munich: Kaiser / Zurich: Theologischer Verlag, 1971–75
TLOT	Ernst Jenni and Claus Westermann (eds.). *Theological Lexicon of the Old Testament.* Translated by Mark E. Biddle. 3 vols. Peabody, Mass.: Hendrickson, 1997
TZ	*Theologische Zeitschrift*
UT	C. H. Gordon. *Ugaritic Textbook.* Analecta Orientalia 38. Rome: Pontifical Biblical Institute, 1965
VAB	Vorderasiatische Bibliothek
VAT	Vorderasiatische Abteilung Tontafel. Vorderasiatisches Museum, Berlin
VS	*Vorderasiatische Schriftdenkmäler der Königlichen Museen zu Berlin*
VT	*Vetus Testamentum*
VTSup	Vetus Testamentum Supplements
WBC	Word Biblical Commentary
ZA	*Zeitschrift für Assyriologie*
ZAW	*Zeitschrift für die Alttestamentliche Wissenschaft*
ZDMG	*Zeitschrift der deutschen morgenländischen Gesellschaft*

Chapter 1

The Inquiry and Its Background

Why should the nations say, "Where is their god?"
Our God is in the heavens—he does all that he pleases.
Their idols are silver and gold—the work of human hands.
Psalm 115:1–4

§1. Introduction

The opening of this liturgical psalm responds to a challenge: the nations taunt Israel, claiming Israel's God is absent but their gods are self-evidently present. The psalmist responds to the challenge. From another perspective, replies the psalmist, our God is the heavenly creator; their idols are earthly creations.

With the destruction of the Jerusalem Temple and the exile of members of that community to the land of its enemies, whose gods were represented as divine statues, the prophet Ezekiel faced a similar challenge. To ask the question Where is God? was to face several complex and tangled problems.

These problems, which are the focus of this study, concern the representation of God, the differentiation of Yahweh from other deities, and the relationship of Yahweh to Israel in exile—all as dealt with by the book of Ezekiel. The unifying element of these three concerns of Ezekiel is the opposition and paradox of divine presence and absence. This expression, *divine presence and absence*, involves multiple levels of meaning and forms a theological construct that runs through the entire book. A summary of central elements in the book of Ezekiel confirms these general observations.

The book of Ezekiel structurally revolves around the Jerusalem Temple and the divine כָּבוֹד. Consider the following sketch of the chapters:

A — From Divine Presence to Divine Absence (1:1–11:25)
  B — Preparation for Destruction (12:1–24:27)
    C — Oracles against the Nations (25:1–32:32)
  B′ — Preparation for Restoration (33:1–39:29)
A′— From Divine Absence to Divine Presence (40:1–48:35)

1

Following the throne vision in chap. 1 and the indictment of Israel in chaps. 6–9, the divine presence of God in the Temple mounts its cherubim throne and leaves the Jerusalem Temple (11:22–25): from divine presence to divine absence. The book concludes with the return of the *kābôd* to the restored sanctuary (43:1–9): from divine absence to divine presence.

Another perspective on this theme occurs in the context of exile. In Babylonia, there is no Jewish temple, not to speak of the fact that God has withdrawn from the Jerusalem Temple, removing his external presence from the midst of Israel. Yet, without physical representation or sanctuary, God is still vitally present; in Babylonia—a foreign land—the prophet receives his call, and there Yahweh himself becomes their 'little sanctuary' (מִקְדָּשׁ מְעַט, or 'a sanctuary for a little while'; 11:16). Israel's deportation to a foreign land and the destruction of the Temple thus do not indicate Yahweh's absence.

Yet a third fundamental aspect of this paradox of divine absence and presence is Ezekiel's aniconic position, apparent in his widespread polemic against idols. Though absent in physical representation Yahweh is present in his actions, while cult statues—idols—are physically present but are powerless. An idol neither locates nor limits God's presence—a particularly effective point for Ezekiel's fellow expatriates in Babylonia.

Finally, consider how Ezekiel's efforts are caught on the horns, as it were, of a dilemma. On the one hand, he enlists various means to describe the presence of God in order to make God mobile and to reassure his audience that Yahweh is present despite his seeming absence. This is clearly the purpose of the *kābôd*-theology, as Samson Levey has observed.

> Viewed from the perspective of history, the prophecy of Ezekiel is a masterpiece of religio-political philosophy which enabled the Jew to weather the crisis of the fall of Jerusalem, the destruction of Judah as a political entity, and the Babylonian exile. . . . He accomplished this by the religio-psychological expedient of the vision of the Merkabah, stressing that though the earthly Temple was destroyed there was a heavenly throne of YHWH beyond the reach of Babylonian might.[1]

On the other hand, in spite of these efforts to *abstract* Yahweh, Ezekiel must provide proof of God's presence. This is accomplished powerfully in the opening vision and call of Ezekiel. There (especially chap. 1) the prophet describes Yahweh in graphic, anthropomorphic terms, and at the same time his language limits if not undercuts this effort at anthropomorphism: in the 'likeness of the appearance of a man' (דְּמוּת כְּמַרְאֵה אָדָם; 1:26).[2] These oppositions—abstract-concrete, iconographic-iconoclastic—compose part of a struggle for

---

1. Samson H. Levey, *The Targum of Ezekiel* (The Aramaic Bible 13; Wilmington, Del.: Glazier, 1987) 3.

2. Note the reserved circumlocution in 1:28: '(this was) the appearance of the likeness of the presence of Yahweh' (מַרְאֵה דְּמוּת כְּבוֹד־יהוה; chiastically related to 1:26).

the appropriate language to describe concretely the divine presence, while demonstrating throughout that Israel's God is not limited. Clearly, describing the presence of God in the context of aniconic theology is intensely difficult.

Even within rather narrow textual confines, the book of Ezekiel incorporates conflicting imagery involving the presence of God. For example, Ezekiel simultaneously uses highly visual language focusing on anthropomorphic and zoomorphic imagery to describe Yahweh's appearance and asserts that the material representation of a deity is an abomination (תּוֹעֵבָה), a detestable thing (שִׁקּוּץ). Chapter 8 is characteristic of this language struggle: the condemnation of a particular object of worship (סֵמֶל) is preceded by the hand of Yahweh falling upon the prophet, who sees a form of the appearance of a man (דְּמוּת כְּמַרְאֵה־אִישׁ)[3] that puts forth the form of a hand (תַּבְנִית יָד) to lift the prophet in visions of God (בְּמַרְאוֹת אֱלֹהִים) to Jerusalem (vv. 1–3). Paradoxically, within the context of condemning idols, Ezekiel graphically describes God in physical terms. Yet, Yahweh is a god limited neither by an image nor by a structure. Again, this portrayal, however perplexing, seems particularly fitting for the exilic experience in which God is absent but present: God does not dwell *in* the sanctuary; he *is* their sanctuary, their מִקְדָּשׁ מְעַט (11:16).

The paradox of divine absence and presence has received some attention in previous studies. For example, Joseph Blenkinsopp captures the character of this issue: "It seems that the teaching of the prophet, as transmitted by his disciples, has been organized in a thematic unity that moves between the poles of exile and return, divine absence and presence."[4] Gary Anderson has recognized this paradox as a principal problem for the exiles: "The overriding theological issue for the postexilic community is that of YHWH's presence. More specifically the concern is with the perceived absence of this presence while Jerusalem and the Temple remain in ruins."[5] This paradox of divine absence and presence, however, has received surprisingly little sustained

---

3. The emendation "man" follows the versions, including the LXX ἀνδρός. Zimmerli suggests that the MT vocalization (אֵשׁ) intended to avoid describing the divine appearance as a man (W. Zimmerli, *Ezekiel 1: [1–24]* [trans. R. E. Clements; Hermeneia; Philadelphia: Fortress, 1979] 216; orig. pub.: *Ezechiel* [2 vols.; BKAT 13/1–2; Neukirchen-Vluyn: Neukirchener Verlag, 1969]). This explanation for the received Hebrew text, indeed, suggests the very point made here, namely, that such anthropomorphic detail and description raised concerns for ancient readers and interpreters.

4. J. Blenkinsopp, *History and Prophecy in Ancient Israel* (Philadelphia: Westminster, 1983) 197. Consider also the integrative theology of Samuel Terrien, who declares this the unifying feature of the biblical conception of God: this (elusive) "presence induces a magnetic field of forces which maintains a dynamic tension . . . between divine self-disclosure and divine self-concealment" (*The Elusive Presence* [San Francisco: Harper & Row, 1978] 43).

5. Gary A. Anderson, *Sacrifices and Offerings in Ancient Israel: Studies in Their Social and Political Importance* (HSM 41; Atlanta: Scholars Press, 1987) 93.

discussion in the book, in spite of various observations that recognize its centrality. Thus the need remains for a thorough analysis of it and its complex set of relations.

The key permutations of the presence-absence motif include the Temple, the divine *kābôd*, and Ezekiel's polemics against idols. The theme of God's absence and presence—which variously explores the issues of his withdrawal, his appearance, his control, and his activity of restoration—is the chord that holds the composition together. It is organic to many of the central features of the book, informing the prophet's own answers, thereby unifying the diverse motifs, topics, and literary forms.

Having identified the variations of the theme of God's absence and presence in the book of Ezekiel, we need to answer three questions: (1) How does Ezekiel develop this paradox? (2) Why does he develop this paradox? and (3) What are the larger significances of this paradox in Israelite and other ancient Near Eastern theology? In answering these questions, I will attempt to demonstrate how deeply Ezekiel is rooted in the context of the exile and the concerns of the Babylonian *golah*. The struggle in the text over the modes of the divine presence is a theological problem precipitated by the exile, for it underlies three fundamental issues: theodicy (Why is Israel in exile?), theophany (Where is God in exile?), and theonomy (What power does God have in exile?). The exile forces Ezekiel to explain defeat, destruction, and deportation and to restrain the loss of national-cultic identity. Surely they were vocal who alleged, "The way of the Lord is not just" (18:25, 29; 33:17, 20), while others turning to foreign gods and claiming Yahweh's own defeat by Babylon complained, "Yahweh does not see us; Yahweh has abandoned the land" (8:12; also 9:9).

The exile concretely raises the question of God's absence. But it also furnishes a means to resolve the problem constructively. Fundamentally, Ezekiel's resolution is not unlike the resolution represented in Ps 115:2–3: "Why should the nations say, 'Where is their god?' Answer: Our God is in the heavens; he does whatever he pleases." The aniconic tradition is subtle. The book of Ezekiel, one of that tradition's most effective voices, is a theological document that helped its audience to survive the destruction of Jerusalem, the razing of the Temple, and exile in Babylonia—with all of the religious and political consequences that these events implied. Ezekiel achieved this by constructing an affirmation of Yahweh's presence that would not fail in the face of foreign idols, loss of sanctuary, and invading victorious nations. Yahweh, though apparently absent, was profoundly present, above and beyond the reach of human military might. The struggle to express the appearance of the divine provides the vehicle for the prophet's message. Using the language and categories of the theological problem of polytheistic idolatry, Ezekiel fashions a constructive and concrete solution: Yahweh alone is God and idols are impotent; though not physically present, Yahweh makes himself known through his actions.

The analysis in the following chapters is based on three premises. First is a recognition of the coherent character and integrated design of the book of Ezekiel. Second is the fact that other Israelite traditions known to us from the Hebrew Bible probably influenced Ezekiel. Third is the likelihood of a Mesopotamian setting for the book and the prophet's conscious interaction with Assyro-Babylonian traditions in exile. Sections 2–4, which follow, will demonstrate that such premises rest on solid historical and textual foundations.

§2. The Coherence of the Book of Ezekiel

An Overview

An investigation of the book of Ezekiel as a basically integrated and coherent text—indeed, with an articulated, artful design—reflecting the context of the exile is a defensible critical position when textual and redactional issues are carefully weighed. The history of this inquiry has been rehearsed many times. I would add here little that has not been reviewed fully elsewhere.[6] However, a brief summary of this history with an emphasis on the main points and current state of the debate is germane to the present study.

The beginning of the twentieth century ushered in the first significant opposition to the unity of the book of Ezekiel, to the association of authorship primarily with Ezekiel, and to the exilic dating of the book.[7] Two works are especially singled out for the impact they delivered to the status quo. The

6. The reader should consult H. H. Rowley, "The Book of Ezekiel in Modern Study," *BJRL* 36 (1953) 146–90; Moshe Greenberg, "Prolegomeon," in *Pseudo-Ezekiel and the Original Prophecy and Critical Articles by Shalom Spiegel and C. C. Torrey* (ed. M. Greenberg; New York: KTAV, 1970) xi–xxxv; Zimmerli, *Ezekiel 1*, 3–8; Brevard Childs, *Introduction to the Old Testament as Scripture* (Philadelphia: Fortress, 1979) 357–70; Henry McKeating, *Ezekiel* (Old Testament Guides; Sheffield: Almond, 1993) 30–61; Katheryn Pfisterer Darr, "Ezekiel among the Critics," *Currents in Research* 2 (1994) 9–24.

7. At the turn of the century, R. Kraetzschmar identified recensional layers in Ezekiel (*Das Buch Ezechiel* [HKAT; Göttingen: Vandenhoeck & Ruprecht, 1900]). See I. M. Duguid, *Ezekiel and the Leaders of Israel* (Leiden: Brill, 1994) 3–8, for the precursors to these most prominent contributions. Note also McKeating, *Ezekiel*, 31; and C. G. Howie, *The Date and Composition of Ezekiel* (JBL Monograph Series 4; Philadelphia: Society of Biblical Literature, 1950) 1–2. Shalom Spiegel ("[Ezekiel or Pseudo-Ezekiel?" *HTR* 24 [1931] 247; repr. in *Pseudo-Ezekiel and the Original Prophecy and Critical Articles by Shalom Spiegel and C. C. Torrey* [ed. M. Greenberg; New York: KTAV, 1970] 125) credits the first modern attack on the homogeneity of the book of Ezekiel to Georg Ludwig Oeder in 1756, who doubted the authenticity of chaps. 40–48; a testimony to this perilous approach was the fact that Oeder's work was published only posthumously in 1771 (*Freye Untersuchung über einige Bücher des Alten Testaments* [Halle]).

first was published in 1924 by G. Hölscher who, using as one criterion the
theory that prophetic messages were expressed in poetic form, identified only
twenty percent of the book as the *ipsissima verba* of Ezekiel.[8] In 1930, the
primarily exilic dating of the book, a direct product of the prophet exiled in
Babylonia, was challenged by C. C. Torrey, who dismissed the stated historical context and argued unequivocally that Ezekiel is a pseudepigraphical
work composed in the Seleucid period and essentially elaborating the portrait
in 2 Kgs 21:1–17.[9]

The debate engendered by these works certainly continued,[10] but the
mainstream current debate still principally wrestles with W. Zimmerli's mon-
umental commentary and study in 1969, which investigated in detail the
text, speech-forms, and traditions in Ezekiel.

Zimmerli's chief contributions to the debate involve observations in two
directions. Moving backward, Zimmerli undertook a detailed text-critical
analysis from which he concluded that the versions "remain at many points a
help that is not to be undervalued for the recovery of a better text."[11] The format of his translation (with nonoriginal text in brackets and an extensive
critical apparatus) bears witness to this labor. Moving forward, Zimmerli
submitted the text to the efforts of tradition-critical analysis, concluding that
the original words of Ezekiel were delivered primarily orally (though not exclusively; for example, chaps. 8–11), which in turn underwent at least two
phases of literary editing and expansion: first by Ezekiel himself and second
by a "school" of disciples. He identified an Ezekiel core (*Grundtext*), with
later additions (*Nachinterpretation*) by this close school of disciples. Thus,
while all of the text may not be original to the prophet, it generally represents
his *ipsissima vox*.

---

8. G. Hölscher, *Hesekiel, der Dichter und das Buch* (BZAW 39; Giessen: Alfred
Töpelmann, 1924). Such a theory was basic to B. Duhm's work on Isaiah (*Das Buch Jesaia*
[HKAT; Göttingen: Vandenhoeck & Ruprecht, 1892]) and Jeremiah (*Das Buch Jeremia*
[KHAT; Tübingen: Mohr, 1901]).

9. C. C. Torrey, *Pseudo-Ezekiel and the Original Prophecy* (New Haven: Yale University Press, 1930; repr., New York: KTAV, 1970) xxxvii–xxxviii, 11–119. For a summary of the opposition that this work met, see Moshe Greenberg, "Prolegomenon," ibid.,
xiii–xvi.

10. For example, J. Garscha attributed only 17:1–10 and 23:2–5 to the prophet Ezekiel and argued that the book is primarily a postexilic redaction, with extensive fifth-century
expansions, though not complete till the end of the third century B.C.E. (*Studien zum
Ezechielbuch: Eine redaktionskritische Untersuchung von Ez 1–39* [Europäische Hochschul-
schriften 23/23; Bern: Herbert Lang / Frankfurt: Peter Lang, 1974]). See especially Rowley, "The Book of Ezekiel in Modern Study," for a critical appraisal of the ensuing
discussion in the quarter century following Hölscher and Torrey.

11. Zimmerli, *Ezekiel 1*, 75.

For Zimmerli, the text moves from an oral form to a written form to expansion by Ezekiel to expansion by his disciples. The final stage of interpretive and reinterpretive expansion is the result of an Ezekiel school, which is responsible for both expanding the composition and maintaining considerable cohesion. That the coherence is generally retained is obvious from Zimmerli's own rather equivocal distinction between the hand of Ezekiel and the hands of traditors.

Since Zimmerli, the debate has moved in two not incompatible directions: (1) a focus on the editorial end of the redaction as a creative and unifying force in itself; and (2) a greater appreciation of the definitive hand of the prophet himself in composing, writing, and organizing his oracles.

This latter position is maintained by Moshe Greenberg through several articles and in his commentary on Ezekiel. [12] Greenberg defends a reliance on the Masoretic Text and questioned even Zimmerli's form-critical methodology. [13] He applies what he calls a "holistic interpretation," finding in the book's complexity, not the contradictions and multiple hands perceived by Zimmerli and others, but a coherent, deliberate text that is nothing short of a work of art. In contrast to Zimmerli, Greenberg ascribes this authorship predominately to the sixth-century prophet. Indeed, even the editorial work was done by Ezekiel himself. [14] Greenberg warns against cultural biases of the modern scholar, far removed in time and place from the literary conventions of the ancient author. As a result of these biases, the effort of the modern commentator to establish an original text is fraught with unproved postulates and inattentiveness to the organic unity.

---

12. M. Greenberg, *Ezekiel 1–20* (AB 22; New York: Doubleday, 1983), *Ezekiel 21–37* (AB 23; New York: Doubleday, 1997).

13. Greenberg outlines his methodological caveats against others' efforts to determine secondary material in the commentary (*Ezekiel 1–20*, 18–27) but especially in "What Are Valid Criteria for Determining Inauthentic Matter in Ezekiel," in *Ezekiel and His Book* (ed. J. Lust; Leuven: Leuven University Press, 1986) 123–35. This discussion should be supplemented with that of Paul Joyce, *Divine Initiative and Human Response in Ezekiel* (JSOTSup 51; Sheffield: Sheffield Academic Press, 1989) 22–27. From the perspective of canonical criticism, Zimmerli's process of reconstruction would be fundamentally flawed, as Childs describes it: "I do not think that he has correctly assessed the canonical shape of the book, but has rested his interpretation on a critically reconstructed pre-canonical form of the book" (*Introduction to the Old Testament as Scripture*, 360). For Childs, consequently, Zimmerli's interpretation of the text rests on the same subjective basis as the reconstruction itself. Indeed, while Childs sees a lengthy period of editorial activity (ibid., 361), this is not commentary but part of the canonical process in which Israel incorporated its experience into the text as biblical witness (ibid., 369–70).

14. Greenberg, "The Design and Themes of Ezekiel's Program of Restoration," *Int* 38 (1984) 115.

Ironically, the redactional study of Ezekiel by Terence Collins results in conclusions not dissimilar to Greenberg's position. Focusing on the literary unity (themes and structure), he attributes both the core material and the overall received scheme of the book to Ezekiel: "The revisions were performed in a restrained manner which ensured that any additions that were made were given the authentic Ezekiel character."[15] To some extent, we return to Zimmerli himself, whose "school" of Ezekiel includes its own variation of the equivocating argument: "Even though a complex redactional work can be recognized in the book of Ezekiel, it preserves for us on the whole the peculiar characteristics of the prophet."[16]

Perhaps one of the freshest contributions to Ezekiel scholarship this century is the study by Ellen Davis, who argues that Ezekiel was primarily a written composition.[17] To be sure, this is not a new position. Ewald described Ezekiel as almost entirely a literary effort.[18] The strength of her proposal, however, lies chiefly in two arguments: (1) while noting the literary qualities of the book of Ezekiel, she also adequately explains the forms and features that have traditionally been cited as evidence of oral delivery; and (2) she situates this shift to written composition within a socioreligious matrix that was served particularly well by this new tool. Thus she argues: "The book as a whole offers testimony to and a subtle apologetic for a fundamentally new kind of prophetic enterprise, whose locus and medium are the text."[19]

What is especially significant is the way Davis develops this shift. She argues that Ezekiel's prophecies accompanied two important developments in Israel. First, it was in the Babylonian exile that the community compiled its sacred traditions into a scriptural corpus, producing versions of the Deuteronomistic History, Torah, and early Prophets.[20] Second, the exile roused the

15. T. Collins, *The Mantle of Elijah: The Redactional Criticism of the Prophetical Books* (The Biblical Seminar 20; Sheffield: Sheffield Academic Press, 1993) 93.

16. W. Zimmerli, "The Special Form- and Traditio-Historical Character of Ezekiel's Prophecy," *VT* 15 (1965) 515.

17. Ellen F. Davis, *Swallowing the Scroll: Textuality and the Dynamics of Discourse in Ezekiel's Prophecy* (JSOTSup 78; Sheffield: Almond, 1989). A summary of her thesis can also be found in "Swallowing Hard: Reflections on Ezekiel's Dumbness," in *Signs and Wonders: Biblical Texts in Literary Focus* (ed. J. C. Exum; Semeia Studies; Atlanta: Scholars Press, 1989) 217–37.

18. H. Ewald, "Jeremia und Hezeqiel," *Die Propheten des Alten Bundes erklärt* (Stuttgart: A. Krabbe, 1840–41). H. Gunkel, too, voiced a similar appraisal: "[Ezechiel] hat das erste Prophetenbuch geschrieben" (see his "Die israelitische Literatur," in *Die Orientalischen Literaturen* [ed. P. Hinneberg; Die Kultur der Gegenwart 1/7; Berlin and Leipzig, 1906] 82.)

19. Davis, *Swallowing the Scroll*, 38.

20. Davis, "Swallowing Hard," 217 and 224. On a similar view of textual formation in exile, see D. N. Freedman, "Son of Man, Can These Bones Live?" *Int* 29 (1975) 171–86.

urgent need to interpret present events in the context of its sacred traditions.[21] The image of the prophet eating the scroll (2:8–3:3) and his enigmatic muteness (3:26–27; 24:27; 33:21–22) are figures that indicate "the new conditions and constraints imposed upon communication by the move toward textualization of the prophetic tradition."[22] Therefore, it should not be unexpected that Ezekiel was influenced by the development of textual traditions that he encountered and by the new opportunities this experience offered his prophetic ministry.

The Functional Method of This Study

Despite the lack of consensus on the form, unity, or redaction of the book of Ezekiel, scholars generally recognize that the book needs to be treated as a literary whole. Even when redaction is conspicuous, most passages resist precise divisions and classifications. Indentifiable literary themes and recurrent phraseology suggest that approaching Ezekiel as a well-integrated, coherent text is warranted. For example, above in §1, I offered an outline of Ezekiel that emphasizes several structuring patterns: sections A and A′ narrate Yahweh's departure and return to the Temple. They in turn envelope sections B and B′, which deal with judgment (the reason for Yahweh's departure) and restoration (the preparation for Yahweh's return). Indeed, the Temple and Yahweh's presence there (*kābôd*) are the text's fundamental structuring elements. Furthermore, characteristic phraseology that occurs through the entire book contributes to a sense of coherence in the Ezekiel text: Yahweh frequently addresses the prophet as *ben-ʾādām* (over 90 times); God is frequently addressed as *ʾădōnāy yhwh* (over 200 times); the divine formula of recognition ("You/They shall know that I am Yahweh")[23] occurs frequently at the end of oracles; and words especially unique to Ezekiel, such as *gillûlîm* 'idols' occur throughout.

Ezekiel was certainly subject to redactional activity. Yet underlying this activity is a characteristic homogeneity to the Ezekiel tradition. Furthermore, the Ezekiel material extends throughout the book, including the program of restoration.[24] Unlike the Isaianic tradition, the accretion that took place in

21. Davis, "Swallowing Hard," 217.

22. Ibid.

23. On the so-called recognition formula (*Erkenntnisformel*), see Walther Zimmerli, *I Am Yahweh* (trans. Douglas W. Stott; ed. Walter Brueggemann; Atlanta: John Knox, 1982), esp. pp. 29–98.

24. The question of the redaction of the ever-elusive chaps. 40–48 has been given a careful and compelling reappraisal by Steven Tuell (*The Law of the Temple in Ezekiel 40–48* [HSM 49; Atlanta: Scholars Press, 1992)]. Tuell argues that Ezekiel 40–48 comprises two sources, one the prophet himself, the second an author portraying a not ideal plan but wrestling with the real problems of postexilic Judea. Still, he concludes that the importance of

Ezekiel occurred between and around the text, one might say, enhancing the prophetic infrastructure. In this sense, to call Ezekiel a composition is most accurate, for the term identifies the composite nature of the book but recognizes the quality of the work as integrated discourse.

§3. Ezekiel and Other Israelite Traditions

I turn now to another matter: the likelihood that the book of Ezekiel explicitly interacts with other Israelite traditions known to us from the Hebrew Bible. As we will see, Ezekiel uses, manipulates, and reacts to these traditions.

An Overview

The relationship of Ezekiel—its content, motifs, and language—to other material in the Hebrew Bible has been a central critical concern in reconstructing the setting, date, and tradition-circle of the prophet and the book. Scholars such as Millar Burrows and Zimmerli, among others,[25] have shown quite clearly that Ezekiel exhibits a conspicuous association with many traditions; and this has initiated a host of investigations into the oral and literary sources and relations of the book. I will provide here only a review of these apparent relationships.

Preclassical Prophetic Traditions

Characteristic features of the book of Ezekiel parallel usage in preclassical prophetic traditions.[26] A list of these motifs should suffice. (1) The formula "and the word of the Lord came to me" is common in Samuel and Kings for describing early prophecy.[27] It appears frequently again in Jeremiah (38 times), but especially as a fixed expression in Ezekiel (50 times). (2) The formula "the hand of the Lord was upon me" is a familiar motif in the Elijah-Elisha cycle (1 Kgs 18:46; 2 Kgs 3:15). It occurs in Isa 8:11 and Jer 15:17,

---

the Temple and the return to this subject are hardly a disturbance in the content and emphasis of the prophet Ezekiel. Tuell characterizes the Ezekiel source of the restoration chapters in terms quite in line with my thesis: "This core vision is concerned with the problem of the divine Presence, which indeed could be said to be the uniting theme of the entire text of Ezekiel" (ibid., 173).

25. See, e.g., M. Burrows, *The Literary Relations of Ezekiel* (Philadelphia: Jewish Publication Society, 1925); K. W. Carley, *Ezekiel among the Prophets* (London: SCM, 1975); also Zimmerli, *Ezekiel 1*, 41–52; and McKeating, *Ezekiel*, 92–98.

26. See the extensive treatment of these associations by Carley, *Ezekiel among the Prophets*, 13–47, 69–71.

27. For example, 1 Sam 15:10 (Samuel); 2 Sam 7:4 (Nathan); 2 Sam 24:11 (Gad); 1 Kgs 6:11 (Solomon); 1 Kings 13 (man of God); 1 Kings 16 (Jehu); 1 Kings 17–21 (Elijah).

but it has more striking frequency in Ezekiel (1:3; 3:14, 22; 8:1; 37:1; 40:1). (3) The use of רוּחַ in Ezekiel again parallels the usage in the Elijah-Elisha cycle (1 Kgs 18:12; 2 Kgs 2:16; compare especially Ezek 3:12, 14; 8:3; 11:24; 43:5) and elsewhere (1 Sam 10:6; 1 Kgs 22:21–24).[28] (4) A quintessential feature of Ezekiel, the proof-saying (*Erweiswort*, "that you/they shall know that I am Yahweh"), was identified by Zimmerli to have a close parallel to usage in 1 Kings 20 and 2 Kings 5.[29]

Deuteronomic Traditions

The traditions in Deuteronomy also have been assessed for their relation to Ezekiel. Consider the following: Ezek 18:6 and Deut 12:2; the Temple program in Ezekiel 40–48 and the Deuteronomic cult centralization; the Deuteronomic phrase "with a mighty hand and an outstretched arm" and Ezek 20:33–34; curse of exile (Deut 4:27; 28:49; and Ezek 11:16) and promise of restoration (Deut 30:3–5; and Ezek 11:17); and the image of the whole heart (Deut 6:5; 26:16; and Ezek 11:20; 36:27; compare its usage in Jer 24:7; 31:33; 32:39). It is not my intention here to answer the critical question that arises, as it does with all of the alleged textual associations, whether similar motifs reflect only shared knowledge or actual dependence. It is worth observing only that similarities exist, and this observation allows further inquiry into this aspect of the book.

Priestly Traditions

A review of Ezekiel's relation to other Israelite tradition would not be complete without a discussion of the Priestly material (P and H). The prophet, a priest, the son of Buzi, incorporates language that clearly reflects the priestly tradition. But how to understand the similarities between Ezekiel and P and H is not easy. Do they mark the dependence of the prophet on the latter traditions or vice versa? Or are they the result of Ezekiel and P and H drawing independently on a broader priestly culture? To gain a sense of the issues here, consider some of these similarities—the clearest ones—in detail.[30]

---

28. See especially, Daniel Lys, *"Rûach": Le Souffle dans l'Ancien Testament* (Études d'histoire et de philosophie religieuses 56; Paris: Presses universitaires de France, 1962).

29. See Zimmerli, *Ezekiel 1*, 36ff. and 43; idem, *I Am Yahweh*, esp. pp. 99–110; see also Carley, *Ezekiel among the Prophets*, 37–40.

30. For a review of the biblical texts and the secondary discussion, see Rudolf Smend, *Der Prophet Ezechiel* (Kurzgefasstes exegetisches Handbuch zum Alten Testament; Leipzig: S. Hirzel, 1880) xxvii–xxviii; Burrows, *Literary Relations*, 47–68; Carley, *Ezekiel among the Prophets*, 57–66; Zimmerli, *Ezekiel 1*, 46–52; and Avi Hurvitz, *A Linguistic Study of the Relationship between the Priestly Source and the Book of Ezekiel* (Cahiers de la Revue biblique 20; Paris: Gabalda, 1982).

For example, the motif of theophany provides a significant area of conjunction between the oracles of Ezekiel and P theology.[31] The כָּבוֹד theophany is central to the imagery of both Sinai (Exod 24:15–18) and the tabernacle (Exod 40:34–38). In Ezekiel the presence of God is also expressed in terms of the divine כָּבוֹד (some 20 times). And certainly Ezekiel's emphasis on the central function of the Temple in the restored land (Ezekiel 40–48), with detailed cultic terminology in chaps. 40–43, reveals a priestly background that intersected with traditions and personnel in the Priestly source.

The Holiness Code (Leviticus 17–26) has been connected even more closely with the terminology and theology of Ezekiel.[32] The following lists some of these items that display at least a surface resemblance:[33] Leviticus 17 and Ezek 14:1–11; the divine self-introduction אני יהוה (*Selbstvorstellungsformel*) in Leviticus 18–19 and throughout Ezekiel, particularly chap. 20; the emphasis on God's holiness and the warning against profaning God's holy name in Leviticus 19–22 and the similar concerns for God's holy name throughout Ezekiel (20:9, 14, 22, 39, 44; 36:20–23; 39:7, 25; 43:7–8). The relation between Ezekiel and Leviticus 26 is most striking. Some of the outstanding parallels are the following: Lev 26:4–13 and Ezek 34:25–31; certain expressions that occur only in Ezekiel and Leviticus 26, such as נתן פנים ב (Lev 26:17; Ezek 14:8; 15:7) and גאון עזכם (Lev 26:19; Ezek 24:21; 30:6, 18; 33:28); the formula for complete destruction (sword, pestilence, and famine) in Lev 26:25–26 and Ezek 5:12, 17; 6:11–12; 7:15; 12:16; 14:21; tearing down of high places and incense altars in Lev 26:30 and Ezek 6:3–6; and occurrences of גלולים for idols throughout Ezekiel and in Lev 26:30.[34]

Since Priestly material will figure especially in the following discussion, a methodological note is warranted here. To be sure, the dating of the Priestly source in relation to other pentateuchal sources has been a matter of intense debate. Methodologically, much of the discussion has involved determining the relative dates of Ezekiel, P, and H. It is important to emphasize, following Menahem Haran, that the composition of P may have been "a preparatory step towards its ensuing promulgation in public."[35] In other words, the

---

31. See J. Milgrom, *Leviticus 1–16* (AB 3; New York: Doubleday, 1991) 58; and the discussion in chap. 3.

32. For distinctions in the vocabulary and style of P and H, see ibid., 35–42; and the more fundamental study of Israel Knohl, *The Conception of God and Cult in the Priestly Torah and in the Holiness School* (Ph.D. diss., Hebrew University, 1988), on which Milgrom is building. See also, now, Knohl's *Sanctuary of Silence: The Priestly Torah and the Holiness Code School* (Minneapolis: Fortress, 1995).

33. See Burrows, *Literary Relations*, 28–36; also Zimmerli, *Ezekiel 1*, 46–52, with a discussion of the differences between these corpora.

34. On גלולים, see chap. 2.

35. M. Haran, *Temples and Temple-Service in Ancient Israel* (Oxford: Clarendon, 1978; repr. Winona Lake, Ind.: Eisenbrauns, 1985) 9. In a similar vein, Avi Hurvitz has

incorporation of P into Israel's life did not necessarily coincide with its literary formation. It is outside the present scope to analyze anew these source-critical questions. However, as I will argue at various points in this study, certain elements in Ezekiel appear to be contemporary with P. In these cases, both P and Ezekiel seem to reflect or respond to identical exilic stimuli. The following is at least a starting point: (1) Ezekiel belonged to a priestly circle prior to his exile but probably also to a circle that continued within the exilic community; and (2) some of the traditions that are encountered in their final literary form in the Priestly sources of the Pentateuch were also available to Ezekiel in some form, oral or written.

Tradition Interaction in the Book of Ezekiel

The incorporation of traditions just reviewed for Ezekiel has long been noted by scholars. Brevard Childs aptly describes this aspect of the book.

> Surely one of the most important aspects of Ezekiel's message was its dependence upon the activity of interpretation within the Bible itself. Not only was Ezekiel deeply immersed in the ancient traditions of Israel, but the prophet's message shows many signs of being influenced by a study of Israel's sacred writings. The impact of a collection of authoritative writings is strong throughout the book.[36]

Ezekiel's incorporation of tradition does not necessarily mean that he knew "writings" per se. Certainly, however, the prophet interacted with the authoritative traditions of various overlapping groups, including priestly, prophetic, and court circles.

Here is one of the contributions of Ellen Davis's excellent work. Her thesis attempts to explain this aspect of Ezekiel based on the emerging written discourse that incorporated the older oral forms. Noting the close connections with language from Jeremiah and the Holiness Code, for example, she comments, "The ways in which Ezekiel modifies the established conventions of prophecy are all the more noticeable because of the extent of his dependence

---

provided a methodical and rigorous analysis of the language of P (*A Linguistic Study of the Relationship between the Priestly Source and the Book of Ezekiel*). From a careful consideration of linguistic criteria, Hurvitz offers the following conclusions: Ezekiel shows linguistic elements that are identifiable as later than P (based on other postexilic works); while Ezekiel shares terminology with P, in places where one might expect P terminology Ezekiel has replaced them with synonyms, and these synonyms occur in postexilic books. Thus, Hurvitz proposes a clear chronological sequence for P and Ezekiel: "Whatever the *absolute* dating of P and Ezekiel, then, it can definitely be stated that P comes first in a *relative* chronological order" (ibid., 155; followed by Milgrom, *Leviticus 1–16*, 3–13; also Mark F. Rooker's recent study, *Biblical Hebrew in Transition: The Language of the Book of Ezekiel* [JSOTSup 90; Sheffield: Almond, 1990], supports Hurvitz's results).

36. Childs, *Introduction to the Old Testament as Scripture*, 364.

on earlier tradition."[37] Ezekiel's oracles mark both the preservation and interpretation of traditions, and these social and religous activities, according to
Davis, are basic to the needs of the exilic community.[38]

In the chapters that follow, I too will focus on Ezekiel's use of traditions
that he incorporates and manipulates to serve his needs and the needs of his
audience. Ezekiel then is both a receiver of *traditum* and a voice of *traditio*.[39]
And it is the context of the exile, with the dynamics of textual conservation
and conversation, that facilitates innovation. Ezekiel and his tradents following closely behind have adopted, adapted, and interacted with contemporary
material and traditions.[40] It is necessarily so, then, that few firm answers for
precisely resolving Ezekiel's orientation to his sources are available.

That Ezekiel could be fluent in the traditions of the Tetrateuch and Deuteronomy is quite possible, especially if one allows some of the redactional activity of these two traditions to be coincident with Ezekiel. But in addition to
isolating these traditions in Ezekiel, it may be equally, perhaps more, urgent
to consider that Ezekiel reflects the same forces and attitudes toward tradition that the redaction of the Pentateuch reveals.[41] If in fact the eclectic nature of the book is not a secondary and late redactional imposition (and I find
no fundamental reason for this conclusion), then reading Ezekiel with close
attention to these traditions will further our appreciation of a vitally important aspect of this prophet and his time.

§4. Ezekiel and Non-Israelite Traditions

Two related issues will also be fundamental to what follows. The first is
the likelihood of a Mesopotamian setting for the book of Ezekiel. The second

---

37. Davis, "Swallowing Hard," 226.

38. Idem, *Swallowing the Scroll*, chap. 2, esp. pp. 29–45.

39. These expressions are especially associated with Michael Fishbane's analysis in
Biblical Interpretation in Ancient Israel (Oxford: Clarendon, 1985), which were taken, in
turn, from scholastic tradition.

40. See also the similar conclusions of Gordon Matties, *Ezekiel 18 and the Rhetoric of
Moral Discourse* (SBLDS 126; Atlanta: Scholars Press, 1990) 17–22.

41. F. M. Cross, e.g., sees the P tradition not as an individual source, but as the redactor of JE, who thus brought the Tetrateuch into being (*Canaanite Myth and Hebrew Epic*
[Cambridge: Harvard University Press, 1973] 318–25). Furthermore, regarding JE-P,
Cross suggests the following: "The traditional arguments for a date later than Deuteronomy and the Deuteronomistic history still hold firm" (p. 324), and "the Priestly Tetrateuch as a completed work must be roughly coeval with Ezekiel's vision of chapters 40–
48"—a period that he places in the sixth century, late in exile (p. 325). In chap. 3, I will
maintain also that a Priestly redactor responds to the exilic crisis in ways similar to Ezekiel;
both P and Ezekiel interact with earlier Israelite traditions and with traditions encountered
in Babylonia.

involves the impact of that setting, particularly the influence of traditions from Mesopotamia on the prophet's presentation.

The Mesopotamian Setting of the Book of Ezekiel

Chapter 1 opens with Ezekiel's receiving a dated vision: "In the thirtieth year,[42] in the fourth month, on the fifth day of the month, I was in the midst of the exiles (*haggôlâ*) by the river Kebar." The conventional understanding of this date is that it points to Ezekiel's having been a part of the first deportation in 597 B.C.E.[43] Ezek 1:2 mentions the "fifth year of the exile of King Jehoiachin," taken generally to be 593 B.C.E., the beginning of Ezekiel's ministry.[44] He is described as living in Tel Abib on the river Kebar (1:1; 3:5), and if the identification of *nĕhal kĕbār* with the canal Shatt en-nil is correct,[45] then Ezekiel would have resided somewhere between Babylon and Uruk, possibly near Nippur.

In spite of this apparent Babylonian locale and the statements that indicate the prophet's presence in exile before 587 B.C.E., some aspects of the book suggest a Judean setting. One aspect is the book's focus on the present and future fate of Jerusalem. Furthermore, the text offers what appear to be eyewitness accounts of specific events in the Temple. Especially significant is the narrative frame begun in chap. 8, which has Ezekiel counseling elders of

---

42. On the various interpretations of the referent of this date, see E. Kutsch, *Die chronologischen Daten des Ezechielbuches* (OBO 62; Freiburg: Éditions Universitaires / Göttingen: Vandenhoeck & Ruprecht, 1985). Two plausible interpretations have been given by Anthony York and James Miller. York ("Ezekiel I: Inaugural and Restoration Visions?" *VT* 27 [1977] 82–98) argues that the thirtieth year mentioned in 1:1 was originally related to the restoration oracle (see 43:3) and therefore would be the last dated oracle (567/8 B.C.E.): "Because this oracle, the vision and the prophecy, was so welcomed and gladly received, it occupied for a time the first place in a collection of Ezekiel's oracles. Later, yielding to principles that guided the collection and final editing of the prophetic books, the restoration prophecy was transposed to its present place, but its introduction and vision remained at the beginning with the consequence that the two similar visions were fused." Miller ("The Thirtieth Year of Ezekiel 1:1," *RB* 99 [1992] 499–503) relates v. 1 to v. 2: "thirtieth year" was the age of the prophet at the time of his first vision in the fifth year of Jehoiachin's exile. The significance of thirty is that at this age Ezekiel would have assumed his priestly responsibilities in Jerusalem (Num 4:3, 23, 30). Moreover, his service as prophet and as priest overlap: the last dated oracle would have coincided with Ezekiel's fiftieth year of age (the twenty-fifth year of the exile; see 40:1), the age when Levites retired from service.

43. The tradition in Josephus also interprets it so (*Ant.* 10.6.3 §98).

44. On the chronological notations in the book of Ezekiel (1:2; 3:16; 8:1; 20:1; 24:1; 26:1; 29:1; 29:17; 30:20; 31:1; 32:1; 32:17; 33:21; 40:1), see Jack Finegan, "The Chronology of Ezekiel," *JBL* 69 (1950) 61–66; also K. Freedy and D. B. Redford, "The Dates in Ezekiel in Relation to Biblical, Babylonian and Egyptian Sources," *JAOS* 90 (1970) 462–85.

45. See E. Vogt, "Der Nehar Kebar: Ez 1," *Bib* 39 (1958) 211–16.

Judah in his house in exile, during which he is taken (8:2) in a vision (8:3) to Jerusalem.[46] In chaps. 8–11 it appears that Ezekiel sees vivid accounts of the apostasy in Jerusalem, after which he is transported back to Babylonia (11:24).[47]

Narrative elements such as these have led scholars to various conclusions. The most radical reconstructions suggest, wholly or in large part, that the oracles were not delivered in exile. As discussed earlier, C. C. Torrey maintained that Ezekiel is altogether a pseudepigraph; its writer was a resident of Jerusalem around 230 B.C.E.[48] A variation of this interpretation came a year later from James Smith, who felt compelled by some of the same texts that led Torrey to his conclusion. Smith argued that the book made better sense in the context of the land of Israel. While it was a product of a prophet Ezekiel, who had been exiled from the Northern Kingdom by the Assyrians prior to 722 B.C.E., this prophet returned to northern Palestine in the early seventh century and delivered his message to those who remained.[49] It was then revised and updated for the experience of the Southern exiles in Babylonia a century later.

Some scholars have argued for a dual venue for the prophet. For example, while extensively denying the conclusions of Torrey and others, Spiegel did concede that some sermons may have come from Ezekiel in Jerusalem, where he would have begun his ministry during the reign of Jehoiakim, but later he continued his mission among the exiles in Babylonia.[50] A more extensive Judean stage was proposed by V. Herntrich, who lengthened Ezekiel's ministry in Jerusalem to the year 586 B.C.E.[51] Chapters 1–39 reflect this location and period. Other material in the book comes from the hand of a redactor, who

---

46. Similar locomotion is reported in 3:12, 14; 11:1; 37:1; 40:1–2; and 43:5. It is a hallmark of the Elijah cycle (1 Kgs 18:11–12; 2 Kgs 2:16).

47. This was a problem for early interpreters. Josephus says only that Ezekiel foretold the destruction of Jerusalem while he was in Babylonia and sent these warnings to Zedekiah in Jerusalem (*Ant.* 10.7.2 §106). The author of the *Lives of the Prophets* simultaneously combines the events in chaps. 8–11 into two interpretations: "While he was there (i.e., in Babylonia) he used to show the people Israel what was happening in Jerusalem and in the Temple. He was snatched up from there and he went to Jerusalem to rebuke those who were faithless" (translation by D. R. A. Hare, "The Lives of the Prophets," *OTP* 2.389).

48. Torrey, *Pseudo-Ezekiel and the Original Prophecy.*

49. J. Smith, *The Book of the Prophet Ezekiel: A New Introduction* (New York: Macmillan, 1931). Smith does suggest that three oracles were delivered in exile to the Northern deportees (20:32–44; 36:16–32; 37:11–14).

50. S. Spiegel, "Toward Certainty in Ezekiel," *JBL* 54 (1935); repr. in *Pseudo-Ezekiel and the Original Prophecy* (see p. 260). Here he cites rabbinic interpretations to this effect (on this, see further below).

51. V. Herntrich, *Ezechielprobleme* (BZAW 61; Giessen: Alfred Töpelmann, 1932) 37–130.

also manipulated chaps. 1–39 to reflect a Babylonian ministry. Similarly, Bertholet and Galling suggested that Ezekiel had two ministries: (1) beginning in 593 B.C.E. in Jerusalem, and (2) continuing in Babylonia in 587 B.C.E. after the fall of Jerusalem.[52]

Proposals that Ezekiel did not prophesy in Babylonia, of course, occasioned opposition. For example, C. G. Howie took on the questions of Ezekiel's date and residence from the vantage of the linguistic and archaeological evidence available to him.[53] Regarding a Mesopotamian provenience, he argued that the details of the text (such as לִבְנָה in 4:1 and תֵּל־אָבִיב in 3:15) justify regarding the setting as authentic. Similarly, he marshaled affirmation from the date formulas and architectural details (in 40:5ff.) that support the position that the prophet conducted his work in Babylonia in the early sixth century. In support of the initial location of Ezekiel in Babylonia, H. Orlinsky noted that if the prophet received his call in Jerusalem instead of in a foreign land, this would be clearly mentioned as a means to legitimize the prophetic message by basing the prophetic commission in the homeland.[54] Certainly, the Jerusalemite details produce no insurmountable obstacle if one allows three points: (1) Ezekiel lived in Jerusalem before the first deportation; (2) correspondence went back and forth between Babylonia and Jerusalem, informing both groups of concerns in each location; and (3) literary license. Indeed, McKeating sees a consensus in current Ezekiel scholarship that returns to the traditional assessment of both the geographical and the chronological context.[55]

This matter does not need to be resolved completely here. The burden of proof, nevertheless, lies more heavily on proving a primarily Judean setting, and the evidence provided has not been persuasive, in contrast to the Babylonian indications. My working position is that Ezekiel was situated in

---

52. A. Bertholet and K. Galling, *Hesekiel* (HAT 13; Tübingen: Mohr, 1936) 82 and 134.

53. C. G. Howie, *The Date and Composition of Ezekiel* (Philadelphia: Society of Biblical Literature, 1950), see chaps. 1 and 2, pp. 5–46.

54. H. M. Orlinsky, "Where Did Ezekiel Receive the Call to Prophesy," *BASOR* 122 (1951) 34–36. Incidentally, the issue of the location of prophetic commission is discussed in rabbinic tradition—specifically, the principle that prophecy cannot take place outside of the land of Israel (*Mekilta, pisqa* 1; see Jacob Z. Lauterbach, *Mekilta de-Rabbi Ishmael* [Philadelphia: Jewish Publication Society, 1933] 1.4, 6). The same tradition explains, however, that if the call to prophesy began in the land of Israel, the person could continue as a prophet outside Israel. Unlike Orlinsky, but certainly reflecting this issue, the *Targum of Ezekiel* adjudicates the problem in chap. 1 by asserting that the word of God first came to Ezekiel in the land of Israel and subsequently in exile (the critical arguments on this position have already been referred to above).

55. McKeating, *Ezekiel,* 44. For further discussion of the various permutations of approaches to the dating and context of Ezekiel, see pp. 32–61.

Babylonian exile, though he may have received correspondence from Judah, and the book may even have been redacted in the early postexilic period. Based not upon this assumption, however, but on elements in the text, I will assert in chaps. 2 and 4 that both the judgment and the restoration oracles interact with the elements that directly relate to this Babylonian context.

The Mesopotamian Socioreligious Traditions and Ezekiel

The effort devoted to defending the Babylonian milieu of Ezekiel also led to discovering apparent Mesopotamian elements in the book. Daniel Bodi has provided the most recent and thorough review of scholarship on this subject, listing important studies on iconographic, philological, and literary questions.[56] Commentaries also have made ample use of these associations to understand hapax legomena[57] and such iconographic images as the flying cherubim-throne in chaps. 1 and 10. These studies are too numerous to mention here. It is necessary to highlight only a few of them and to consider their implications.

Doubts about the authenticity of the Babylonian setting of the prophet Ezekiel met resistance from scholars who investigated Akkadian contacts with the book of Ezekiel. As mentioned above, the thesis of C. C. Torrey sparked Shalom Spiegel's response, which included an attempt to demonstrate the precise connections between Ezekiel and Assyriological evidence, thereby setting the prophet directly within this sphere of influence.[58]

Linguistic influences in a book with a lion's share of lexical difficulties have received special scrutiny. For example, S. P. Garfinkel, after reviewing previous studies on the Akkadian influences on Ezekiel, investigated both the Akkadian etymologies and the broader impact from Akkadian literature, such as the muteness motif (3:22–27; 33:21–22).[59] His results support an exilic provenience of the prophet Ezekiel, who appears to have had some familiarity with Akkadian literature.

Specific literary works in Akkadian have been mined for their possible impact on the book of Ezekiel. Among these, the Babylonian Poem of Erra

---

56. See Daniel Bodi, *The Book of Ezekiel and the Poem of Erra* (OBO 104; Freiburg: Universitätsverlag / Göttingen: Vandenhoeck & Ruprecht, 1991), chap. 2, "Survey of Research of the Babylonian Influence on the Book of Ezekiel," 35–51. On iconographic evidence of Ezekiel's familiarity with Babylonia, esp. Ezekiel 1, see pp. 42–45. See also Othmar Keel, *Jahwe-Visionen und Siegelkunst* (Stuttgarter Bibelstudien 84/85; Stuttgart: Katholisches Bibelwerk, 1977) 361–83.

57. Over 130 words are found only in Ezekiel, according to Zimmerli (*Ezekiel 1*, 23).

58. Spiegel, "Ezekiel or Pseudo-Ezekiel?" 244–321; *Pseudo-Ezekiel and the Original Prophecy,* 123–99.

59. S. P. Garfinkel, *Studies in Akkadian Influences in the Book of Ezekiel* (Ph.D. diss., Columbia University, 1983); see the review of studies on pp. 1–11.

has long been singled out as an excellent resource for understanding Ezekiel.[60] Bodi offers the most extensive demonstration of these influences, suggesting that the relationship between Ezekiel and the Poem of Erra should be described as "literary emulation."[61] He does this by investigating twelve motifs that exhibit this relationship. Four of these motifs are peculiar to Ezekiel in the Hebrew Bible and appear in Erra in comparable usages. Eight motifs are common to the other biblical books, but Bodi argues they have been modified under the influence of Erra. Bodi's thesis is certainly most convincing when he evaluates the four motifs unique in the Bible to Ezekiel and present in Erra: (1) the Hebrew שאט and Akkadian *šēṭu/leqû šēṭūtu* ('to have scorn for'); (2) the Hebrew חשמל and the Akkadian *elmēšu* ('amber'); (3) the seven executioners (Ezekiel 9) and the Divine Seven (*Sebetti*); and (4) the motif of preservation from the Flood.[62]

Bodi's conclusions remain rather broad but generally persuasive. For example, consider the following cautious summary:

> We would argue that the influence of the Poem of Erra on the Book of Ezekiel was operating at the level of the prophecy's origin and should not be seen as being introduced only at the redactional level. However since the primary goal of the present research was to demonstrate the probable relationship between the Book of Ezekiel and the Poem of Erra, the method which we have used was not conceived in such a way as to provide an answer concerning the author of the book of Ezekiel. Therefore, throughout the present work we have referred to the author or the redactor of the Book of Ezekiel.[63]

Simultaneously, Bodi widens the picture by noting that the Poem of Erra itself draws on major themes in Akkadian literature, and thus he also concludes that "the author or redactor of the Book of Ezekiel has employed some of these themes and motifs in a form modified to suit his purpose."[64] In other words, because Erra is itself an eclectic work, it is sometimes difficult to say whether the similarities between it and Ezekiel are due to Ezekiel's borrowing directly from Erra or from a broader Mesopotamian tradition, of which Erra is simply one manifestation.[65]

---

60. See, e.g., R. Frankena, *Kanttekeningen van een Assyrioloog bij Ezechiël* (Leiden: Brill, 1965); M. Anbar, "Une nouvelle allusion à une tradition babylonienne dans Ézéchiel (XXII 24)," *VT* 29 (1979) 352–53; and B. Maarsingh, "Das Schwertlied in Ez 21,13–22 und das Erra-Gedicht," in *Ezekiel and His Book* (ed. J. Lust; Leuven: Leuven University Press, 1986) 350–58.

61. Bodi, *Ezekiel*, 315.

62. Ibid., chap. 4. On the Flood motif, see the discussion in chap. 2 below.

63. Ibid., 318.

64. Ibid., 13, 318–20.

65. Ibid., esp. p. 27. In this regard, he cites the comments of J. H. Tigay, *The Evolution of the Gilgamesh Epic* (Philadelphia: University of Pennsylvania Press, 1982) 162:

In the final analysis, Bodi has at least demonstrated probable cause for considering that such an acquaintance existed between Ezekiel and Erra. And it seems certain that he has demonstrated a clear relationship between Mesopotamian traditions and Ezekiel, in general. This conclusion should not be underestimated. Bodi's observations contribute to our understanding of the impact that the exile had at both the compositional and the ideological levels. This aspect of Bodi's work will receive particular attention in the chapters that follow.

A critical question arises: To what extent was the prophet able to exploit Mesopotamian traditions? According to the biblical tradition, the social status of exiles was not uniform: exiled persons included the skilled and educated members of the population (2 Kgs 24:14–17) as well as the poorest people (Jer 52:15).[66] We can draw the working assumption that, as a priest, a member of an elite class, Ezekiel was literate, as were members of his support group and immediate audience.

Still another critical question arises: to what extent were the language and concepts of Assyrian and Babylonian royal and religious texts known beyond limited palace, temple, and scribal circles? The possibility of much influence has been denied, for example, by Leo Oppenheim.[67] He argued that since building inscriptions were either buried or displayed in inaccessible locations within palaces and temples, they were intended for the patron gods or the monarchs that would succeed them and not for the general, contemporary audience. The evidence that supports a wider acquaintance, however, should

---

"Ancient writers drew extensively upon larger components, such as topoi, motifs, groups of lines, and episodes, which had their original settings in other compositions. Sometimes they composed passages imitating such elements, and at other times they simply transferred such elements verbatim into their own compositions."

66. At least regarding the makeup of the exiles, it appears that Bustenay Oded's study of the Neo-Assyrian policy of deportation offers corroborating evidence: "It is . . . clear that the Assyrians did not restrict themselves to a particular class or social group, but deported assorted elements of the population of a conquered country" (*Mass Deportations and Deportees in the Neo-Assyrian Empire* [Wiesbaden: Reichert, 1979] 22). In other respects, however, Neo-Babylonian and Neo-Assyrian deportation policies do not match. For example, Neo-Assyrian policy regularly replaced deportees of one region with deportees of other regions, thereby weakening local resistance to imperial control, while Neo-Babylonian policy appears not to have done this.

67. A. L. Oppenheim, *Ancient Mesopotamia* (rev. Erica Reiner; Chicago: University of Chicago Press, 1977) 147. But consider Oppenheim's remarks regarding the "terrifying mask" of Assyria that was deliberately and effectively "turned toward the outward world" ("The Neo-Assyrian and Neo-Babylonian Empires," in *Propaganda and Communication in World History, Vol. I: The Symbolic Instrument in Early Times* [ed. H. D. Lasswell, D. Lerner, and H. Speier; Honolulu: University Press of Hawaii] 133–34); in other words, Oppenheim does allow that Assyrian propaganda made its mark on the local populations.

be considered. I will review two studies that suggest the possibility of access on a broader scale.

Peter Machinist has argued that knowledge of Mesopotamian literary tradition in Israel can be demonstrated in the eighth-century prophecies of First Isaiah.[68] He analyzes six examples of motifs in Isaiah that reveal a relationship to Neo-Assyrian texts. While cautious in his conclusions, he suggests that Isaiah's use of these motifs, common especially to Neo-Assyrian royal inscriptions, indicates that it is reasonable to infer that they became known to Isaiah through Neo-Assyrian channels. Indeed, these common idioms reflect "the impact of a literary and military tradition brought by Neo-Assyria."[69] This would not be an unexpected outcome from what we know of the imperial ambitions of the Assyrian Empire.

> Whether, then, for Isaiah himself or for the circle that followed, it appears to be no accident that the image of Assyria to which they were responding was also that defined and promulgated in the official literature of the Neo-Assyrian kings. In other words, in Isaiah we are evidently dealing with the effects of Assyrian propaganda.[70]

The source of this image of Assyria is more difficult to assess with certainty. One cannot rule out reports from ambassadors who may have seen such visual displays in the Assyrian capitals.[71] Written means of Assyrian expressions can be included as well. The erection of royal stelae, especially at boundaries and extremities of the empire, is a well-known practice.[72] And finally, such official propaganda may have been channeled through translation into Aramaic—both oral and written delivery—which by the eighth century was the lingua franca in the western regions of the Near East.[73] That Neo-Assyrian rulers sought any available avenue by which to inform their prey of the futility of either rebellion or escape is certain.

68. P. Machinist, "Assyria and Its Image in the First Isaiah," *JAOS* 103 (1983) 719–37.

69. Ibid., 726.

70. Ibid., 729.

71. Ibid., 730–31. Note also the studies by Irene J. Winter of the impact of palace iconography: "Royal Rhetoric and the Development of Historical Narrative in Neo-Assyrian Reliefs," *Studies in Visual Communication* 7 (1981) 1–31; and "The Program of the Throneroom of Assurnasirpal II," in *Essays on Near Eastern Art and Archaeology in Honor of Charles Kyrle Wilkinson* (ed. P. O. Harper and H. Pittman; New York: Metropolitan Museum of Art, 1983) 15–32.

72. Machinist, "Assyria and Its Image," 731. Ann T. Shafer has exhaustively analyzed these examples in *Repetition, Reiteration, and Empire: Victory Stelae and Rock Reliefs on the Assyrian Periphery* (Ph.D. diss., Harvard University, 1998).

73. Ibid., 733, with literature; also Machinist, "Assyrians on Assyria in the First Millennium B.C.," in *Anfänge politischen Denkens in der Antike* (ed. K. Raaflaub; Schriften des Historischen Kollegs Kolloquien 24; Munich: Oldenbourg, 1993) 94 n. 107.

A recent study by Barbara Porter carries similar implications.[74] She investigates the reign of Esarhaddon and the official images of the king that he proclaimed through his public-works projects. Esarhaddon used building inscriptions, she argues, as a tool of propaganda and a vehicle of presenting the different images of this king to both a Babylonian and an Assyrian audience. But she notes, "In order to be used for such a purpose, however, the inscriptions had to be accessible to a contemporary audience."[75] Her analysis includes a lengthy discussion of indirect evidence that suggests that some indigenous knowledge of the content and language of royal inscriptions reached contemporary audiences in the late Neo-Assyrian period.[76]

Porter presents several reasons that would encourage making available the message of these texts to contemporary audiences of Esarhaddon (and, by extension, to the larger Assyro-Babylonian period). For example, the Nineveh A text of Esarhaddon fits the pattern of what Hayim Tadmor has called an "autobiographical apology," whose purpose was to describe how a particular ruler attained legitimate power, as well as to make straight the path for his intended successor.[77] Porter states unequivocally that the reason the account of Esarhaddon's succession is not included in earlier building inscriptions is that it was written for a contemporary audience. Similarly, the omission in Nineveh A of Sennacherib's murder was also motivated, Porter proposes, by a sensible political consideration: it was not wise to raise that example as a means of succession. If Porter is correct, it certainly would make little sense if such care were taken only for future kings or gods; rather Esarhaddon's building inscriptions did reach a contemporary audience and achieved political objectives through this transmission. Certainly, too, the exploits of an imperial ruler contained in royal inscriptions would be effective as a means of broadcasting the message of the divine sanction by which he both gained and maintained power over renegade lands.

Porter, like Machinist, considers also the means by which royal inscriptions reached contemporary audiences, especially building inscriptions, which were buried in the foundation of municipal buildings. She offers some suggestions. Perhaps the content of texts composed by scribes would circulate among the administrative elite. Furthermore, there is evidence that copies of

74. B. N. Porter, *Images, Power, and Politics: Figurative Aspects of Esarhaddon's Babylonian Policy* (Philadelphia: American Philosophical Society, 1993).

75. Ibid., 105.

76. Ibid., 105–16.

77. Hayim Tadmor, "Autobiographical Apology in the Royal Assyrian Literature," in *History, Historiography and Interpretation* (ed. H. Tadmor and M. Weinfeld; Jerusalem: Magnes, 1984) 36–57. The text is dated to 673 B.C.E., near the end of Esarhaddon's reign and just before he named his two sons to succeed him—Assurbanipal over Assyria and Shamash-shum-ukin over Babylonia.

foundation texts were made and deposited at other locations or in an archive.[78] These mechanisms, however, are indirect and admittedly provide limited general exposure. Also, admittedly, the reconstruction of direct means, such as public speeches or ceremonies for the dedication of buildings, remains conjectural.[79] We can surely envision, however, that the royal sponsors of such public works had every intention of making their efforts known, admired, and revered.[80]

§5. Summation and Outline

With this review of scholarship (in §§2–4 above), I advance three preliminary judgments for my study of the presence and absence of God in the book of Ezekiel. First, I see a consensus in Ezekiel scholarship that endorses further inquiry into the coherent and integrated nature of the text. With proper regard for both redactional and text-critical concerns, I will pay close attention to elements that represent central motifs throughout the book. Second, Ezekiel's relationship to other Israelite traditions is a significant feature of the book at the compositional level, however broadly that may be defined. Third, the Babylonian setting of Ezekiel offers critical avenues of investigation, not only for understanding the religious and intellectual context of the exiles, but also for considering the ideological arguments presented in the book of Ezekiel. That the destruction of Jerusalem should end for some in removal to the land of its conquerors is plainly a theological dilemma begging for prophetic response.

The body of this analysis will present what might be called "case studies," that is, evidence that supports the argument that the presence and absence of God is a central paradox for the prophet and appears in the book through the interrelationship of (1) the representation of Yahweh, (2) the dissociation of Yahweh's power and presence from other (images of) deities, and (3) the relationship between Yahweh and Israel in exile. This last element involves two themes, a defense of the exile as punishment and the promise of return, and is directly indebted to the images developed in items (1) and (2).

Throughout his book, the prophet struggles with this complex conceptual dilemma involving the mode of God's appearance and the proper portrayal of him. At the same time, it defines Ezekiel's problem and his answer.

---

78. See Porter, *Images*, 111–12.

79. Ibid., 113–15, where she discusses what can be gleaned from ancient sources on oral delivery of official instruction.

80. See, e.g., the Banquet Stela of Ashurnasirpal II (ca. 883–859) on the dedication of the new capital city of Kalah (northwest palace; Nimrud); translation in *ARI* 2.172–76. Room EA, where the stela was found, appears to have been built for the text's presentation since it is little more than a niche facing a great hall.

Thus, chap. 2 will explore what the prophet considers to be illegitimate representations of God, what makes them so, and what impact they have on Israel. Chapter 3 will evaluate representations of God that the prophet considers to be legitimate, especially expressions of God's presence that involve the Jerusalem Temple. Chapter 4 will demonstrate that the prophet directly interacts with Israelite and Mesopotamian religious imagery when he predicts restoration but in terms that both underscore the cause of the exile and demonstrate the sole, transcendent presence of Yahweh.

A final chapter will suggest how the individual studies relate and contribute to understanding the book of Ezekiel, both its content and unity of structure and its place in the history of Israelite religious thought. For example, this study will demonstrate that the prophet's own representation of God produces contrasts, tensions, and paradoxes that highlight Yahweh's supremacy and power in relation to Israel and the nations. Specifically, we will see that the book of Ezekiel plays a central and previously unappreciated role in the development of Israelite theology. The conceptualization of Yahweh in the book redefines the power and position of Israel's God in distinctively universal terms, indeed, monotheism in the strictest sense. Along the way, we will see how the prophet emerges as a skillful interpreter of Israel's traditions, and in his encounter with Assyro-Babylonian traditions he proves an exceptionally subtle analyst, polemicist, and literatus.

Chapter 2
Idolatry and Theodicy:
Illegitimate Expressions for God's Presence

The House of Israel says, "The way of the Lord is not just."
Ezekiel 18:29

§1. Idolatry as a Main Cause of the Exile

A late Second Temple text that claims to record the lives of the prophets—or more precisely, the circumstances of their deaths—says of Ezekiel,
"He died in the land of the Chaldeans during the captivity. . . . The ruler of
the people of Israel killed him there as he was being reproved by him concerning the worship of idols."[1] This tradition recognizes a central and pervasive
element in the book of Ezekiel: more dramatically than either Jeremiah or
Second Isaiah (indeed, than any single book of the Hebrew Bible, including
the Deuteronomistic corpus), Ezekiel targets the sin of idolatry. According to
this prophetic text, idolatry is the quintessential cause of the Babylonian exile.

A brief review of Ezekiel's introduction confirms this general statement.
The opening chapters progressively narrow their focus to the subject of idolatry. The prophetic call narrative (1:28b–3:27) begins with a broad indictment that Israel rebelled against God. The charge is driven home with the
repetition of the verbs מרד and מרה and the noun מְרִי (2:3, 5, 6, 7, 8; 3:9, 26,
27). This general charge is narrowed in chap. 5 (vv. 6–11): Jerusalem has
rejected Yahweh's statutes and defiled the Temple with detestable things
(שִׁקּוּצִים) and abominations (תּוֹעֵבוֹת), two common expressions in Ezekiel
for idolatry. In chap. 6 the focus narrows still further: Israel has worshiped on
high places (בָּמוֹת), on hills (גִּבְעָה רָמָה and רָאשֵׁי הֶהָרִים), and under trees
(אֵלָה עֲבֻתָּה and עֵץ רַעֲנָן)—all of which were forms of worship that the
prophet considered improper. Chapter 6 introduces Ezekiel's preferred term

---

1. Translation by D. R. A. Hare, "The Lives of the Prophets," in *OTP* 2.388 (3:2). The
ruler of Babylonian Jewry is left unidentified.

for idols: גִּלּוּלִים (vv. 4, 5, 6, 9, 13). Yahweh warns that he will destroy these idols and even the land itself (vv. 3–6, 13–14). The focus on idolatry reaches its height in chap. 8, where the prophet is transported in a vision to the Temple precincts and there witnesses a series of offenses: an image of jealousy (vv. 3, 5), a room full of idols and idolatrous representations (vv. 10–12), women weeping for the god Tammuz (v. 14), and men worshiping the sun (v. 16). The vision ends with the pronouncement in v. 17: "Do you see this, O human? Is it such a minor thing that the House of Judah commits the abominations that they commit here?" The inescapable punishment draws near (chap. 9), as does the departure of the presence of Yahweh (10:1–22; 11:22–25). [2]

Certain sections of Ezekiel focus on idolatry with particular intensity (for example, chaps. 6, 8, 14, 18, 20, 23). Moreover, the charge is present in every major division of the book (see table 1, p. 29). In short, and to reemphasize, idolatry is the single most consistent reason the prophet offers for the exile.

The repercussions of idolatry—namely, divine withdrawal and exile—constitute Ezekiel's message of theodicy. As Ackroyd has observed, "Ezekiel's attention is entirely concentrated upon the reality of disaster. He is concerned in this situation to justify the ways of God to man." [3] Apropos of this emphasis, consider again Davis's understanding, that the signs of ingesting the scroll (2:8–3:3) and the subsequent prophetic muteness (3:26–27; 24:27; 33:21–22) are indications of new constraints on the prophet in both medium and message. God has established one-way communication to the people through a particularly textual means. The prophet is not a channel for the peoples' appeals to God. While this type of message may not be without precedent (for example, Isa 6:9–10), Ezekiel raises it to a new level.

> With Ezekiel, the goal of prophecy undergoes a profound shift. No longer is it aimed at opening the ears of the people, at repentance and avoidance of disaster (cf. Jer 25:3–7; 26:2–6; 36:2–3). That possibility is foreclosed; the disaster is decreed, and now the function of the prophet is simply to make known to Israel the author of that judgment and the just grounds for its execution (cf. 16:2; 20:4). The divine recognition formula ("that you/they may know that I am YHWH") which recurs continually throughout the book and the related formula, "that they may know there has been a prophet in their

---

2. The departure of God's presence as the consequence of idolatry is a theme repeated in pseudepigraphical literature from the Second Temple period (e.g., *3 Enoch* 5).

3. Peter R. Ackroyd, *Exile and Restoration: A Study of Hebrew Thought of the Sixth Century B.C.* (OTL; Philadelphia: Westminster, 1968) 104. Thomas M. Raitt discusses the central message of theodicy (through the "Oracle of Judgment") in *A Theology of Exile: Judgment/Deliverance in Jeremiah and Ezekiel* (Philadelphia: Fortress, 1977), esp. pp. 83–105.

midst" (2:5; 33:33), show how completely the role of the prophet and the course of history are determined by that primary intention of God.[4]

Ezekiel is the vehicle of a divine indictment, the mouthpiece of a monologue set in motion when the die was cast, and the prophet argues that Judah cast the die by its spurious worship. The prophet delivers the evidence and the verdict from the divine court, and idolatry is the most incriminating evidence introduced during the testimony. Indeed, it is elementary that the misrepresentation of God provokes a dual punishment: the destruction of the people and the departure of its God. The lines of communication have been cut, and admission to God's presence is jeopardized. Restoration is possible only after a proper understanding of that presence is reached.

The Socioreligious Function of Ezekiel's Idol Polemic

Ezekiel's answer to the question of theodicy very plainly involves the paradox of the presence and absence of God. Idolatry, the misrepresentation of God's image, the illegitimate expression of his presence, results in the removal of God's presence and the destruction of his symbolic dwelling place. Ezekiel's condemnation of the physical representation of divine presence was essential to reconstructing exilic theology. Furthermore, the very vehicle of the message is significant: in exile, even without territory and Temple, Yahweh still speaks through a prophet, who delivers a message that both justifies the punishment and subverts any apparent explanation that God's absence indicated God's powerlessness.

In this physical and ideological milieu, Ezekiel offers an extensive argument that Yahweh alone is God, despite all appearances. While exile clearly intensified the problem, the prophet rose to the challenge by constructively employing the paradox of God's absence and presence. The problem provided the paradigm for the solution: by emphasizing the absence of God, namely, his lack of physical representation, Ezekiel enabled his audience to perceive God's presence in exile. Ironically, the judgment against their idolatry provided the conceptual means for survival and for expectation of return.

This chapter investigates the evidence of idolatry in Ezekiel, including its characteristic motifs, vocabulary, and cultural background. Of course, Ezekiel is not a lone voice condemning idolatry. Deuteronomic texts, for example, warn that such worship especially will be the cause of destruction and exile

---

4. E. F. Davis, "Swallowing Hard: Reflections on Ezekiel's Dumbness," in *Signs and Wonders: Biblical Texts in Literary Focus* (ed. J. C. Exum; Semeia Studies 18; Atlanta: Scholars Press, 1989) 230. It is in this sense, too, that the book is radically theocentric, as both W. Zimmerli (*I Am Yahweh* [trans. Douglas W. Stott; Atlanta: John Knox, 1982]) and more recently P. M. Joyce (*Divine Initiative and Human Response in Ezekiel* [JSOTSup 51; Sheffield: Sheffield Academic Press, 1989], esp. pp. 89–105) have shown.

(Deut 4:25–27; 6:10–15; 7:1–5; 8:17–20; 11:16–17). What is notable about Ezekiel, however, is that the polemic against idolatry is fundamental to the prophet's overall message and to his hearers' experience, both past and present.

First, it is plain that the destruction of Judah posed the urgent question: Why? Four times Ezekiel quotes the people's charge that God's way was not just (18:25, 29; 33:17, 20).[5] In so doing, the prophet matches the charge with the theme and variations of their improper allegiance and the frequent refrain "That you/they may know that I am the Lord."

Second, the prophet's setting raised another question: Where is God? The deity's city and sanctuary were facing, or already had experienced, destruction. Had he abandoned them for good? Could Yahweh be worshiped on foreign soil? Deuteronomistic material includes narratives that may suggest territorial limitations to the deity (Deut 4:28; 28:64; Judg 11:24 [note also Mic 4:5]; 1 Sam 26:19; 2 Kgs 5:17; even topographical restraints in 1 Kgs 20:23, 28), concerns perhaps voiced by the exilic psalmist: "How can we sing the song of Yahweh upon foreign land?" (Ps 137:4). Indeed, Ezekiel must have taken this question quite personally, when he, a priest, was deprived of the tools of his trade.

Third, we will see that the prophet interacted with both Israelite and Mesopotamian traditions in order to demonstrate that the worship of idols was incompatible with the worship of Yahweh. The polemic against idolatry in the book of Ezekiel, as well as its oracles of judgment (where we meet much of this polemic), ultimately serves a constructive function. The folly of idols is that they represent non-gods. Thus the exile was a result of a confrontation not between Babylon and Judah or between the gods of Babylon and Yahweh but between Yahweh and his people.

The Terminology in Ezekiel's Idol Polemic

Table 1 presents the terms and their occurrences in Ezekiel's polemic against idolatry. The most important terms for condemned practices are the following: גִּלּוּלִים, תּוֹעֵבוֹת, שִׁקּוּצִים, סֶמֶל, צֶלֶם, and זְנוּת(תַּ). Including all objections to improper worship, such as open-air sites, there are about eighty references to such proscribed activity in the book of Ezekiel. While the vocabulary is concentrated especially in chaps. 6, 8, 14, 16, 18, 20, 22, and 23, its usage is distributed throughout the book (including the program of restoration).

---

5. On the so-called disputation speech, which is especially common in Ezekiel, see Adrian Graffy, *A Prophet Confronts His People: The Disputation Speech in the Prophets* (AnBib 104; Rome: Pontifical Biblical Institute, 1984).

Table 1
Charges of Idolatry in Ezekiel: Occurrences and Terminology

5:9	תּוֹעֵבוֹת
5:11	תּוֹעֵבוֹת, שִׁקּוּצִים
6:3, 6	improper worship[a]
6:4, 5, 6	גִּלּוּלִים
6:9	תּוֹעֵבוֹת, גִּלּוּלִים
6:13	גִּלּוּלִים (2 times), improper worship
7:20	שִׁקּוּצִים, צַלְמֵי תוֹעֵבוֹת
8:3, 5	סֵמֶל הַקִּנְאָה (הַמַּקְנֶה)
8:6, 9, 13, 15, 17	תּוֹעֵבוֹת (6 times)
8:10	תַּבְנִית . . . מְחֻקֶּה עַל־הַקִּיר, גִּלּוּלִים
8:12	חַדְרֵי מַשְׂכִּית
8:14	weeping for Tammuz
8:16	worshiping the sun
14:3, 4, 5, 7	גִּלּוּלִים (5 times)
14:6	תּוֹעֵבוֹת, גִּלּוּלִים
16:15–22	תּוֹעֵבוֹת (צַלְמֵי זָכָר), idolatry, תַּזְנוּת
16:36	תּוֹעֵבוֹת, גִּלּוּלִים, תַּזְנוּת
18:6	improper worship, גִּלּוּלִים
18:12	תּוֹעֵבוֹת, גִּלּוּלִים
18:13	תּוֹעֵבוֹת
18:15	improper worship, גִּלּוּלִים
20:7, 8	שִׁקּוּצִים, גִּלּוּלִים
20:16, 18, 24	גִּלּוּלִים
20:28–29; 21:3	improper worship
20:30	שִׁקּוּצִים
20:31	גִּלּוּלִים
20:32	worshiping wood and stone
20:39	גִּלּוּלִים (2 times)
21:15	worshiping wood
22:3, 4	גִּלּוּלִים
22:9	improper worship
23:7, 30, 37, 39, 49	גִּלּוּלִים, תַּזְנוּת
23:27	זְנוּת
30:13	אֱלִילִים, גִּלּוּלִים (of Egyptians!)
33:25	גִּלּוּלִים
36:18, 25	גִּלּוּלִים
37:23	שִׁקּוּצִים, גִּלּוּלִים
43:7	פִּגְרֵי מַלְכֵיהֶם בָּמוֹתָם (of kings), זְנוּת
43:8	תּוֹעֵבוֹת
43:9	פִּגְרֵי מַלְכֵיהֶם, זְנוּת
44:10, 12	גִּלּוּלִים

a. Various stereotypical offenses are included under the label "improper worship," such as performing ritual practices upon בָּמוֹת, גִּבְעָה רָמָה, and רָאשֵׁי הֶהָרִים; and under אֵלָה עֲבֻתָּה and עֵץ רַעֲנָן.

The vocabulary in Ezekiel for idols is rather limited. Three terms occur most often: גִּלּוּלִים, תּוֹעֵבוֹת, and שִׁקּוּצִים.[6]

Outside of the book of Ezekiel, שִׁקּוּצִים especially relates to idols (Deut 29:17; 2 Kgs 23:24; Jer 16:18) or objects that defile the Temple (Jer 7:30; 32:34). Indeed, more than half of the 28 occurrences of this term in the Hebrew Bible refer to idols, and 5 of the 8 occurrences of this term in Ezekiel are explicit references to idolatry.[7]

The word תּוֹעֵבָה occurs some 117 times in the Hebrew Bible. It is especially concentrated in Deuteronomic-Deuteronomistic texts (22 times), Jeremiah (8 times), and Ezekiel (42 times). Outside of Ezekiel, תּוֹעֵבָה refers to various offenses. Deuteronomy, for example, includes a wide range: cultic infractions (17:1), divination (18:12), gender violations (22:5), dishonesty (25:16), but also idolatry (7:25; 13:15; 27:15; note also Jer 16:18).[8] Deutero-Isaiah describes both the worshiper of other gods (41:24) and the idols themselves (44:19) as תּוֹעֵבָה. Some references to תּוֹעֵבוֹת in Ezekiel are ambiguous: 6:11; 7:3–4, 8–9; 9:4; 11:18, 21; 16:2, 50–51; 18:24; 20:4; 33:29; 36:31; 16:47, 51, 58. I have not included these in table 1. In other cases תּוֹעֵבָה is used as a general term for an offensive act, but in context it includes idolatry (these are cited in parentheses): Ezek 18:20 (see vv. 10–11, 13); 22:2 (see vv. 3–4); 23:36 (see vv. 37–39); 33:26 (see v. 25); 44:6–7, 13 (see vv. 7–12).

The imagery of adultery is another feature in Ezekiel (תַּזְנוּת occurs only in Ezekiel 16 and 23; compare Hosea 1–4 and Jeremiah 2–3). In chap. 16, the harlotry of the adopted and wedded maiden picks up the theme of following other gods.[9] Here Ezekiel develops an argument that I will develop below in §2. This argument starts from the assertion that Israel has misperceived the notion of God and his creation. Yahweh clothes and cares for his people, who are the image of God (vv. 10–13a). Israel, however, has gone after other gods, constructing them from materials (vv. 16–18) and forming them into mere 'images of men' וַתַּעֲשִׂי־לָךְ צַלְמֵי זָכָר (v. 17). We will see below that divine statues in Mesopotamian theology could be described as images of gods (*ṣalam ilāni*). If Ezekiel is drawing on this tradition, v. 17 is a resourceful wordplay that contains both a motif of idols being made from

---

6. Other common terms that denote or are associated with idols in the Hebrew Bible include אֲשֵׁרִים, מַסֵּכָה, מַצֵּבָה, תְּרָפִים, בַּעַל, פֶּסֶל, אֵלָה/אֱלוֹהַּ, עֶצֶב, אֱלִיל. Not all of these occur in Ezekiel.

7. Christopher North ("The Essence of Idolatry," in *Von Ugarit nach Qumran* [ed. J. Hempel and L. Rost; Berlin: Alfred Töpelmann, 1958] 155) suggests שִׁקּוּץ is a causative (*Shaphel*) derivative of קוּץ.

8. See P. Humbert, "Le substantif *tôʿēbâ* et le verbe *tʿb* dans l'AT," *ZAW* 72 (1960) 217–37.

9. The *Targum of Ezekiel* explicitly interprets harlotry as idolatry in both Ezekiel 16 and 23.

man's image (צֶלֶם)—as opposed to God's—and a motif of the unfaithful maiden pursuing other men (זכר).

Ezekiel 23 continues the motif of cuckoldry.[10] Here the prophet describes Samaria and Jerusalem as two sisters, Oholah and Oholibah.[11] The motif of harlotry is intricately bound up with both cultic and political unfaithfulness. Samaria and Jerusalem—and by extension, Israel and Judah—pursue the Assyrians and Chaldeans and are enticed by their idols (23:7, 30, 37, 39, 49). Again we find in Ezek 23:14 a mix of metaphors similar to the one in 16:17: וַתּוֹסֶף אֶל־תַּזְנוּתֶיהָ וַתֵּרֶא אַנְשֵׁי מְחֻקֶּה עַל־הַקִּיר צַלְמֵי כַשְׂדִּים חֲקֻקִים בַּשָּׁשַׁר 'She added to her prostitution even more: she gazed at (figures of) men carved upon the wall, images of Chaldeans engraved with vermilion'.[12] The passage proceeds quite graphically to describe Judah's lust for the Babylonians, equaled only by Israel's previous lust after the Egyptians in the days of her youth.[13]

10. This chapter provides a good example of W. Zimmerli's reconstruction of the stages involved in the creation of the text—what he calls *Fortschreibung* ('literary development'). The basic oracle of chap. 23 includes vv. 1–27. However, some verses are cited as additions (4b, 7b, 8, 9b, 10b, 12–14a, 18, 21, 23aβb, 25b, 26); the result produces a passage with metric features that W. Zimmerli displays and describes as "an exalted narrative style, which sometimes approximates closely a firm metric rhythm, but then slips back again into a freer movement" (*Ezekiel 1* [trans. R. E. Clements; Hermeneia; Philadelphia: Fortress, 1979] 481). He analyzes the unit 23:28–49 as follows: vv. 28–30 are a weak summary of previous material; vv. 32–34 form an independent unit; vv. 36–49 are secondary; and vv. 31 and 35 are transitional. Zimmerli compares the growth of this chapter to that of its compositionally related passage, chap. 16. Neither developed from collections of short independent oracles. Instead, they have been "formed in a process of successive supplementation of a kernel element, the ideas of which have been developed and expanded" (p. 334). Later interpretation may be conjectured where prose speech interrupts the elevated narrative language. Furthermore, because of the general fidelity of the additions, the identity of the interpreter remains obscure. Zimmerli readily admits this: "To what extent the hand of Ezekiel himself is to be seen in these additions cannot be determined with certainty, at least for the whole" (p. 348).

11. Oholah and Oholibah are identified specifically as Samaria and Jerusalem in v. 4c, which Zimmerli attributes to an interpretive gloss (*Ezekiel 1*, 471). While we are not certain if v. 4c is a gloss, the use of Samaria and Jerusalem synecdochally for the Northern and Southern Kingdoms seems clear. Zimmerli correctly observes, "Since 'Israel' in Ezekiel is the emphatic name for the whole people of God, the antithesis Israel–Judah is impossible" (ibid., 483; and see his excursus, "'Israel' in the Book of Ezekiel," *Ezekiel 2* [trans. J. D. Martin; Hermeneia; Philadelphia: Fortress, 1983] 563–65).

12. Reading כשׂדים with vv. 15, 16, 23. The construction אנשי מחקה על הקיר is difficult and seems to be related to 8:10. Zimmerli, without any support from the versions, supports the emendation to אנשים מחקים or אנשים חקקים (*Ezekiel 1*, 473).

13. Ezekiel associates Egypt with the lure of idols (20:7–8) and chronicles this as an ominous beginning in Israel's history.

By far the most striking expression that Ezekiel uses to characterize idol-atry is גִּלּוּלִים. The noun *gillûlîm* occurs 48 times in the Hebrew Bible, always in the plural.[14] Ezekiel contains 39 of the 48 occurrences (see table 1). Out-side of Ezekiel, the term appears in Lev 26:30; Deut 29:16; 1 Kgs 15:12; 21:26; 2 Kgs 17:12; 21:11, 21; 23:24; Jer 50:2—all texts whose authorship or redaction is generally considered exilic or postexilic.[15] Thus the term does not seem to be attested in literature prior to the exilic period.[16] This evidence has led Zimmerli to suggest that the term was coined in the period of the Jo-sianic reform and was associated particularly with the Jerusalem priesthood, a circle to which Ezekiel belonged.[17] Bodi even argues, "L'émergence du terme *gillûlîm* chez Ézéchiel aurait influencé son emploi dans les 9 références généralement datées après son époque."[18] Nevertheless, there is not sufficient evidence to conclude that Ezekiel invented the term,[19] only that it was his term of choice to denote idols and idolatry. Perhaps, then, the least we can say is that *gillûlîm* cannot date much before the late seventh century B.C.E.

The Septuagint exhibits little consistency in translating the Hebrew word, as the following examples show:[20]

εἴδωλα 'idols' (Ezek 6:4, 6, 13; 8:10; 16:12; 23:39; 36:25; 37:23; 44:12; Lev 26:30; Deut 29:17 [MT 16]; 4 Kgdms 17:12; 21:12, 21; 23:24)

ἐνθυμήματα 'thoughts, inventions, devices' (Ezek 14:7; 16:36; 18:6, 15; 20:16, 24, 31; 22:3, 4; 23:7, 30, 37, 49; 44:10)

ἐπιτηδεύματα 'practices, habits' (Ezek 14:6; 20:7, 8, 18, 39; 3 Kgdms 15:12)

διανοήματα 'thoughts, ideas' (Ezek 14:3, 4)

διάνοια 'thoughts, intelligence' (Ezek 14:5)

βδελύγματα 'abominations' (3 Kgdms 20:26 [MT 1 Kgs 21:26])

This list reveals that the variation in interpretation is most dramatically evi-dent in the book of Ezekiel, where only 9 of the 39 occurrences of *gillûlîm* are

---

14. It occurs once in the singular in Sir 30:19. It is always used in the plural in Qum-ran texts (e.g., 1QS 2:11, 17; 4:5; 1QH 4:15, 19; 4QFlor 1:17; see H. D. Preuss, "גִּלּוּלִים, *gillûlîm*," *TDOT* 3.1).

15. See ibid.

16. Daniel Bodi, "Les *gillûlîm* chez Ézéchiel et dans l'Ancien Testament, et les dif-férentes pratiques cultuelles associées à ce terme," *RB* 100 (1993) 482.

17. Zimmerli, *Ezekiel 1*, 186.

18. Bodi, "Les *gillûlîm*," 482–83.

19. As North suggested ("The Essence of Idolatry," 155); followed by H. W. Wolff, "Jahwe und die Götter in der alttestamentlichen Prophetie," *EvT* 29 (1969) 397–416.

20. The LXX does not reflect the MT passages that contain the term *gillûlîm* in Ezek 6:5; 30:13; 33:25; 36:18; Jer 27:2 (MT 50:2).

translated εἴδωλα.[21] Most often *gillûlîm* is reflected by the less concrete 'thoughts' (ἐνθυμήματα, διανοήματα, or διάνοια) and 'practices' (ἐπιτηδεύματα). Such a repertoire provides little help in determining the meaning of the Hebrew term.

While most agree that the vocalization of *gillûlîm* is artificial, formed on the basis of *šiqqûṣîm*,[22] the etymology of the term still holds some ambiguity. Two suggestions have been offered for the derivation of *gillûlîm*. First, *g-l-l* (I) 'to roll', with an attested nominal form *gal* (I) 'heap of stones' (Gen 31:46; 2 Kgs 19:25 pl.), was suggested by Baudissin as the root, *gillûlîm* being a *qiṭṭûl* construction.[23] Baudissin supported this suggestion with extrabiblical evidence, particularly the Aramaic *gll'* found in a bilingual Palmyrene inscription, whose Greek equivalent is στήλη λιθίνη.[24] Thus, the prophet may have used *gillûlîm* to indicate sacred standing stones (*maṣṣēbôt*).[25]

A second proposed derivation is from *g-l-l* (II) 'to be dirty' (only *Polal* ptc. Isa 9:4; and *Hithpolel* ptc. 2 Sam 20:12), with attested nominal forms *gālāl* 'dung-pellets' (1 Kgs 4:10; Zeph 1:17) and *gelēlê/gelālô* (*gēl* 'dung'; respectively: Ezek 4:12, 15; Job 20:7).[26] H. D. Preuss argued that the clearly abusive meaning of *gillûlîm* in Ezekiel and its frequent association there with *ṭāmē'*[27] weigh in favor of a derivation from *g-l-l* II.[28] Preuss argued further that *gillûlîm* was coined in the exilic period, patently for this invective.[29]

---

21. As opposed to the targumim, which consistently render גלולים with טעות, a common expression for idol (on this, see further below).

22. Zimmerli, *Ezekiel 1*, 187; also Greenberg, *Ezekiel 1–20* (AB 22; Garden City, N.Y.: Doubleday, 1983) 132; and Bodi, "Les *gillûlîm*," 483.

23. See W. W. Graf Baudissin ("Die alttestamentliche Bezeichnung der Götzen mit *gillūlīm*," ZDMG 58 [1904] 395–425), who essentially follows Gesenius's *Thesaurus*. Greenberg (*Ezekiel 1–20*, 132) advocates Baudissin's view.

24. See G. A. Cooke, *A Textbook of North-Semitic Inscriptions* (Oxford: Clarendon, 1903) 321, 314, 334. Note also the Ugaritic forms *gll* ('to roll', *UT* no. 581) and *gl* ('cup', *UT* no. 575), and Akkadian *galālu(m)* II ('to roll', AHw 273b).

25. Baudissin, "Die alttestamentliche Bezeichnung der Götzen mit *gillūlīm*," 405–6. Furthermore, the Aramaic *'eben gĕlāl* in Ezra 5:5, 8 and 6:4 has the meaning 'blocks of stone'. Incidentally, however, the Greek versions never translate the word *gillûlîm* with a meaning reflecting 'stone' (see above).

26. See, for example, North, "The Essence of Idolatry," 151–60; and Wolff, "Jahwe und die Götter in der alttestamentlichen Prophetie," 397–416. Essentially, this etymology was proposed as early as the eleventh- and twelfth-century Medieval scholars Ibn Yanaḥ, Ibn Ezra, and David Qimḥi (see Bodi, "Les *gillûlîm*," 489–90).

27. Ezek 20:7, 18, 31; 22:3–4; 23:7, 30; 36:18, 25; 37:23.

28. Preuss, "גִּלּוּלִים, *gillûlîm*," 1–5.

29. By Ezekiel himself (ibid., 2). Similar positions are held by North, "The Essence of Idolatry," 155, though without conviction; and Zimmerli, *Ezekiel 1*, 187.

Recently, Bodi has fully reviewed the arguments for these two derivations, as well as for a less likely one from Akkadian *gallû*(*m*) (Sumerian loan-
word *gal₅-lá*) 'demon' and *gullulu*(*m*) 'crimes, hostile acts'.[30] He suggests
that the different etymologies should not be perceived as antithetical.[31] That
is, instead of proposing two separate roots, namely, *gal/gālal* 'to be round'/
'heap of stones', and *gēl/gēlel* (constr. pl. *gelēlê*) 'excrement', and associating
only the latter root with *gillûlîm*, Bodi suggests that it might be more accurate to reconstruct one root *gl/gll* with a semantic field to which both possible
meanings belong. The basic sense of this common root would be "roundness" or "being round," characteristic of stones and boulders. The derived
meaning, with "roundness" still in mind, would be "excrement."

Bodi has correctly identified the double entendre Ezekiel conveyed
through *gillûlîm*. Certainly, the basic meaning of idols as (merely) a stone—
a neutral description with perhaps a suggestion of their efficacy—may lie behind the term *gillûlîm*, but Ezekiel intended the derived meaning especially
to resonate with his audience. In other words, he exploited the dual association of (idol-)stone and excrement in order to imply that pagan idols are, in
Wolff's words, "Scheissgötter."[32] Besides the obvious mocking tone this expression evokes, it additionally conveys the sense of impurity, both physical
and cultic (note Ezek 4:12, 15). Bodi aptly describes Ezekiel's acute theological usage of this term as "surcharge sémantique."[33]

On one level, the term *gillûlîm* is a description of pagan gods as merely
coarse objects.[34] On another level, the word implies scorching mockery. We
should not overestimate the force of the latter connotation (namely, a meaning associated with dung), since the former connotation (that is, a heap of
stones) is a very significant polemic in itself. Fundamentally, this quintessential Ezekielan term plainly avoids any reference to divine associations, repre-
sentational merit, or even craftsmanship that such expressions as אלהים,
אלים, עצב, מסכה, פסל, or צלם might imply. Such terms as these find little or
no usage in Ezekiel.

The terminology for idolatry is distributed throughout the book of Ezekiel
and is employed to deliver the most consistent charge against Judah, both

30. See respectively: AHw 275a (which von Soden remarks has the same semantic field
as *galālu*) and AHw 297–98. For discussion of these derivations, see Bodi, "Les *gillûlîm*,"
485–87. Bodi observes, however, that the frequency of the term *gillûlîm* especially in Ezekiel is surprising and poses a stumbling block to positing an Akkadian derivation, since the
well-known Babylonianisms in Ezekiel do not ever manifest such a frequency (p. 487).

31. Ibid., 490.

32. Wolff, "Jahwe und die Götter in der alttestamentlichen Prophetie," 407.

33. Bodi, "Les *gillûlîm*," 510.

34. This contemptuous characterization may be intended in the common Deuteronomic phrase "gods (אֱלֹהִים) . . . of wood and stone" (e.g., Deut 4:28; 28:36, 64; 2 Kgs
19:18; Isa 37:19).

prior to the destruction of Jerusalem and among the exiles of Babylonia. The prophet's terminology itself emphasizes a clear judgment against the practice (for example, גִּלּוּלִים, תּוֹעֵבוֹת, שִׁקּוּצִים, and תַּזְנוּת). Furthermore, Ezekiel avoids expressions that imply divine potential. Despite their physical presence no divine power dwells within them. For Ezekiel they are not symbols of the gods' presence but arguments for their absence. The next section of the discussion will show how Ezekiel's discourse extends this strategy even further.

The Omission of the Term *ʾĕlōhîm*

The above comments regarding the use of the term *gillûlîm* for pagan gods in Ezekiel lead us to a further observation about the book's attitude toward idolatry: it never uses the term *ʾĕlōhîm*—the generic term for 'gods' as well as for the God of Israel—to describe divine images or foreign gods.[35] I take this absence of *ʾĕlōhîm* as deliberate, all the more because it directly contrasts with the usage in Deuteronomy, the Deuteronomistic History, Jeremiah, and Deutero-Isaiah. What the absence suggests is that Ezekiel refuses to acknowledge even a verbal identity of other objects of worship as gods.

Consider this issue in more detail. Table 2 (p. 36) lists particular usages of גִּלּוּלִים and אֱלֹהִים that include venerating such objects of worship (אַחֵרִי) or that involve the qualification אֲחֵרִים.

In considering table 2, I would suggest first that because *ʾĕlōhîm* could refer to either pagan gods or Yahweh (as a routine proper name for the God of Israel) its usage created the potential for confusion. For example, in Lev 19:4, idols could be called *ʾĕlōhîm*, alongside the same term for Yahweh: "Do not turn to idols (אֱלִילִים), do not make for yourselves molten gods (אֱלֹהִים): I am Yahweh your God (אֱלֹהִים)." With reference to idols, then, this verse appears to endorse a category, *ʾĕlōhîm*, to which they did not belong. Given such confusion, it is not surprising that biblical texts applied various techniques to correct any misunderstanding that the use of *ʾĕlōhîm* might have caused. One of these techniques—qualifying the term so that it plainly did not refer to Yahweh—was the expression 'other gods' (אֱלֹהִים אֲחֵרִים). Sections A and B in table 2 list these occurrences. The phrase is especially common in Deuteronomy, Joshua–2 Kings, and Jeremiah.

We can observe more radical modifiers for *ʾĕlōhîm* when it refers to either idols or pagan gods. One strategy was to apply the phrase מַעֲשֵׂי יְדֵי אָדָם or מַעֲשֵׂה יְדֵי חָרָשׁ, accented occasionally with עֵץ וָאָבֶן or כֶּסֶף וְזָהָב: Deut 4:28;

---

35. The four occurrences of *ʾĕlōhîm* in chap. 28 (vv. 2 [2 times], 6, 9) are distinct in that they are direct boasts of the prince of Tyre that he is (a) god (cf. the taunt against the king of Babylon, esp. Isa 14:14). They are used as such to exploit the image of the Tyrian hubris.

Table 2
Uses of the Terms אֱלֹהִים and גִּלּוּלִים

A. *All occurrences of* '(to follow) after gods' (אַחֲרֵי אֱלֹהִים)[a]

Exod 34:15, 16 (3 times)	זנה אַחֲרֵי אֱלֹהִים
Deut 6:14	הלך אַחֲרֵי אֱלֹהִים אֲחֵרִים
Deut 8:19	הלך אַחֲרֵי אֱלֹהִים אֲחֵרִים
Deut 11:28	הלך אַחֲרֵי אֱלֹהִים אֲחֵרִים
Deut 13:3	הלך אַחֲרֵי אֱלֹהִים אֲחֵרִים
Deut 28:14	הלך אַחֲרֵי אֱלֹהִים אֲחֵרִים
Deut 31:16	זנה אַחֲרֵי אֱלֹהֵי נֵכַר־הָאָרֶץ
Judg 2:12, 19	הלך אַחֲרֵי אֱלֹהִים אֲחֵרִים
Judg 2:17	זנה אַחֲרֵי אֱלֹהִים אֲחֵרִים
1 Kgs 11:2	נטה אֶת־לְבַבְכֶם אַחֲרֵי אֱלֹהִים
1 Kgs 11:4	נטה אֶת־לְבָבוֹ אַחֲרֵי אֱלֹהִים אֲחֵרִים
1 Kgs 11:10	הלך אַחֲרֵי אֱלֹהִים אֲחֵרִים
1 Chr 5:25	זנה אַחֲרֵי אֱלֹהֵי עַמֵּי־הָאָרֶץ
Jer 7:6, 9; 11:10; 13:10; 16:11; 25:6; 35:15 (7 times)	הלך אַחֲרֵי אֱלֹהִים אֲחֵרִים

B. *All occurrences (in addition to A) of* 'other gods' (אֱלֹהִים אֲחֵרִים)
    Deuteronomy: 5:7; 6:14; 7:4; 8:19; 11:16, 28; 13:3, 7, 14; 17:3; 18:20; 28:14, 36,
        64; 29:25; 30:17; 31:18, 20
    Deuteronomistic texts: Josh 23:16; 24:2, 16; Judg 2:12, 17, 19; 10:13; 1 Sam 8:8;
        26:19; 1 Kgs 9:6, 9; 11:4, 10; 14:9; 2 Kgs 5:17; 17:7, 35, 37, 38; 22:17
    Jeremiah: 1:16; 7:6, 9, 18; 11:10; 13:10; 16:11, 13; 19:4, 13; 22:9; 25:6; 32:29;
        35:15; 44:3, 5, 8, 15
    Other: Exod 20:3; 23:13; Hos 3:1; 2 Chr 7:19, 22; 28:25; 34:25

C. *All occurrences of* '(to follow) after idols' (אַחֲרֵי גִּלּוּלִים)

Ezek 6:9	זנה אַחֲרֵי גִּלּוּלִים
Ezek 20:16	אַחֲרֵי גִּלּוּלִים לִבָּם הֹלֵךְ
Ezek 20:24	אַחֲרֵי גִּלּוּלֵי אֲבוֹתָם
Ezek 44:10	תעה אַחֲרֵי גִּלּוּלִים
1 Kgs 21:26	הלך אַחֲרֵי הַגִּלֻּלִים

D. *Additional (selected) usages of* אֱלֹהִים *for* 'gods'
    Priestly texts: Exod 12:12; 18:11; 20:23; 23:24, 32, 33; 32:4, 8, 23, 31; 34:17; Lev
        19:4 (H); Num 25:2; 33:4
    Deuteronomy: 4:28; 7:16, 25; 10:17; 12:3, 30, 31; 20:18; 29:17; 32:17, 37
    Deuteronomistic texts: Josh 23:7; 24:14, 15, 20, 23; Judg 2:3, 12; 3:6; 5:8; 6:10; 9:9,
        13; 10:16, 14, 16; 18:24; 1 Sam 4:8; 6:5; 7:3; 17:43; 2 Sam 7:23; 1 Kgs 11:8;
        12:28; 2 Kgs 17:29, 31, 33; 19:18
    Jeremiah: 2:11, 28; 5:7, 19; 10:11; 11:12, 13; 14:22; 16:20; 43:12, 13; 46:25
    Deutero-Isaiah: 41:23; 42:17 (44:6; 45:5, 21)

---

    a. For similar expressions (using אחרי) that substitute the name of a pagan god for אלהים, see
Deut 4:3 (בעל־פעור); 1 Kgs 11:5 (עשתרת and מלכם); 1 Kgs 18:18, 21; Jer 8:23, 25; 9:13 (הבעלים;
note also Hos 2:7, 15); Jer 8:2 (צבא השמים); 2 Kgs 13:2 (compare v. 6); Lev 17:7 (שעירם); Lev 20:5
(מלך; note also v. 6).

27:15; 2 Kgs 19:18 (= Isa 37:19); Jer 10:3 (compare Jer 1:16; 25:6–7; 44:8); Ps 115:4; 135:15; 2 Chr 32:19; also compare Isa 2:8; Hos 14:4; and Mic 5:12.[36] In this strategy, such "gods" are patently and simply human products—"the work of human hands," mere "wood and stone." Another common strategy involved expressions that directly challenged the category אֱלֹהִים as appropriate for idols or pagan gods: לֹא אֱלֹהַּ (Deut 32:17), לֹא־אֵל (Deut 32:21), and לֹא־אֱלֹהִים (2 Kgs 19:18 = Isa 37:19; Jer 2:11; 5:7; 16:20; Hos 8:6). In this view, such gods are really "non-gods." The authors of these texts appear to imply a degree of unease with the designation "gods," not only because it may be confused with Yahweh, but because the existence of gods other than Yahweh was being challenged.

Biblical scholars have most commonly identified Deutero-Isaiah as the Hebrew Bible's first sustained and explicit voice claiming that Yahweh, the God of Israel, is not one god among many but the only God, a universal deity. Such a routine conclusion is offered by John Scullion in his review of monotheism in the Hebrew Bible: "It is Deutero-Isaiah who expresses most clearly that Israel's God is one and unique, in short, monotheism in the strictest sense."[37] To be sure, Deutero-Isaiah explicitly describes Yahweh as the sole god in existence. He does so in two ways that we have already seen in some form in Deuteronomic texts. First, he ridicules the process by which idols are formed, as well as the persons who trust in these so-called gods: 40:18–20; 41:6–7; 42:17; 44:9–20; 45:16. No divine power resides in them. Second, Deutero-Isaiah contains a series of quite definitive statements about Yahweh's sole existence as God using the expressions אֵין 'none' and אֵין עוֹד 'no other' (see Isa 44:6–8; 45:5–7; 45:18–22; 46:9;[38] compare also 43:10–12).[39]

36. Note also the similar form of contempt in Ps 96:5 (= 1 Chr 16:26).

37. J. J. Scullion, "God," *ABD* 2.1043. Or consider the more general comments of Fritz Stolz: "Doch mit dem Exil tritt die Entwicklung des monotheismus in eine völlig neue Phase ein, die für sich betrachtet werden muss" ("Monotheismus in Israel," in *Monotheismus im alten Israel und seiner Umwelt* [ed. O. Keel; BibB 14; Fribourg: Schweizerisches Katholisches Bibelwerk, 1980] 179). Bernhard Lang traces five stages in the movement from polytheism to actual monotheism in the exilic period (see "Die Jahwe-allein-Bewegung," in *Der einzige Gott: Die Geburt des biblischen Monotheismus* [ed. B. Lang; Munich: Kösel, 1981] 47–83). Most recently, Robert Karl Gnuse focuses on the gradual development of monotheism in Israel (*No Other Gods: Emergent Monotheism in Israel* [JSOTSup 241; Sheffield: Sheffield Academic Press, 1997], esp. p. 207 on Deutero-Isaiah).

38. The expression of incomparability employing אֵין עוד is apparently a Deuteronomistic influence, based on the recognition formula that emphasized the exclusivity of Yahweh (note Deut 4:35, 39; 1 Kgs 8:60; similarly Deut 32:39; see S. Schwertner, "אַיִן," *TLOT* 1.96–97). Its usage alone is probably not a monotheistic formula (see B. Hartmann, "Es gibt keinen Gott ausser Jahwe," *ZDMG* 110 [1961] 229–35), but within the context of Deutero-Isaiah's larger polemic it can certainly be interpreted as such.

39. In a comparable strategy found in biblical texts other than Deutero-Isaiah, the attributive term הֶבֶל is used, suggesting the nonexistence or emptiness of other gods or the

I would suggest, however, that no matter how much the expression *'ĕlō-hîm* was qualified in order to disavow its potency, through hackneyed use it implied the very reality that Deutero-Isaiah struggled to deny. This observation emerges from evidence in the book of Ezekiel. I find compelling the fact that Ezekiel, despite his consistent polemic against idols, eschews the above strategies; rather, he appears to struggle with the very use of the term *'ĕlōhîm* and undertakes a more direct means to reject its efficacy.

The most categorical strategy and the most unequivocal means to deny power to idols is simply to assert that idols are idols. Idols are never gods. This is precisely what we find in the book of Ezekiel. The word *'ĕlōhîm* is never employed to refer to idols or pagan gods. Considering the centrality and frequency of idol polemics in Ezekiel, this is a wholly unique and significant omission. In other words, Ezekiel does not use *'ĕlōhîm* to refer to other gods, because to employ the term, even qualified, would give credence to the category. He omits the usage altogether and thereby leaves no doubt as to the vacuity of idols. [40] Instead, the prophet relies on the terms listed above in table 1, particularly the highly pejorative *gillûlîm*.

Initially, the proposal that Ezekiel intentionally avoids *'ĕlōhîm* for the gods may appear to be an argument from silence. On the basis of indirect evidence, however, I suggest that there was a deliberate strategy. First, consider the possibility that Ezekiel coins an expression that indicates he purposefully substituted his preferred term *gillûlîm* for the problematic *'ĕlōhîm*. The evidence for this argument is in table 2, sections A and C. Note in section A the frequent expression אַחֲרֵי אֱלֹהִים ('[to follow] after gods'), prominent especially in Deuteronomistic texts. There it appears to have become a rather

---

foolishness of activities associated with idols (particularly in Jeremiah): Deut 32:21; 1 Kgs 16:13, 26; 2 Kgs 17:15; Jer 2:5; 8:19; 10:3, 8, 15; 14:22; 16:19; 51:18; Jonah 2:9; Zech 10:2; Ps 31:7. Another similar evaluation, sometimes used alongside הֶבֶל, characterizes idols and their worshipers as שֶׁקֶר; here the biblical occurrences do include Deutero-Isaiah (Isa 44:20; Jer 10:14; 16:19–20; 51:17; Hab 2:18; Zech 10:2). Both of these strategies occur in predominantly late-seventh- or sixth-century B.C.E. texts.

40. Compare the generic use of the word *'ĕlōhîm* for gods: in the Pentateuch—about 67 times (J/E = 23, P = 4, D = 40), Deuteronomistic History—more than 90 times, Jeremiah—33 times, Deutero-Isaiah—only 5 times, and Ezekiel—none. The comparison of Jeremiah and Ezekiel is most effective, since these two books are of comparable length. But, clearly, we can observe a decreased usage of *'ĕlōhîm* for pagan gods in Ezekiel and, to a lesser extent, in Deutero-Isaiah (note אֵל for a pagan god in Isa 43:10; 44:10, 15, 17 [2×]; 45:20; 46:6 [cf. 46:9]). It appears that both prophets reflect a similar unease over using the ambiguous *'ĕlōhîm*. (As an aside, note the marked decline in Ezekiel's use of *'ĕlōhîm* as a title for God: the Deuteronomistic History contains some 415 uses of this term for Yahweh, Jeremiah about 115 occurrences, and Deutero-Isaiah and Ezekiel have only 32 each.)

fixed expression.[41] The verb varies to a small degree, but the basic sense is the same. If we compare this with what we find in section C—זנה/הלך/תעה אַחֲרֵי/גִּלּוּלִים (Ezek 20:24 omits the verb but closely parallels 20:16)—it appears quite possible that *gillûlîm* has been substituted for *ʾĕlōhîm*, creating an expression that can be attributed primarily to Ezekiel.[42] The surrogate phrase is somewhat awkward—namely, that the people seek after inanimate objects.[43] It is original to Ezekiel, an intentional product of his strategy to eliminate even the mere mention of *ʾĕlōhîm*.

A second observation involves another common expression apparently modified by Ezekiel. In Deut 4:28, 28:36, and 28:64 we find the phrase עבד אֱלֹהִים . . . עֵץ וָאָבֶן 'to serve gods . . . of wood and stone'.[44] There is a peculiarly similar passage in Ezek 20:32: שרת עֵץ וָאָבֶן 'to worship wood and stone'.[45] By comparison with the phrase in the Deuteronomy passages, the phrase in Ezekiel is patently awkward, for Ezekiel has removed all allusion to any intended divine referent. Even Deutero-Isaiah's lampoon of the craftsman and his material describes the idols as gods (44:15, 17), preceding a finale that closely resembles Ezekiel's "god-less" derision (44:19).

וְהָיָה לְאָדָם לְבָעֵר וַיִּקַּח מֵהֶם וַיָּחָם אַף־יַשִּׂיק וְאָפָה לָחֶם אַף־יִפְעַל־אֵל
וַיִּשְׁתָּחוּ עָשָׂהוּ פֶסֶל וַיִּסְגָּד־לָמוֹ . . . וּשְׁאֵרִיתוֹ לְאֵל עָשָׂה לְפִסְלוֹ [יִסְגּוֹד]
יִסְגָּד־לוֹ וְיִשְׁתַּחוּ וְיִתְפַּלֵּל אֵלָיו וְיֹאמַר הַצִּילֵנִי כִּי אֵלִי אָתָּה . . . וְלֹא־יָשִׁיב

41. Franz Josef Helfmeyer discusses the idiom הלך אחרי and its synonyms, particularly focusing on expressions involving following other (pagan) gods and following Yahweh (*Die Nachfolge Gottes im Alten Testamentum* [Bonn: Hanstein, 1967]).

42. There is good evidence, too, that (in table 2, section C) 1 Kgs 21:26 is a late editorial gloss—an addendum that, along with other such appraisals of the kings (e.g., Deut 29:17; 1 Kgs 16:33; 2 Kgs 17:11–12; 21:11, 21; 23:24), contains summary remarks by the Deuteronomistic redactor (so J. Gray, *I & II Kings* [2d ed.; OTL; Philadelphia: Westminster, 1970] 436, 443; M. Weinfeld, *Deuteronomy 1–11* [AB 5; New York: Doubleday, 1991] 18; and G. H. Jones, *1 & 2 Kings* [NCB; Grand Rapids, Mich.: Eerdmans, 1984] 1.283, 360).

43. Jeremiah appears to make a similar awkward substitution in the expression: וַיֵּלְכוּ אַחֲרֵי הַהֶבֶל וַיֶּהְבָּלוּ (Jer 2:5; compare Jer 2:8; 10:14–15; 16:19). It is likely that this expression is picked up by a later Deuteronomistic redactor in 2 Kgs 17:15 (so J. A. Montgomery, *The Book of Kings* [ICC; Edinburgh: T. & T. Clark, 1951] 469). On the charge that they have followed their own hearts by following other gods, compare Jer 9:13 with Jer 3:17, 16:12, and 18:12. Also note the more ambiguous expressions in Hos 5:11 (צו) and Amos 2:4 (כזב).

44. For the frequent allegation 'to serve gods' (עבד אֱלֹהִים), see also Exod 23:24, 33; Deut 7:4, 16; 8:19; 11:16; 12:30; 13:2, 6, 13; 28:14; 29:18; 30:17; 31:20; Josh 23:7, 16; 24:16, 20; 1 Sam 16:19; 1 Kgs 9:6; 2 Kgs 17:35; Jer 5:19; 11:10; 13:10; 16:13; 25:6; 35:15; 44:3; 2 Chr 7:19.

45. In the Hebrew Bible, the term שרת is used almost exclusively for the Temple service and the worship of Yahweh.

אֶל־לִבּוֹ וְלֹא דַעַת וְלֹא־תְבוּנָה לֵאמֹר חֶצְיוֹ שָׂרַפְתִּי בְמוֹ־אֵשׁ וְאַף אָפִיתִי
עַל־גֶּחָלָיו לֶחֶם אֶצְלֶה בָשָׂר וְאֹכֵל וְיִתְרוֹ לְתוֹעֵבָה אֶעֱשֶׂה לְבוּל עֵץ אֶסְגּוֹד:[46]

(15) Then for the man it becomes fuel; he takes some of it and warms
himself, starts a fire, and bakes bread. *He also makes a god and worships
it; he makes an idol and falls down before it.* . . . (17) *The rest of it he
makes into a god, his idol; he falls down before it,* worships it, and prays
to it saying, "Save me, for you are my god.". . . (19) He does not recall
this (how he made it), without awareness or understanding (enough)
to say, "Half of it I burned in the fire; I baked bread on its coals,
roasted meat, and ate it. And with what's left shall I make into an
abomination? *Shall I fall down before a block of wood?*"

In sum, while Deuteronomy and Deutero-Isaiah disparage idolatry, Ezekiel is
downright blunt about it: devotees of idols do not worship wood and stone
gods; they worship mere wood and stone.

Third, the aversion to describing idols as gods is a theological position
that post-Ezekiel tradition clearly and intentionally adopts. Consider a comparison between Ezekiel's avoidance of *'ĕlōhîm* and the same strategy in the
targumim. Three separate pentateuchal traditions (*Neofiti, Onqelos, Pseudo-
Jonathan*) unanimously and consistently substitute an Aramaic word for idols
(טעות, *tā'ăwāt*) in place of אלהים.[47] *Pseudo-Jonathan* and *Onqelos* uniformly
translate the Hebrew אחרים with Aramaic עממיא (*'ammĕmāyā'*), understanding "other gods" as "idols of the nations," removing any ambiguity inherent
in the Hebrew.[48] Any impression that idols are real or have existence as gods
of other peoples is eliminated. Compare, for example, Deut 8:19 in the MT,
"If you forget the Lord your God (אלהים) and go after other gods (אלהים
אחרים)," with the same passage in *Onqelos*, "If you forget the fear of the Lord
your God (אלוה), and go after the idols of the nations (טעות עממיא)." The
targumim thus prevent any implication that "other gods" exist, leaving no

46. The *Kethiv* of סגד in v. 17b is in brackets. BHS suggests the reading וְיִשְׁתַּחֲוֶה in
vv. 15 and 17c, though this is not necessary, considering that the received form frequently
occurs elsewhere (e.g., Gen 18:2; 19:1; 23:7, 12; Exod 18:7). Similarly, the insertion of לֹ
after דעת in v. 19, as suggested by BHS, is not imperative.

47. See Alexander Sperber, *The Pentateuch according to Targum Onkelos* (The Bible in
Aramaic 1; Leiden: Brill, 1959). The Aramaic is derived from טעא, טעי 'to go astray' (see
Jastrow, p. 542). Note also that the targum renders all occurrences of גלולים in Ezekiel with
טעות.

48. *Neofiti*, a more literal rendering, translates אחרים with אחרניין, thereby producing
the potential for an extremely awkward expression; for example, in some passages (such as
Deut 8:19), this creates the impression that God is an idol: "If you forget the Lord your
God and go after other idols. . . ."

impression that idols have any divine reality.[49] All three traditions reveal an interpretational strategy designed to remove any association between gods and God.[50]

It is this identical theological motivation, I reemphasize, that operated for Ezekiel in his aversion to using *'ĕlōhîm* for pagan gods and idols. This aversion, this avoidance of any association that might legitimize a god other than Yahweh[51] has far-reaching implications, for it suggests that Ezekiel was clearly

49. As an aside, note an analogous example of targumic theological sensitivity. Above, I parenthetically mentioned the decreasing use of *'ĕlōhîm* for the God of Israel in Ezekiel (and also in Deutero-Isaiah). I would suggest now that this was intentional—that the exilic prophets were uneasy about the confusion inherent in the term. Similarly, *Targum Onqelos* takes all biblical occurrences in which *'ĕlōhîm* refers to God and renders them explicitly with the Tetragrammaton. E. T. Rasmussen (*Relationship of God and Man: According to a Text and Targum of Deuteronomy* [Ph.D. diss., Brigham Young University, 1967] 12) understands this aversion in the way described here: *Onqelos* is concerned that the generic term could be misunderstood as referring to gods of other peoples rather than the God of Israel. Using the personal name of God eliminates this possibility.

50. It is interesting to consider the implications that a Second Temple interpreter drew from this same conclusion. The fact that idols represent nothing, that there exists no reality to the gods of the nations, allowed Pseudo-Philo to rewrite the account of Jephthah to declare that the Ammonites had no claim to the land, since their claim was based on the inheritance of a god that did not exist (compare Judg 11:24 with *Bib. Ant.* 39:9).

51. Scholars have contrasted the peculiar absence of the divine epithet *yhwh ṣĕbā'ôt* in Ezekiel with Jeremiah's frequent usage (82 times in the MT; but only 10 times in the LXX). It appears that Ezekiel has replaced this common epithet of his contemporary with *'ădōnāy yhwh* (217 times). W. Kessler suggested that the phrase recollects numinous powers that might be associated with pagan gods ("Aus welchen Gründen wird die Bezeichnung 'Jahwe Zebaoth' in späteren Zeit gemieden?" *Wissenschaftliche Zeitschrift* 7 [1957–58] 767–72). Ezekiel then excludes any use of this expression "weil er die Alt-Judäer ja ganz von einer Beziehung zu solchen dunklen Mächten lösen und sie zur alleinigen Verehrung Jahwes zurückführen wollte" (ibid., 771). Such a connection might be suggested by the expression *ṣĕbā' haššāmayim*, which occurs especially in Deuteronomistic texts and refers most often to astrological objects of idolatrous worship (Deut 4:19; 17:3; 2 Kgs 17:16; 21:3, 5; 23:4–5; Zeph 1:5; Jer 8:2; 19:13; 2 Chr 33:3, 5; as God's enemy in Isa 34:4, compare 24:21; used neutrally in 1 Kgs 22:19 = 2 Chr 18:18; Jer 33:22; Neh 9:6). On the larger context of the biblical usage of *ṣĕbā'ôt* and its replacement in Deuteronomistic texts with *šēm* and in Ezekiel with *kābôd*, see T. N. D. Mettinger, *The Dethronement of Sabaoth: Studies in the Shem and Kabod Theologies* (trans. Frederick H. Cryer; ConBOT 18; Lund: CWK Gleerup, 1982).

As a further but related aside, Jacob Milgrom argues that the Priestly theology negates the basic premises of pagan religion and polytheism: "It (Priestly theology) posits the existence of one supreme God who contends neither with a higher realm nor with competing peers. The world of demons is abolished; there is no struggle with autonomous foes because there are none" ("Priestly ['P'] Source," *ABD* 5.454).

monotheistic, accomplishing his goal in ways different from Deutero-Isaiah but consciously carrying his conviction to a radical extreme in his terminology. Unlike Deutero-Isaiah, the prophet Ezekiel is rarely invoked as a theological voice contributing to the development of monotheism in the religion of Israel. Quite the opposite is true, however; he is one of its loudest voices.[52]

We can also speculate why Ezekiel earnestly mocks idolatry and how his polemic directly engages the paradox involving the presence and absence of God. Ezekiel offers the exiles a proposition: the physical presence of idols indicates their powerlessness. In so doing, Ezekiel provides one element to the argument that the absence of Yahweh's presence indicates God's power.[53] Through this argument, Ezekiel frees the exiles from the conclusion that absence means divine abandonment or defeat. Ironically, then, the judgment against idolatry, which is central to Ezekiel's reason for exile, provides the conceptual means for social-spiritual survival and for hope of return.

Toward a Definition of Idolatry

Having examined Ezekiel's indisputable polemic against idols, we are now in a position to determine the dimensions of idolatry at the time of Ezekiel. This and the following sections will explore the historical context of Ezekiel's opposition to idolatry. I begin by defining idolatry within the biblical tradition. The task is difficult, of course, because of the composite nature of the sources, to which even relative dates can be applied only with a degree of speculation.[54]

---

52. These observations markedly differ from the appraisal of Christopher North, for example, who contrasts Ezekiel with both Hosea (13:2) and Deutero-Isaiah: "Ezekiel is too filled with indignation to busy himself with any rationale or 'philosophy' of idolatry. But when we come to Deutero-Isaiah, Hosea's theme is elaborated in a series of pictures in which the utter fatuity of idolatry and idol-manufacture is exposed" ("The Essence of Idolatry," 158).

Indeed, in none of the following comprehensive studies and collections of studies on monotheism in Israel does Ezekiel figure significantly in the discussion: Keel (ed.), *Monotheismus im alten Israel und seiner Umwelt*; Lang (ed.), *Der einzige Gott*; Ernst Haag (ed.), *Gott, der einzige: Zur Entstehung des Monotheismus in Israel* (Freiburg: Herder, 1985); Walter Dietrich and Martin A. Klopfenstein (eds.), *Ein Gott allein? JHWH-Verehrung und biblischer Monotheismus im Kontext der israelitischen und altorientalischen Religionsgeschichte* (OBO 139; Freiburg: Universitätsverlag / Göttingen: Vandenhoeck & Ruprecht, 1994); and Fritz Stolz, *Einführung in den biblischen Monotheismus* (Darmstadt: Wissenschaftliche Buchgesellschaft, 1996), esp. the section on pp. 168–72 devoted to Ezekiel; and Gnuse, *No Other Gods*.

53. I will develop this point in chaps. 3 and 4 below.

54. The following studies review the biblical evidence and especially seek to understand the development of the prohibition: R. H. Pfeiffer, "The Oldest Decalogue," *JBL* 43

The Decalogue contains the most categorical definition of proscribed worship in the Hebrew Bible (Deut 5:7–9a and Exod 20:3–5a).

לֹא יִהְיֶה־לְךָ אֱלֹהִים אֲחֵרִים עַל־פָּנָי: לֹא־תַעֲשֶׂה־לְךָ פֶסֶל כָּל־תְּמוּנָה אֲשֶׁר בַּשָּׁמַיִם מִמַּעַל וַאֲשֶׁר בָּאָרֶץ מִתָּחַת וַאֲשֶׁר בַּמַּיִם מִתַּחַת לָאָרֶץ: לֹא־ תִשְׁתַּחֲוֶה לָהֶם וְלֹא תָעָבְדֵם כִּי אָנֹכִי יְהוָה אֱלֹהֶיךָ אֵל קַנָּא [55]

(1924) 294–310; idem, "The Polemic against Idolatry in the Old Testament," *JBL* 43 (1924) 229–40; Karl-Heinz Bernhardt, *Gott und Bild* (Berlin: Evangelische, 1956); North, "The Essence of Idolatry," 151–60; J. Faur, "The Biblical Idea of Idolatry," *JQR* 69 (1978) 1–15; Julien Ries, "Idolatry," *Encyclopedia of Religion* (ed. Mircea Eliade; trans. Kristine Anderson; New York: Macmillan, 1986) 7.72–82; and Charles A. Kennedy, "The Semantic Field of the Term 'Idolatry,'" in *Uncovering Ancient Stones: Essays in Memory of H. Neil Richardson* (ed. Lewis M. Hopfe; Winona Lake, Ind.: Eisenbrauns, 1994) 193–204. As a rule, these presentations fail to deal adequately with material remains. Other studies have focused on the archaeological record, such as John S. Holladay, Jr., "Religion in Israel and Judah under the Monarchy: An Explicitly Archaeological Approach," in *Ancient Israelite Religion* (ed. Patrick D. Miller Jr. et al.; Philadelphia: Fortress, 1987) 249–99. A recent study has attempted to remedy the neglected dialogue between biblical and extrabiblical (written and nonwritten) evidence, at least to a limited degree; see Susan Ackerman, *Under Every Green Tree: Popular Religion in Sixth-Century Judah* (HSM 46; Atlanta: Scholars Press, 1992). Most recently, T. N. D. Mettinger has examined the question of Israelite aniconism through a systematic comparative analysis of other cultures in the ancient Near East (see *No Graven Image? Israelite Aniconism in Its Ancient Near Eastern Context* [ConBOT 42; Stockholm: Almqvist & Wiksell, 1995]).

55. The wording in these verses differs slightly in vv. 8/4: כל־תמונה (Deuteronomy) and וכל־תמונה (Exodus). Moshe Weinfeld considers this only a minor, stylistic variation (*Deuteronomy 1–11*, 290–91). This opinion is contrary to Frank-Lothar Hossfeld (*Der Dekalog* [OBO 45; Göttingen: Vandenhoeck & Ruprecht, 1982] 21–26), who argues that the Deuteronomic version connects "worshiping and serving" back to the "other gods," while the later Exodus version connects these verbs with "graven image and likeness." (Hossfeld's exacting source-critical study of the two versions considers the most minor variation a matter of significance.) While Hossfeld is convincing in his relative dating of the two versions, Deuteronomy being the earlier version, Weinfeld is also correct that both the Exodus version and the Deuteronomic version closely associate foreign gods and their respective idols (*Deuteronomy 1–11*, 291; see further below). Weinfeld rightly sees the asyndetic expression in Deut 5:8 as a stylistic variation and notes this usage in Deut 4:16, 23, and 25. The syndetic version in Exodus merely tried to express explicitly that the direct object ('them') in vv. 9/5 referred to both אלהים אחרים (7/3) and פסל כל־תמונה (8/4). Furthermore, note that Exodus 34, which Hossfeld sees as the ancestor of the Deuteronomic version, closely connects the prohibition against worshiping other gods (v. 14) with injunctions against physical representations of pagan gods (vv. 13 and 17). (For Hossfeld, though, Exod 34:17 is a secondary insertion [*Der Dekalog*, 268].)

For a review of the issues involved in the redaction of the Decalogue and the origin of Israelite legal traditions, consult Hossfeld, ibid.; also J. J. Stamm and M. E. Andrew, *The Ten Commandments in Recent Research* (SBT n.s. 2; Naperville, Ill.: Allenson, 1967) 13–75.

(7/3) You shall have no other gods besides me.[56] (8/4) You shall not make for yourself a graven image, a likeness of anything that is in the heavens above, that is on the earth beneath, or that is in the water under the earth. (9/5) You shall not worship them or serve them, for I am the Lord your God, a jealous god.

This passage in both Deuteronomy and Exodus combines a prohibition against worshiping other gods (vv. 7/3) with a prohibition against fashioning images in the likeness of any natural objects (vv. 8/4). That the worship of other gods is forbidden is clear, but the second prohibition has two possible implications. First, it may bear close connection with the first prohibition and therefore refer to the making of images of pagan gods.[57] Second, it may indicate a ban on images altogether. On the one hand, Weinfeld argues that both commandments (vv. 7/3 and 8/4) are essentially restatements of each other: "There is no distinction in the Bible and in the ancient Near East between 'gods' and their representatives, the 'idols.' Having gods means having idols."[58] He suggests further that vv. 8/4 reflect a general aniconic tendency in Israel (citing Exod 34:17; Lev 19:4; 26:1; Deut 4:15; 27:15) and says that this "seems to have its roots in the Israelite tradition from its beginning."[59] However, the Sinai prohibition alone does not support this conclusion. Indeed, considering the reference to Yahweh's jealousy (vv. 9/5), the commandment more plainly presumes a prohibition against worshiping other gods and their images (whatever forms they may take). Thus it is not certain that a prohibition of images of Yahweh is implied in the Decalogue.

A more comprehensive prohibition of all images, including those of Yahweh, is emphatically expressed in Deut 4:15–19 (note also v. 12).

וְנִשְׁמַרְתֶּם מְאֹד לְנַפְשֹׁתֵיכֶם כִּי לֹא רְאִיתֶם כָּל־תְּמוּנָה בְּיוֹם דִּבֶּר יְהוָה
אֲלֵיכֶם בְּחֹרֵב מִתּוֹךְ הָאֵשׁ: פֶּן־תַּשְׁחִתוּן וַעֲשִׂיתֶם לָכֶם פֶּסֶל תְּמוּנַת כָּל־סָמֶל
תַּבְנִית זָכָר אוֹ נְקֵבָה: תַּבְנִית כָּל־בְּהֵמָה אֲשֶׁר בָּאָרֶץ תַּבְנִית כָּל־צִפּוֹר כָּנָף

---

56. The *crux interpretum* in this verse is the meaning of עַל־פָּנַי 'before me'. See Weinfeld, *Deuteronomy 1–11*, 276–77; and A. S. van der Woude, "פָּנִים," *TLOT* 2.1013. BDB 818b offers several suggestions: 'before me', literally as 'in front of me' and figuratively as 'in preference to me'; also 'in addition to me'. The term may combine the range of meanings ('besides me'), emphasizing, to be sure, the exclusive nature of the command.

57. See above, n. 47. Exod 34:11–17 provides a covenant tradition (note v. 28), perhaps a more ancient one, that prohibits both the worship and manufacture of gods. See the discussion in Pfeiffer, "The Oldest Decalogue," 294–310; and Hossfeld on Exod 34:12–15a (*Der Dekalog*, 262–63).

58. Weinfeld (*Deuteronomy 1–11*, 291) seems to suggest that this equivalence is verbally made in the expression אלהי מסכה (Exod 34:17 and Lev 19:4; note also Exod 20:23).

59. Ibid., 291. Stamm and Andrew present a similar argument that aniconic worship was the original intent of the commandment (*The Ten Commandments*, 83–86).

אֲשֶׁר תָּעוּף בַּשָּׁמָיִם: תַּבְנִית כָּל־רֹמֵשׂ בָּאֲדָמָה תַּבְנִית כָּל־דָּגָה אֲשֶׁר־בַּמַּיִם
מִתַּחַת לָאָרֶץ: וּפֶן־תִּשָּׂא עֵינֶיךָ הַשָּׁמַיְמָה וְרָאִיתָ אֶת־הַשֶּׁמֶשׁ וְאֶת־הַיָּרֵחַ
וְאֶת־הַכּוֹכָבִים כֹּל צְבָא הַשָּׁמַיִם וְנִדַּחְתָּ וְהִשְׁתַּחֲוִיתָ לָהֶם וַעֲבַדְתָּם אֲשֶׁר
חָלַק יְהוָה אֱלֹהֶיךָ אֹתָם לְכֹל הָעַמִּים תַּחַת כָּל־הַשָּׁמָיִם:

(15) Take careful heed for yourselves: since you did not see any form
on the day Yahweh spoke to you at Horeb from the midst of the fire,
(16) do not act ruinously by making for yourselves a graven image in
the form of any image, the shape of either a man or a woman, (17) the
shape of any beast that is on the earth, the shape of any bird that flies
in the sky, (18) the shape of any crawling things on the earth, the
shape of any fish that is in the water under the earth; (19) do not lift
your eyes toward heaven, that when you see the sun and the moon
and the stars and the the hosts of heaven, you go astray and you worship them and serve them, those things that Yahweh your God has al-
lotted to all the peoples under the heaven.

Christopher North characterizes this passage as "a further amplification" on
Exod 20:4 and Deut 5:8.[60] The beginning of the passage (as well as v. 12)
suggests that, since the Israelites saw no form of Yahweh, the use of an idol in
the form of any earthly creature was forbidden. The text then ends with a
prohibition against worshiping heavenly bodies as substitutes for Yahweh. In
other words, for the Deuteronomist it seems quite clear that idolatry included both the fashioning of an idol as an object with which to worship Yahweh and the worship of other gods (and their images).[61] Indeed, this suggests
to Labuschagne that, for the later Priestly tradition as well, idolatry would
have included the worship of other gods and the use of physical representations (image or portrait) to represent the divine.[62]

60. North, "The Essence of Idolatry," 151. G. von Rad similarly calls it a "theological
exposé" on the commandment and dates it to the exile (*Old Testament Theology* [2 vols.;
trans. D. M. G. Stalker; Edinburgh: Oliver & Boyd, 1962–65] 1.216).

61. In passing, note C. J. Labuschagne's observations regarding the idol polemics in
Deuteronomy 32 and Jeremiah 10, which include statements of Yahweh's incomparability
(Deut 32:31, 39; Jer 10:16); he comments that these "expressions of his incomparability
emerged from the struggle against idolatry" (*The Incomparability of Yahweh in the Old Testament* [Leiden: Brill, 1966] 72). Additionally, he suggests that these types of passages in
Deuteronomy (along with, e.g., Deut 4:7, 34, 35, 39) should be dated to just before or during the exile (ibid., 73–74). It is also an exilic redactor of the Deuteronomistic History that
plainly equates Israel's demand for a king with idolatry in 1 Sam 8:8 (see H. Wildberger,
"בחר," *TLOT* 1.218–19, here and on Joshua 24, which also in exilic context demands that
Israel transfer any allegiance to other gods to Yahweh alone).

62. Labuschagne, *The Incomparability of Yahweh,* 72. Such an approach would trace a
progression in Israelite proscription of images but would place the complete ban on images

That Ezekiel considered these two elements of idolatry one is uncertain. He may well have, given the contemporary textual evidence for the matter discussed above (Deuteronomic and Priestly). Moreover, it is reasonable to presume that Ezekiel saw no physical representation of Yahweh in the Temple. He nowhere makes reference to a legitimate object depicting Yahweh's presence itself (except for the cherubim, which form a platform for that presence). If such an image of Yahweh did exist, it may have more readily fallen within Ezekiel's category of idol. The offensive items mentioned as objects of worship in Ezek 8:10–12—the גִּלּוּלִים and the representations in the חַדְרֵי מַשְׂכִּיתוֹ—are not identified with any specificity but certainly recall Deut 4:17–18.

The problem of identifying and classifying images is known elsewhere. For example, the distinction between objects involved in worship and objects of worship may be confused in 1 Kgs 12:28–32. The bulls Jeroboam allegedly set up at Dan and Bethel were perhaps intended to represent the thrones of an invisible Yahweh, similar to the cherubim in the Temple. The Deuteronomistic writer, however, clearly interprets them as substitute gods.[63] Whether or not this was an intentional misinterpretation is beside the point; the meaning of the objects themselves was not self-evident and risked misidentification.[64]

---

in the period contemporary with Ezekiel. For example, Pfeiffer's schematization of the pentateuchal sources sees phases in the history of idolatry in Israel ("The Polemic against Idolatry in the Old Testament"). The stage encompassing the period of the Deuteronomic reform, Ezekiel, and the Priestly legislation altogether prohibits images of God. See also Julien Ries, "Idolatry," 73. Both H. T. Obbink ("Jahwebilder," *ZAW* 47 [1929] 264–74) and H. G. Reventlow (*Gebot und Predigt im Dekalog* [Gütersloh: Mohn, 1962] 29–31) argue that the commandment at first did not pertain to images of Yahweh. Nevertheless, a consensus considers the exilic period the terminus ad quem for a complete ban on images.

63. See Carl D. Evans, "Cult Images, Royal Policies and the Origins of Aniconism," in *The Pitcher Is Broken: Memorial Essays for Gösta W. Ahlström* (ed. Steven W. Holloway and Lowell K. Handy; JSOTSup 190; Sheffield: Sheffield Academic Press, 1995) 192–212. Hosea's reference to the עֵגֶל שֹׁמְרוֹן (8:5), which is clearly treated as idolatrous, may be an example of a similar misrepresentation.

64. Perhaps the iconography of cherubim, as opposed to bulls, was quite unequivocal as a throne and was therefore less subject to misinterpretation (see T. N. D. Mettinger, *In Search of God* [Philadelphia: Fortress, 1988] 127–31; and idem, *The Dethronement of Sabaoth*, 19–24, for the iconographic convention of cherub-decorated thrones). Recently, Mettinger has described the cherubim-throne iconography as "empty-seat aniconism" (*No Graven Image?* 139).

Curiously, Ezekiel reports quite casually on the images of cherubim on the walls of the Temple in 41:17–18, 20, 25. This aspect of apparently acceptable imagery led José Faur to distinguish between decorative, legitimate iconolatry (e.g., Exod 25:18–22; 26:1, 31; 36:8, 35; 37:7–9; 1 Kgs 6:21–29, 32, 35; 7:29, 36; 8:5–9; 2 Chr 3:7, 10–14) and illegitimate idolatry, that is, the actual worship of images ("The Biblical Idea of Idolatry," 1–15).

Even considering the potential for misinterpreting an object's intended meaning, it is clear that the visions in Ezekiel 1–11 mention no object from which the presence of God withdraws; rather, the כָּבוֹד is described as resting over the כְּרוּבִים (9:3 sg.; 10:18, 19 pl.; 11:22 pl.). As with the Priestly description of the אֲרוֹן, the cherubim represent the seat of the divine (compare the description in Exod 25:10–22 P). The scene in Ezekiel recollects quite closely the statement in the so-called Ark Narrative, in which the ark is called אֲרוֹן בְּרִית־יְהוָה צְבָאוֹת יֹשֵׁב הַכְּרֻבִים 'the ark of the covenant of Yahweh-of-hosts, who is enthroned on the cherubim'.[65] The same situation holds in the vision of the restored Temple: the כָּבוֹד does not return to dwell within any physical object. As with the theophanic visions in the Priestly tradition, the emphasis is on the overwhelming dimension of God's presence in the Temple (Ezek 43:5b): וְהִנֵּה מָלֵא כְבוֹד־יהוה הַבָּיִת.[66] In the visions of God's departure from the Temple, the emphasis is on the removal of the supernatural manifestation of the divine כָּבוֹד. The description served to portray God's absence from the Temple. It was all the more appropriate that Yahweh should not be described as removing his presence from any physical image. Nothing remained behind. There could be no denying his absence, though his presence was a matter of conviction.

We have broadly reviewed testimony more or less contemporary with Ezekiel. Considering Ezekiel's own monotheistic position, as well as his widespread polemic against idolatrous worship, it seems certain that Ezekiel would have associated idolatry with other gods and the material representation of other gods. From our brief review of Ezekiel's emphasis on the divine כָּבוֹד that departs the Temple, we can suggest that Ezekiel would have considered the material representation of Yahweh idolatrous, though, admittedly, on this matter the evidence is less certain.

Idolatry as Historical Reality

A fundamental basis for Torrey's thesis that Ezekiel is a pseudepigraph is his assertion that the sins recounted in Ezekiel (especially chap. 8) are reflections of sins during Manasseh's age (evidence of which comes from 2 Kings)

65. 1 Sam 4:4; also 2 Sam 6:2; 1 Chr 13:6; 2 Sam 22:11 = Ps 18:11; 2 Kgs 19:15 = Isa 37:16; Ps 80:2; Ps 99:1.
66. Note also 2 Sam 7:5; 1 Kgs 8:27 (= 1 Chr 6:18); Ps 99:5; Ps 132:7, 13–14; Lam 2:1; 1 Chr 2:5–6; 28:2; Isa 66:1. Perhaps an aspect of the inadequacy of a temple for representing God's presence is expressed in Hos 8:1, where בֵית־יהוה refers to the land of Israel, not a temple (though occurrences of Yahweh's "house" elsewhere generally refer to a temple: Hos 2:10; 9:8, 15; Jer 12:7; Zech 9:8; see also Hans Walter Wolff, *Hosea* [Hermeneia; Philadelphia: Fortress, 1974] 137).

and were not practiced during the early sixth century. While Yehezkel Kaufmann and Moshe Greenberg disagree with Torrey's conclusions, they generally support the view that Ezekiel's condemnation of contemporary idolatrous practices had no basis in historical reality.[67]

Kaufmann's views are well known.[68] He draws a sharp line between royally sanctioned cults and popular religion. Moreover, even within this distinction, Israelite religion was monotheistic and nonmythological from its inception. When the Hebrew Bible speaks of Yahweh's confronting foreign gods, the gods are mere idols, not living, divine beings: "Idolatry is the worship of an anonymous idol, an idol that represents no god at all, but is itself to be worshiped."[69] While biblical evidence suggests an occasional royal sanction of pagan deities, especially during the reign of Manasseh, this sort of influence was altogether slight.[70] In still other cases, argues Kaufmann, objects and actions labeled idolatrous in the Bible are evidence of fetishism involving Yahweh, not other gods.[71] Especially in popular practice, Yahweh may have been worshiped in pagan ways—with idols—but idols do not reflect a belief in pagan gods. Kaufmann calls this form of worshiping Yahweh—that is, with practices that incorporate pagan ways—"vestigial idolatry," which he distinguishes from the pagan practice of worshiping an idol qua idol.[72]

According to Kaufmann, the time of Jeremiah and Ezekiel is no exception to this picture.[73] Jeremiah condemns his contemporaries for worshiping idols (8:19; 10:5, 8, 14; 16:18), worshiping at high places (13:27; 17:1–4), and worshiping astral bodies (19:13)—primarily marks of vestigial idolatry. The official sanction of paganism by Manasseh was never repeated after the reforms of Josiah. Kaufmann considers Ezekiel 8, the vision of Temple abominations, to be a clear aberration, particularly when compared with the eyewitness testimony of Jeremiah: "Jeremiah was accustomed to speak in the

---

67. See Y. Kaufmann, *The Religion of Israel: From Its Beginnings to the Babylonian Exile* (trans. Moshe Greenberg; Chicago: University of Chicago Press, 1960) 401–46; and Greenberg, "Prolegomenon," in *Pseudo-Ezekiel and the Original Prophecy and Critical Articles by Shalom Spiegel and C. C. Torrey* (ed. M. Greenberg; New York: KTAV, 1970) xviii–xxviii. Compare, however, G. Fohrer, *Die Hauptprobleme des Buches Ezechiel* (BZAW 72; Berlin: Alfred Töpelmann, 1952) 164–77; and V. Herntrich, *Ezechielprobleme* (BZAW 61; Giessen: Alfred Töpelmann, 1932) 52–55.

68. Kaufmann, *Religion of Israel,* esp. pp. 7–20, 133–47.

69. Ibid., 13.

70. Ibid., 140–41.

71. By *fetishism* he means "the belief that divine and magical powers inhere in certain natural or man-made objects and that man can activate these powers through fixed rituals" (Kaufmann, *Religion of Israel,* 14).

72. Ibid., 142.

73. Ibid., 401–46.

temple and visited it on other occasions during the reigns of Jehoiakim and Zedekiah. Yet he never sees in it the abominations mentioned in Ezekiel 8."[74] Ezekiel prophesied solely to the exiles, delivering an uncompromising message of doom for Jerusalem. The exiles must separate themselves from that fate. In this context, for this purpose, the vision in chap. 8 is altogether a "fantasy," a "parable," not a report of current practices in the Temple.

> What Ezekiel sees are shadows of the past. He had heard in his youth of the dreadful abominations that took place in the Temple during Manasseh's time. . . . Retribution still clamors for satisfaction, and its claim will not be met until the city and Temple are destroyed.[75]

Thus, according to Kaufmann, there was no true post-Josianic relapse into idolatry among Ezekiel's audience.

Greenberg draws similar conclusions: "Ezekiel's visions must therefore be discounted as untrustworthy witnesses to current Temple practice."[76] Greenberg ascribes the idolatry in Ezekiel to secret pagan practices, not public, officially sponsored cults. Such clandestine practices may have occurred here and there. But after Josiah's death no officially sponsored idolatrous activities were reinstituted in the Temple, where they could not have persisted without royal approval.[77] This distinction is fundamental to Greenberg's argument, since he constrasts Ezekiel with Jeremiah, who certainly witnesses idolatrous practices (e.g., Jer 7:17–18; 11:13; 13:27; 17:1–4; 19:2–13; 32:35; 44:15–16) but who observed them outside the Temple. Thus they are "unofficial private cults."[78] Based on this argument, Greenberg concludes that Ezekiel offers unreliable testimony to the official religious climate just prior to the exile.

Is this strict distinction between popular and official religion justified? Moreover, it seems that vestigial idolatry covers a multitude of sins, so to speak. Susan Ackerman pursues some of these issues when she examines the evidence of popular religion in late-seventh- and sixth-century Judah.[79] Introducing the nature of the question, she asserts,

> Beliefs and rituals which are a part of the religion of the king may just as easily be "popular" as those which belong to the cult of the commoner; similarly the Temple may as likely contain "popular" religion as the high places of the *bāmôt*.[80]

---

74. Ibid., 407.
75. Ibid., 430.
76. Greenberg, "Prolegomenon," xxii.
77. Ibid., xxiii.
78. Ibid., xxi.
79. Ackerman, *Under Every Green Tree.*
80. Ibid., 1.

Furthermore, it seems that the elements of pagan and idolatrous practices that Ezekiel's contemporary, Jeremiah, decries could not have been possible without at least the tacit approval of the monarchy (for example, 17:16–8:3; 19:1–5). Certainly their continuation questions the effectiveness of any alleged reforms. That they continued even in surreptitious fashion indicates less than success.

Consider, for example, Ezekiel 8, which has been a focal point in this debate. Greenberg argued that the scene of pagan practices represents a "montage of whatever pagan rites ever were conducted at the Jerusalem temple," not a description of actualities in 592 B.C.E.[81] And as we saw, Kaufmann admitted only to the possibility of private practices, not public activity with royal support. However, it is not clear that the activities that Ezekiel 8 describes are public practices. While no doubt the distinction between officially sanctioned public ritual and private practice is overdrawn, as we have just asserted, some of the rites listed in chap. 8 are explicitly described as private. For example, in order for Ezekiel to see כָל־תַּבְנִית רֶמֶשׂ וּבְהֵמָה שֶׁקֶץ וְכָל־גִּלוּלֵי בֵית יִשְׂרָאֵל מְחֻקֶּה עַל־הַקִּיר (8:10), he has to burrow through a wall (8:7–8). Moreover, the elders of Israel are said to be doing these things "in the dark" (8:12).

It is outside the scope of this study to detail the material and epigraphic evidence for idolatry at the time of Ezekiel. Suffice it to say that the issue does not so much involve the evidence as it does its interpretation. Recent discussion of Israelite religion as it was practiced in monarchic Israel, particularly as it involved the worship of non-Yahwistic deities, is quite extensive.[82] The extrabiblical evidence, generally, falls within four categories: architectural, artifactual, artistic, and epigraphic.[83] The first category, which includes the re-

---

81. Greenberg, *Ezekiel 1–20*, 201.

82. Generally, see the review of evidence in Ackerman, *Under Every Green Tree*, 46–99. Note also the data and discussion in Holladay, "Religion in Israel and Judah under the Monarchy," 249–99; and William G. Dever, *Recent Archaeological Discoveries and Biblical Research* (Seattle: University of Washington Press, 1990) 119–66. The evidence for the cult of the goddess Asherah in ancient Israel has been a particularly well-worn trail. Sources for this evidence and analysis include the following: J. B. Pritchard, *Palestinian Figurines: In Relation to Certain Goddesses Known through Literature* (AOS 24; New Haven: American Oriental Society, 1943); Walter A. Maier III, *ʾAšerah: Extrabiblical Evidence* (HSM 37; Atlanta: Scholars Press, 1986); Saul Olyan, *Asherah and the Cult of Yahweh in Israel* (SBL Monograph Series 34; Atlanta: Scholars Press, 1988); Richard J. Pettey, *Asherah, Goddess of Israel* (American University Studies Series 7, Theology and Religion 74; New York: Peter Lang, 1990); and Steve A. Wiggins, *A Reassessment of "Asherah"* (Kevelaer: Butzon & Bercker / Neukirchen-Vluyn: Neukirchener Verlag, 1993).

83. We are here following Holladay's categories ("Religion in Israel and Judah under the Monarchy," 252).

mains of sanctuaries (such as at Ta ʿanach and Arad), offers evidence of cultic practice but often provides little information about the identity of deities or how they were worshiped. Artifactual data, such as altars and incense stands provide more detailed evidence of cultic practice, though again they generally do not supply a means to identify the deities worshiped. Of this artifactual data, however, a relatively large body of evidence can be gathered for the fig-ureless standing stones (*maṣṣēbôt*), which the Hebrew Bible quite clearly as-sociates with idolatry.[84] Of these four categories, epigraphic and artistic remains provide the most explicit evidence for understanding idolatrous and non-Yahwistic worship.[85] In light of this manifold testimony, no real gap ex-ists between Ezekiel's portrayal of idolatrous practices (as listed in above in table 1) and either Jeremiah's depictions or other material and epigraphic re-mains.[86] Indeed, when Greenberg concedes that the "secret cults" in Ezek 8:10–12 "are another story and may have been practiced in Ezekiel's time,"[87] it seems that Greenberg has drawn a distinction that ultimately undermines his conclusion that Ezekiel's idol polemic was not based in historical reality.

Here, however, we must consider Jeffrey Tigay's important onomastic study of Iron Age Israel and its implications for understanding Israelite reli-gion during the monarchic period.[88] From an exhaustive analysis of theo-phoric names (Yahwistic versus non-Yahwistic),[89] Tigay computes the ratio of Yahwistic names to pagan names as 94.1% to 5.9%, which not inciden-tally is close to that found in the Hebrew Bible (96% to 4%). While he no-tices tokens of pagan influence, such as in peripheral zones (for example, Kuntillet ʿAjrud) and capital cities, the evidence presents a historical picture

84. Exod 23:24; 34:13; Lev 26:1; Deut 7:5; 16:22; 1 Kgs 14:23; 2 Kgs 3:2; 10:26–27; 17:10; 18:4; 23:14; Hos 10:1–2; Mic 5:12 (but cf. Gen 35:14; Exod 24:4; Isa 19:19). This evidence is the central focus of Mettinger's thesis (*No Graven Image?* 135–97), which will be discussed below. See also Karel van der Toorn, "Worshipping Stones: On the Deification of Cult Symbols," *JNSL* 23 (1996) 1ff.

85. For a review of this evidence, see P. Kyle McCarter Jr., "Aspects of the Religion of the Israelite Monarchy: Biblical and Epigraphic Data," in *Ancient Israelite Religion* (ed. Patrick D. Miller Jr. et al.; Philadelphia: Fortress, 1987) 137–55; and Dever, *Recent Archae-ological Discoveries and Biblical Research*, 119–66.

86. To a large extent, it seems that Kaufmann's label "fetishism" was aimed at weak-ening a straightforward interpretation of the archaeologically recovered physical evidence.

87. Greenberg, *Ezekiel 1–20*, 202.

88. J. Tigay, *You Shall Have No Other Gods before Me: Israelite Religion in the Light of Hebrew Inscriptions* (HSS 31; Atlanta: Scholars Press, 1986); for a précis of this larger work, see idem, "Israelite Religion: The Onomastic and Epigraphic Evidence," in *Ancient Israelite Religion* (ed. Patrick D. Miller Jr. et al.; Philadelphia: Fortress, 1987) 157–94. Most of Tigay's evidence is concentrated within the eighth–sixth centuries B.C.E.

89. See esp. his appendixes A–E.

of an "overwhelmingly Yahwistic society in the heartland of Israelite settlement."[90] Such a conclusion appears to support the views of Kaufmann and Greenberg, namely, that the Deuteronomistic and prophetic polemic against idolatry and the worship of foreign gods stems "largely from prophetic hyperbole and the historiographic need to explain a catastrophe that would otherwise seem inexplicable."[91]

While Tigay certainly demonstrates that a strong heritage of Yahwism was in place, his assessment of the biblical witness is not indisputable. It is just as likely to see a developing monotheism and an aniconic tradition as the context for the invective of Jeremiah, Ezekiel, and the Deuteronomist. Indeed, it is precisely in the context of a strong heritage of Yahwism—a Yahweh-alone movement—that Ezekiel's polemic fits most neatly.[92] Ezekiel's demand for exclusive commitment to Yahweh was not unique. Ezekiel was insisting quite emphatically that Israel have no other gods before—or alongside of—Yahweh. As Tigay admits, "Northwest Semitic personal names, even those employed in polytheistic groups, rarely invoke more than one deity in a single name."[93] An extensive picture of the worship of gods in addition to Yahweh, then, might not be available in the onomastic evidence (regardless of the size of the database), particularly if the general culture was strongly influenced by Yahwism and other deities were secondary. For the Deuteronomist, Jeremiah, and Ezekiel, Yahwism was exclusive and did not tolerate any other deities, and this is the emphasis we perceive in Ezekiel's polemic. Furthermore, Mettinger's recent investigation of the aniconic tradition has suggested a similar portrait of a strong Yahwistic heritage in Israel.[94] Investigating the question of Israelite aniconism especially from the archaeological record, he suggests that the *maṣṣēbâ* is an aniconic symbol and that Israel's explicit and programmatic aniconism ("sacred emptiness") developed from a general West Semitic de facto aniconism. In other words, these unfolding ideological convictions are the theological standards out of which Ezekiel forms his message. Ezekiel's polemic is most effective if we view it in the context of convictions that already have some legitimacy, acceptance, and support.

90. Tigay, *You Shall Have No Other Gods before Me,* 36.

91. Tigay, "Israelite Religion," 158.

92. For the expression "Yahweh-alone movement," see Bernhard Lang's outline of five stages in the development from polytheism to an eighth-century B.C.E. Yahweh-alone movement, culminating in actual monotheism during the exilic period ("Die Jahwe-allein-Bewegung," in *Der einzige Gott,* 47–83; also chap. 1 of Lang's, *Monotheism and the Prophetic Minority: An Essay in Biblical History and Sociology* [SWBA 1; Sheffield: Almond, 1983]; and note Morton Smith's *Palestinian Parties and Politics That Shaped the Old Testament* (New York: Columbia University Press, 1971), upon which Lang builds.

93. Tigay, *You Shall Have No Other Gods before Me,* 6.

94. Mettinger, *No Graven Image?* esp. chap. 7.

Finally, one still faces the problem that Torrey raised: Why did the Deuteronomistic historian go back to Manasseh's time in order to explain Jerusalem's destruction (2 Kgs 21:10–15, note *gillûlîm* in v. 11; 23:26–27; 24:3–4)? This issue is inexorably intertwined with matters involving Deuteronomistic redaction. The levels of composition suggest that the fall of Jerusalem was not the only motivation for that work. One might even hazard the opinion that the Deuteronomist's expectation and hope for the future of the Davidic monarchy influenced the neglect in updating the work to include royal sanction of current heathen practices. There would be less resignation to condemning the monarchy completely when such heinous sins were relegated to the hoary past.[95]

Certainly, the primary explanation for the fall of Jerusalem in the Deuteronomistic History appears to be the sins of Manasseh.[96] Thus, Ezekiel's assertion that "the son shall not suffer for the iniquity of the father" (18:20b; see also Jer 31:29–30; Ezek 18:25; 33:17, 20) may be aimed directly at the Deuteronomistic interpretation of the fall of Jerusalem. The people's response in 33:10 may represent Ezekiel's accomplishment in convincing his audience. But we need not conclude that he achieved this persuasion at the expense of the evidence.

§2. Divine Images in the Book of Ezekiel

Section 1 analyzed Ezekiel's terminology for idols, especially in the context of Israelite thought and practice. We saw that Ezekiel crafts some of his own vocabulary, terminology that expresses the exclusivity of Yahweh in relation to any presumed divine powers of idols. For Ezekiel, illegitimate expressions of God's presence lie at the very heart of the exile, for the offensive practices allied with these expressions precipitate destruction. In short, Ezekiel describes and condemns the worship Israel practiced at home.

Section 2 will look at the rhetoric Ezekiel develops in the context of the exile. With ironic and potentially ruinous effect, a segment of the Judean population is deported to Babylonia—a land where divine images were a legitimate and an official feature of the cult. It was one task to find an adequate

---

95. Morton Smith argues that Josiah's death contradicted the Deuteronomistic theology and created the need to cast back to Manasseh for the culprit ("The Veracity of Ezekiel, the Sins of Manasseh, and Jeremiah 44:18," *ZAW* 87 [1975] 13–14).

96. Nevertheless, the Deuteronomistic History is not completely silent on the religious sins of kings following Josiah. (On this, see especially Fohrer, *Die Hauptprobleme des Buches Ezechiel*, 164–71.) The stereotypical phrase in the Deuteronomistic History, "to do evil in the eyes of Yahweh," indicts kings of Israel and Judah for religious apostasy and therefore indicates that Jehoahaz, Jehoiakim, Jehoiachin, and Zedekiah (respectively, 2 Kgs 23:32, 37; 24:9, 19) allowed illicit practices to continue.

explanation for defeat and exile: Ezekiel accused Israel of cultic unfaithfulness. It was quite another task, however, to defend Yahweh against an ideology that associated both international loss and victory with the gods. As the
nation goes, so go the gods—an argument the *rab-shakeh* employs (2 Kgs
18:33–35).[97] While the prophets might argue that Yahweh was using Babylon as an instrument of vengeance on Israel,[98] one wonders how theologically
effective this message was. If Israel had been defeated by Babylon, perhaps it
was not Yahweh who was running the show but the Babylonian gods themselves, who would then appear superior to Yahweh. How could Ezekiel claim
idolatry was the cause of their present plight when the victor worshiped his
deities with idols? Thus Ezekiel faced another challenge on the Babylonian
religiopolitical front, a place of exiled defeat where the Babylonian gods of
the conquering nation were officially and publicly worshiped with wood and
stone.

Having already discussed Ezekiel's rhetoric of theodicy (that exile was the
punishment for worshiping lifeless objects rather than Yahweh), I will now
present the argument Ezekiel develops to discredit altogether the existence of
divine presence within cult statues, a concept propagated by Babylonian religious language and practice. We will see that Ezekiel and his audience were
aware of the concepts associated with the construction of cult statues, a well-
documented subject in Mesopotamian texts. Furthermore, while Ezekiel
never directly used the phrase *image of God*, he knew of a usage similar to that
found in the Priestly tradition (Gen 1:26–27; 5:1–3; 9:6). With this knowledge the prophet contrasted the Mesopotamian concept of a divine statue as
the image of god (*ṣalam ili/ilāni*) with the Priestly theology that man is made
in the image of God (*ṣelem ʾĕlōhîm*). In so doing he achieves a measure of victory by blunting the effectiveness of Babylonian theology. Ezekiel's polemic
goes to the heart of the issue: if idols are not the image of God, then worship
of them is in vain.

The Construction and Consecration of Divine Images

Both biblical and extrabiblical texts record the care taken to construct and
decorate divine statues. Prophetic literature in particular contains such accounts, especially in contexts denying the efficacy of idols. Craftsmen make
idols from wood and stone, adorn them with precious metals and gems, and
array them in fine fabric (Jer 10:1–9; Isa 40:19–20; 41:7; 44:9–20; 46:6;
Hos 2:10; 8:4; Hab 2:18–19; note also Dan 5:4). Ezekiel, too, is well aware

97. See chap. 4 below for the extensive evidence of this theology in the ancient Near
East.
98. For example, Jer 20:4; 21:7; 25:9 (though the king of Babylon would have his
turn, v. 12); Ezek 21:18–23.

of the effort that goes into the construction of idols. He mentions the use of ornaments to make images (7:20) and describes the creation, care, and feeding of idols (16:17–19).

וַתִּקְחִי כְּלֵי תִפְאַרְתֵּךְ מִזְּהָבִי וּמִכַּסְפִּי אֲשֶׁר נָתַתִּי לָךְ וַתַּעֲשִׂי־לָךְ צַלְמֵי זָכָר
וַתִּזְנִי־בָם: וַתִּקְחִי אֶת־בִּגְדֵי רִקְמָתֵךְ וַתְּכַסִּים וְשַׁמְנִי וּקְטָרְתִּי נָתַתְּ לִפְנֵיהֶם:
וְלַחְמִי אֲשֶׁר־נָתַתִּי לָךְ סֹלֶת וָשֶׁמֶן וּדְבַשׁ הֶאֱכַלְתִּיךְ וּנְתַתִּיהוּ לִפְנֵיהֶם לְרֵיחַ
נִיחֹחַ וַיֶּהִי נְאֻם אֲדֹנָי יְהוִה:

(17) "You took your beautiful ornaments of my gold and of my silver, which I gave to you, and you made for yourself images of men; and you played the harlot with them. (18) You took your fancy garments to cover them, and my oil and my incense you set before them. (19) My food which I gave to you—fine flour, oil, and honey (which) I had you eat—you set before them for a pleasing odor." So it was, says the Lord Yahweh.

Ancient Near Eastern sources amply document the activity associated with creating and maintaining divine images (*ṣalmu*).[99] In Akkadian texts, the king frequently cites his piety by claiming to fashion cult statues, as was recorded for Sennacherib (704–681 B.C.E.): *epiš ṣalam ilišu bān bīt damiqtašu* 'he who made the image of his god (Aššur) (and) built his (Aššur's) favorite temple'.[100] The care and expense lavished on these divine images are illustrated by the extensive descriptions of their apparel. While the iconographic remains are more limited, the philological evidence displays a wealth of terminology describing the details of garments (for example, *muṣîptu, têdiqu, pišannu, kusîtu*), their ornaments (for example, *aiaru, tenšia, nipḫu, šipṭu, ḫašu*), and their cleaning (*ḫâbu, mesû*).[101]

99. Edward M. Curtis provides a thorough review of the divine images in Mesopotamia (*Man as the Image of God in Genesis in the Light of Ancient Near Eastern Parallels* [Ph.D. diss., University of Pennsylvania, 1984] 97–142). See also A. L. Oppenheim, *Ancient Mesopotamia* (rev. Erica Reiner; Chicago: University of Chicago Press, 1977) 183–98; and W. G. Lambert, "Donations of Food and Drink to the Gods in Ancient Mesopotamia," in *Ritual and Sacrifice in the Ancient Near East* (ed. J. Quaegebeur; Leuven: Peeters, 1993) 191–201. Although published too late to make adequate use, see now Angelika Berlejung, *Die Theologie der Bilder: Herstellung und Einweihung von Kultbildern in Mesopotamien und die alttestamentliche Bilderpolemik* (OBO 162; Freiburg: Freiburg University Press, 1998); and M. B. Dick (ed.), *Born in Heaven, Made on Earth: The Making of the Cult Image in the Ancient Near East* (Winona Lake, Ind.: Eisenbrauns, 1999).

100. Cited from CAD E 200a (OIP 2 146:31). Note that Ezek 16:16 begins with a reference to building bedecked high places (*bāmôt*) that apparently would house the idols.

101. For a discussion of the iconographic and philological evidence, see E. Douglas Van Buren, "The *ṣalmê* in Mesopotamian Art and Religion," *Or* 10 (1941) 65–92, esp. pp. 68–69; A. Leo Oppenheim, "The Golden Garments of the Gods," *JNES* 8 (1949)

The constant and costly labor over divine images reflects the theological role they played.[102] The image of the god required regular maintenance, care, and feeding, since, as Oppenheim remarks, "Fundamentally, the deity was considered present in its image."[103] One source of how the Babylonians understood this issue is the poem of Erra, a text composed sometime in the early first millennium B.C.E.[104] The poem describes a situation in which the statue's condition reflects the degree of divine control.[105] When the god Erra inveigles Marduk to leave his statue (described as "putting off the lordly turban"), chaos ensues. Indeed, Marduk warns that when he removed his presence from his statue in the past it caused "the very heavens to tremble" and the position of the stars to change.[106] The religious concept underlying such effects, W. G. Lambert notes, is the belief that "the god in a very real sense resided in the statue"; thus, for instance, "if the statue was carried off as spoils of war, the residence of the god changed."[107] An example of this belief occurs in an inscription by Nabu-apla-iddina (ca. 900 B.C.E), which records a Sutean invasion of Sippar that resulted in the spoliation or destruction of the statue of Shamash. With the statue out of commission, the god's privileges were no longer available—a situation the priests were eager to remedy.

172–93; Agnes Spycket, *Les statues de culte dans les textes Mesopotamiens des origines à la Ire Dynastie de Babylone* (Cahiers de la Revue biblique 9; Paris: Gabalda, 1968); G. Pettinato, "Review of Spycket, *Les statues*," *BiOr* 26 (1969) 212–16; and William W. Hallo, "Cult Statue and Divine Image: A Preliminary Study," in *Scripture in Context II: More Essays on the Comparative Method* (ed. W. W. Hallo, J. C. Moyer, and L. G. Perdue; Winona Lake, Ind.: Eisenbrauns, 1983) 3. In chap. 4, §2 ("Repair of Divine Images Captured in War"), I will return to aspects of this topic. The reader should further consult the surveys in Oppenheim, *Ancient Mesopotamia*, 183–98; and Thorkild Jacobsen, "The Graven Image," in *Ancient Israelite Religion* (ed. Patrick D. Miller, Jr. et al.; Philadelphia: Fortress, 1987) 23–28. See also Curtis's review of the iconographic and textual evidence involving divine images in *Man as the Image of God in Genesis*, 97–113.

103. Oppenheim, *Ancient Mesopotamia*, 184.

104. See especially W. G. Lambert, "Review of F. Gössmann, *Das Era-Epos*," *AfO* 18 (1957–58), esp. pp. 398–400.

105. Generally, the composition of the poem is related historically to a period of crisis created by the Sutean raids in the eleventh or tenth century B.C.E. (ibid., 398), though there remains some dispute (see W. von Soden, "Etemenanki vor Asarhaddon nach der Erzählung vom Turmbau zu Babel und dem Erra-Mythos," *UF* 3 [1971] 253–63). L. Cagni rehearses some problems associated with dating the poem and concludes, "the question thus arises as to whether a certain elasticity and historical imprecision were not in fact meant as part of the historical perspective and the poetic language" (*The Poem of Erra* [Sources from the Ancient Near East 1/3; Malibu: Undena, 1977] 21).

106. I 34. Citation from Stephanie Dalley's translation in *Myths from Mesopotamia* (Oxford: Oxford University Press, 1991) 290.

107. Lambert, "Review," 399; see also Hallo, "Cult Statue and Divine Image," esp. pp. 11–14. This aspect of Near Eastern ideology will be discussed further in chap. 4.

Nevertheless, an artisan could not merely replace the old statue with a new one. Fortuitously, however, a priest turned up a clay model, and from this a legitimate statue was reproduced that bore the imprimatur necessary to replace the defunct original.[108]

The consecration of statues was a crucial step in the animation of a divine image. Thus, Mesopotamian texts also record the processes and ceremonies involved in the final stage of creation, namely, the so-called *mīs pî / pīt pî* ('washing/opening of the mouth') rituals. The literature on the subject is extensive and well known, and it is unnecessary to review these rituals here.[109] Rather, I mention it to emphasize the significance of the divine statue in Mesopotamian theology and the extensive ceremony involving its transformation into a platform through which the supplicant could approach the deity. In Jacobsen's words, the care and custom expended on the physical object produced a statue that "ceases to be mere earthly wood, precious metals and stones, ceases to be the work of human hands. It becomes transubstantiated, a divine being, the god it represents."[110]

To what extent the biblical record is aware of this elaborate preparation of divine images (beyond the physical construction of the statues) is difficult to discern. Deutero-Isaiah's lampoons do seem to be aware, although they appear as quite crass misrepresentations of the subtle ideology involved. Faur, for example, suggests that the consecration of images, such as the *mīs pî / pīt pî* ceremonies, were known among the ancient Israelites but that biblical authors intentionally denied any intrinsic power to the rite in inducing the

---

108. L. King, *Babylonian Boundary Stones and Memorials in the British Museum* (London: British Museum, 1912) no. 36, col. III, lines 11ff. Furthermore, while such extreme circumstances of reproduction are rare, Mesopotamian royal annals frequently mention the renovation of extant but decrepit statues and temples as a matter of public policy vaunting the religious devotion of the king. On this see especially Barbara Nevling Porter, *Images, Power, and Politics: Figurative Aspects of Esarhaddon's Babylonian Policy* (Philadelphia: American Philosophical Society, 1993). See also A. Kapelrud, "Temple Building, a Task for Gods and Men," *Or* 32 (1962) 56–62; and my discussion in chap. 4.

109. Descriptions of this ritual, with references to the primary material and further literature, can be found in Oppenheim, *Ancient Mesopotamia*, 183–98; Jacobsen, "The Graven Image," 23–28. See also C. B. F. Walker, *Material for a Reconstruction of the* mīs pî *Ritual* (B.Phil. thesis, Oxford University, 1966). For a recent discussion of matters in Egypt, see Ann Macy Roth, "The *pss-kf* and the 'Opening of the Mouth' Ceremony: A Ritual of Birth and Rebirth," *JEA* 78 (1992) 113–47. A comprehensive treatment of this ritual has now been published by Michael B. Dick and C. B. F. Walker, "The Induction of the Cult Image in Ancient Mesopotamia," in *Born in Heaven, Made on Earth: The Creation of the Cult Image* (ed. M. B. Dick; Winona Lake, Ind.: Eisenbrauns, 1999) 55–121.

110. Jacobsen, "The Graven Image," 22–23. See also van der Toorn, "Worshipping Stones," 1ff.; and Knut Holter, *Second Isaiah's Idol-Fabrication Passages* (BBET 28; Frankfurt am Main: Lang, 1995).

spirit of the gods to reside in the image (e.g., Isa 30:22; 42:8): "The Biblical polemics against idolatry were intended to undermine the belief in living idols and in the ritual efficacy of the pagan consecration."[111] In other words, cult statues remained mere wood and stone.

In the following sections I will suggest that, even if Ezekiel and his audience were aware of this more subtle theology affecting the image of a god, Ezekiel tackled the problem on a far deeper level.

The Image of a God in Mesopotamia

Mesopotamian texts describe divine cult statues with the expression *ṣalmu*, and less frequently with *lānu*, *maṭṭalātu*, and *zikru*.[112] This section focuses on the term *ṣalmu*, because it is the most common word denoting the physical image of a god (*ṣalam ili/ilāni*), and it offers a striking parallel to the Priestly phrase *ṣelem ʾĕlōhîm* (Gen 1:27; 9:6).

Ṣalmu (ALAM) often specifies the sculptured statue of a god, as *ṣelem* does in the Hebrew Bible (Amos 5:26; 2 Kgs 11:18 = 2 Chr 23:17; Ezek 7:20; Num 33:52). For example, Sennacherib boasts that 'he made the image of the great lord Šamaš (*ṣa-lam* ᵈUTU *bēli rabî*)' out of various precious metals and stones.[113] An artisan writes the king, "I have made the images (ALAM. MEŠ) which the king my lord ordered, (and) the crown of Anu which the king my lord ordered I have (also) made."[114] The expression *ṣalam* / ALAM + DN (divine name) most often indicates the cult image of a god,[115] or *ṣalam* / ALAM could stand as a second element of a divine name, also indicating the physical object of worship (for instance, ᵈ*Ištar*.ALAM, ᵈ*Nu-ru*-ALAM, or ᵈ*Iš-ḫa-ra*-ᵈALAM).[116] In a related usage a sanctuary of the goddess Aja at Sippar, called É.ALAM, was restored by Nabonidus (559–539 B.C.E.).[117]

---

111. Faur, "The Biblical Idea of Idolatry," 12.

112. E. M. Curtis, "Images in Mesopotamia and the Bible," in *The Bible in the Light of Cuneiform Literature: Scripture in Context III* (ed. W. W. Hallo, B. W. Jones, and G. L. Mattingly; ANETS 8; Lewiston, N.Y.: Mellen, 1990) 31–56. For *ṣalmu*, see CAD Ṣ 79a–80a, 84b–85a; AHw 1078b; and Van Buren, "The *ṣalmê* in Mesopotamian Art and Religion," 66–70. For *lānu*, see CAD L 79. For *maṭṭalātu*, see CAD M/1 428a. For *zikru*, see CAD Z 116b.

113. CAD Ṣ 79. Chapter 4 below will discuss examples of epithets of Sargon and Sennacherib that describe the kings as "maker of images of the great gods."

114. *ABL* 498 (K. 646), obv. lines 6–7: *ṣalmāni*ᵐᵉˢ *šá šarru bêli-a iq-ba-a e-te-pu-uš agû* ᵈ*A-nim šá šarru be-lí-a iq-ba-a etepuš* (see R. H. Pfeiffer, *State Letters of Assyria* [AOS 6; New Haven: American Oriental Society, 1935] 176–77).

115. CAD Ṣ 79; AHw 1078b. It could also less often function as an attribute of the king, as will be shown (AHw 1079a; CAD Ṣ 85).

116. CAD Ṣ 80a; also Van Buren, "*ṣalmê*," 67.

117. See ibid. Compare the *bīt ṣalmê* built by Shalmanezer I (ca. 1273–1244 B.C.E.; *ARAB* 1.64–65, §132).

Moreover, divine statues could be quite literally rendered with the expression 'image(s) of (a) god(s)', as we saw in Sennacherib's claim that he made 'the image of his god' (*ṣalam ilišu*), or the royal epithet, *epiš ṣalam Anšar u ṣalam ilāni rabūti.*[118] Examples of this occur most notably in the reigns of the Neo-Assyrian kings Sennacherib, Esarhaddon, and Ashurbanipal (from 704 to 627 B.C.E.).[119]

The Image of God in the Priestly Tradition

Scholars have proposed numerous interpretations of צֶלֶם אֱלֹהִים in Gen 1:27 and 9:6. G. A. Jónsson, in an extensive review of this literature, is particularly concerned with the two main avenues the question has taken in the twentieth century: "What role has the theory of the P document played in the interpretation of the *imago Dei*?" and "What role have the Near Eastern comparative material and the concept of an earlier tradition lying behind the final form of the *imago Dei* texts played?"[120] It is beyond the scope of this study to review at length these questions; rather, this section will outline two issues that provide the foundation for my own analysis: (1) the interpretation of *ṣelem ʾĕlōhîm* in the context of Mesopotamian ideology; and (2) the exile as the likely setting for *ṣelem ʾĕlōhîm*'s inclusion in the Priestly material.

As already seen, *ṣalmu* frequently refers to the physical representation, the cult statue, of a god.[121] Besides cult statues, Mesopotamian texts apply the expressions *ṣalam ili* / DN to both kings and, what is least attested, officials (an *āšipu*-priest).[122] The significance of these three uses of *ṣalam ili* / DN for understanding the biblical Priestly idiom was first recognized by Johannes Hehn.[123]

118. See Hallo, "Cult Statue and Divine Image," 15 n. 118.

119. See CAD Ṣ 79b; and AHw 1078b.

120. G. A. Jónsson, *The Image of God: Genesis 1:26–28 in a Century of Old Testament Research* (ConBOT 26; Lund: Akademisk, 1988) 9. See also Claus Westermann, *Genesis 1–11* (Minneapolis: Augsburg, 1984) 142–60 (commentary and an excursus on the history of exegesis); and Curtis, *Man as the Image of God in Genesis*, 4–39 (review of ancient interpretations) and pp. 40–59 (review of modern). James Barr offers an especially thorough interpretation of the phrase in the context of the Priestly source ("The Image of God in the Book of Genesis: A Study in Terminology," *BJRL* 51 [1968] 11–26).

121. See also the references to this usage in CAD I–J 102–3 (*ilu* 7); ibid., 90 (*iltu* d); and ibid., 274 (*ištaru* 3).

122. For this text, see G. Meier, "Die zweite Tafel der Serie *bīt mēseri*," *AfO* 14 (1941–44) 150–51, lines 225–26: *šip-tum ši-pat* ᵈ*Marduk a-ši-pu ṣa-lam* ᵈ*Marduk* 'the incantation is the incantation of Marduk; the incantation priest is the image of Marduk'. Consult discussions of this usage of *ṣalam* DN in Curtis, *Man as the Image of God in Genesis*, 85–86, 161–63; and Peter Machinist, *The Epic of Tukulti-Ninurta I: A Study in Middle Assyrian Literature* (Ph.D. diss., Yale University, 1978) 197.

123. J. Hehn, "Zum Terminus 'Bild Gottes,'" in *Festschrift Eduard Sachau* (ed. G. Weil; Berlin: Reimer, 1915) 36-52.

Of these usages, biblical scholars have especially focused on the divine image as a royal title or description.[124] Evidence of this royal status finds expression as early as the Middle-Assyrian Tukulti-Ninurta epic. This text describes the king (ca. 1244–1208 B.C.E.) as the embodiment of the god Enlil.

(16′) *ina ši-mat* ^d*Nu-dím-mud-ma ma-ni it-tí šēr ilāneli mi-na-a-šu*
(17′) *ina purussûlê(î) bēl mātāteli ina ra-a-aṭ šlsassuruli(šaturruli) ilāneli ši-pi-ik-šu i-te-eš-ra*
(18′) *šu-ú-ma ṣa-lam* ^d*E/Illil da-ru-ú še-e-mu pi-i nišēli mi-lik mmāteli*

(16′) By the fate (determined by) Nudimmud, his mass is reckoned with the flesh of the gods. (17′) By the decision of the lord of all the lands, he was successfully engendered through/cast into the channel of the womb of the gods. (18′) He alone is the eternal image of Enlil, attentive to the voice of the people, to the counsel of the land.[125]

But it is the Neo-Assyrian and Neo-Babylonian periods that provide the most examples of the king's being lauded as the image of particular gods. For example, Adad-šum-uṣur flatters Esarhaddon and his parentage in a letter: *abušu ša šarri bēlija ṣa-lam* ^dEN *šu u šarru bēlī ṣa-lam* ^dEN-*ma šû* 'The father of the king, my lord, was the very image of Bēl, and the king, my lord, is likewise the very image of Bēl'.[126]

In addition to the Mesopotamian evidence, Hehn also considered Egyptian texts that describe the king as the image of god. Indeed, the Egyptian evidence quantitatively outweighs the Mesopotamian material. Since Hehn's initial treatment, Hans Wildberger renewed interest in the extrabiblical evidence of the king's status as the image of a god in both Egypt and Mesopotamia. While recognizing that the Akkadian texts offered the closest cognate to the Hebrew *ṣelem*, Wildberger emphasized heavily the Egyptian background to the biblical expression.[127] Similarly, Werner Schmidt saw the biblical expression in the light of a Near Eastern royal background, also noting the frequent description of the king as the image of a god especially in New

---

124. For this evidence, see AHw 1079a; CAD Ṣ 85b. For a lengthy discussion of this usage in Mesopotamia, see Curtis, *Man as the Image of God in Genesis*, 80–86, 155–60, 163–72; and see also the review in Westermann, *Genesis 1–11*, 151–54.

125. Col. I.A obv. lines 16′–18′. Text and translation from Machinist, *Epic of Tukulti-Ninurta I*, 68–69. For a discussion of the difficult *mi-ni-a-šu*, see pp. 193–94. For a discussion of the themes of the king's birth and nurturing by the gods and especially the reference to the king as the image of Enlil, see pp. 193–98.

126. *ABL* 6 (K. 595), obv. lines 18–19 (see Pfeiffer, *State Letters of Assyria*, 119–20; or *LAS* 125, part 1, pp. 98–99). For this and other texts, see CAD Ṣ 85b; and Curtis, *Man as the Image of God in Genesis*, 81–86.

127. H. Wildberger, "Das Abbild Gottes Gen 1:26–30," *TZ* 21 (1965) 245–59, 481–501; see esp. p. 489.

Kingdom Egypt.[128] Although Schmidt does not propose a specific background to the biblical tradition (namely, Egypt or Mesopotamia), he does suggest that the Priestly source democratized the Near Eastern royal usage. Whereas other ancient sources identified a king or a priest as a divine representative on earth, P broadened the usage to include all humans.[129]

Most recently, Edward Curtis and Boyo Ockinga have analyzed the evidence for the Egyptian background of *ṣelem ʾĕlōhîm*.[130] Both argue that the biblical *imago Dei* concept originated within Egyptian royal ideology. Curtis is especially interested in the means through which the biblical phrase was adopted from Egypt.[131] Emphasizing the positive use of the phrase as a description of humans, he reasons that because a "negative attitude toward images was clearly in place by the eighth century B.C.E., . . . it seems doubtful that a word with the negative connotations that surely were associated with the word *ṣelem* at the time of the Exile [namely, idol] would . . . have been accepted into Israel's tradition as late as the Exile."[132] In order to explain the origin of the expression's transfer into Israelite ideology, Curtis resorts to the tradition of Moses' being educated in pharaoh's court (Exod 2:1–10) and the period of Egyptian bondage.[133]

While a thorough evaluation of Curtis's argument is not possible here, I would raise two points that suggest that an Egyptian background is not the most likely source for the biblical *ṣelem ʾĕlōhîm*. First, the Akkadian cognate *ṣalam ili/ilāni* offers a more solid prospect for the origin of the biblical *ṣelem ʾĕlōhîm*. This and the previous sections included some of the considerable evidence for the usage of *ṣalam ili/ilāni* in Mesopotamian religiopolitical ideology. Both etymological and functional equivalences can be argued from the Mesopotamian cognate. Second, the negative view of images found in the Bible is an obstacle that Curtus attempts to overcome through a strained

---

128. Werner H. Schmidt, *Alttestamentlicher Glaube in seiner Geschichte* (2d ed.; Neukirchener Studienbucher 6; Neukirchen-Vluyn: Neukirchener Verlag, 1975); English translation: *The Faith of the Old Testament* (trans. John Sturdy; Philadelphia: Westminster, 1983) 195.

129. See ibid., 138. On this observation, see also W. W. Hallo, "Problems in Sumerian Hermeneutics," *Perspectives in Jewish Learning* 5 (1973) 2, 11 n. 4. This has been picked up in the commentaries; for example, see Nahum Sarna, *Genesis* (Philadelphia: Jewish Publication Society, 1989) 12.

130. Curtis, *Man as the Image of God in Genesis*, esp. pp. 86–96, 97–102, and 113–19; and Ockinga, *Die Gottebenbildlichkeit im Alten Ägypten und im Alten Testament* (Wiesbaden: Harrassowitz, 1984).

131. Curtis, *Man as the Image of God in Genesis*, 358.

132. Ibid., 342; also p. 331.

133. Ibid., 344–58. Note also that Hans Wildberger harkened back to the Egyptian bondage to explain the Egyptian influence ("Auf dem Wege zu einer biblischen Theologie," *EvT* 19 [1959] 89).

historical argument.[134] His thesis rests heavily on finding a window of opportunity, as it were, in Israelite history that would allow a prenegative connotation of *ṣelem* to enter Israelite theology. However, this reliance on the Moses traditions as providing that window of opportunity raises serious historical difficulties.

To determine *ṣelem 'ĕlōhîm*'s origin we must first and foremost find a motive for its usage, not merely a window of opportunity for its entrance into the biblical tradition. Toward this objective, consider Phyllis Bird's suggestion that the influence on Priestly terminology came particularly from Mesopotamian royal ideology.[135] Bird offers an essential insight into the purpose of our phrase.

> The extent that the Genesis creation account may be viewed as an alternative, or counter, myth, either in its original Yahwistic formulation or in its final Priestly edition, the elements with which it most clearly compares and contrasts are found in traditions known from Mesopotamia. Since the final editing of the work is also located there, a polemical reading of the account may be suggested, even if the terms of the polemic do not originate with the final composition.[136]

The polemical nature of the Priestly expression is the key factor; when this is recognized, we are not confined to finding a prenegative milieu. Quite the opposite is true: the Priestly formulation intended to contradict its common usage.

J. Maxwell Miller's discussion of the *imago Dei* passages in Genesis also supports Bird's point.[137] Miller correctly observes that Genesis 1–11 is imbued with Mesopotamian mythic traditions modified by the Priestly writer for various ideological purposes,[138] and this holds true also for P's use of *ṣelem 'ĕlōhîm*. Furthermore, the extensive Mesopotamian elements found especially in Genesis 1–11 suggest to Miller the location of the final redaction of P in the exilic or immediate postexilic period.[139] Certainly the Priestly

134. See Curtis, *Man as the Image of God in Genesis*, 246–329.

135. Phyllis Bird, "'Male and Female He Created Them': Gen 1:27b in the Context of the Priestly Account of Creation," *HTR* 74 (1981) 129–59.

136. Ibid., 143.

137. J. M. Miller, "In the 'Image' and 'Likeness' of God," *JBL* 91 (1972) 289–304.

138. See ibid., 290–91, 294–97, 303–304, for a references to Creation and Flood material. The discussion of the mythic elements in Genesis 1–11 is enormous, and even a review of the material would take us far afield. For this discussion, consult the following: E. A. Speiser, *Genesis* (AB 1; Garden City, N.Y.: Doubleday, 1964); J. W. Rogerson, *Myth in Old Testament Interpretation* (BZAW 134; Berlin: de Gruyter, 1974); Westermann, *Genesis 1–11*; Sarna, *Genesis*; and Joseph Blenkinsopp, *The Pentateuch: An Introduction to the First Five Books of the Bible* (ABRL; New York: Doubleday, 1992) 54–97.

139. Miller, "In the 'Image' and 'Likeness' of God," 289.

stratum is complex and cannot be attributed to a single source or to a single period. The rather diverse body of material that falls within the Priestly rubric incorporates preexilic traditions, which in turn have been supplemented and modified in the transmission process. Indeed, while the Priestly material is arguably the most debated source, this brief description is generally acknowledged.[140] While a full analysis of this debate is not possible here, suffice it to say that the Priestly material encompasses a lengthy period of compositional and editorial activity. The Babylonian exile was a particularly important stage in P's final development—the penultimate, if not the ultimate stage of redaction.

Thus I am inclined, as will be shown further in the next section, to doubt arguments for a preexilic Israelite *ṣelem ʾĕlōhîm* tradition. Two points can be noted. First, as Miller has observed, "this supposed older tradition concerning the creation of man *in which ṣelem was the crucial term* has yet to be verified,"[141] that is, the phrase finds limited usage in P and finds no usage in any other preexilic biblical traditions. Second, Curtis has rehearsed well the biblical evidence that suggests that a positive connotation to *ṣelem* would not have been likely in the preexilic period.[142] To reemphasize the previous point, understanding the *purpose* of the phrase *ṣelem ʾĕlōhîm* is critical to accounting for its heritage. The conditions had to be extreme in order to warrant the adoption and adaptation of the *ṣelem* concept. Thus the more probable explanation for this Priestly phrase is Bird's: the circumstance that attracted the Priestly writer to this phrase was precisely its usage as a response to Near Eastern ideology, and the more likely origin of the biblical *imago Dei* was the Mesopotamian theology Israel encountered in exile.

Image of God and Idolatry in Ezekiel

This section will present what may be either an alternative or a more complex substitute for explaining the biblical concept that humans are created in the image of God. While there is certainly extensive evidence for the royal background of the concept, it is fundamentally connected with a polemic against idolatry. Furthermore, though *ṣelem ʾĕlōhîm* is not used in Ezekiel, it is foundational to the book's idol polemics. Two important discussions of the

---

140. For example, Israel Knohl argues for preexilic and exilic strata, with a final editing in the postexilic return to Judah (*The Sanctuary of Silence: The Priestly Torah and the Holiness Code School* [Minneapolis: Fortress, 1995] 200–204); see also Blenkinsopp, *The Pentateuch*, esp. pp. 25–26. Frank Crüsemann presents a more traditional Wellhausenian dating of the entire Priestly corpus to the exilic period in *The Torah: Theology and Social History of Old Testament Law* (trans. Allan W. Mahnke from the 1992 German original; Minneapolis: Fortress, 1996) 277–301.

141. Miller, "In the 'Image' and 'Likeness' of God," 294.

142. Curtis, *Man as the Image of God in Genesis*, esp. pp. 246–86.

imago Dei passages will help develop this point before we turn to passages in Ezekiel that suggest the manner of its usage there.

Unlike the interpretations reviewed in the section above, James Barr deals little with the etymological origin of the term *ṣelem*.[143] Rather, he is interested in the literary, theological, and social context of the Priestly source, the document that contains the *imago Dei* passages. Barr maintains that Deutero-Isaiah deeply influenced the Priestly writer's choice of terminology to describe the creation of humans in the image of God.[144] In this connection he notes some important similarities between Deutero-Isaiah and the Priestly source, such as "the emphasis on creation, the universality of vision, the emphatic monotheism, the assurance of the incomparability and uniqueness of the God of Israel."[145] Two Isaianic passages denouncing the crafting of idols are especially significant: וְאֶל־מִי תְּדַמְּיוּן אֵל וּמַה־דְּמוּת תַּעַרְכוּ לוֹ (40:18, 'To whom will you liken God, or what likeness compare with him?'); and לְמִי תְדַמְיוּנִי וְתַשְׁווּ וְתַמְשִׁלוּנִי וְנִדְמֶה (46:5, 'To whom will you liken me, or make me equal, or compare me, that we may be alike?'). The answer to these questions is "surely not idols," as well as "not humans." In other words, Deutero-Isaiah emphasized Yahweh's universality and incomparability, and in the divine realm Yahweh had no likeness. In contrast to Deutero-Isaiah, Barr maintains that P's purpose—in the context of creation—was to call attention to man's unique position among all the created order.[146] Barr suggests, however, that the occurrence of the word *dĕmût* in the *imago Dei* passages, which P uses to define and limit the word *ṣelem*, is intrinsic to the expression, having entered through Deutero-Isaiah's influence.[147]

J. Maxwell Miller has sketched the importance of the book of Ezekiel for the *imago Dei* debate.[148] Regarding the use of *dĕmût* in Ezek 1:26–28, he observes,

> Although Ezekiel is extremely cautious and leaves us with the overall impression that the appearance of God's glory defies adequate description, he uses *dĕmût* very effectively to suggest that this appearance was in a form more like that of a man than of any other creature.[149]

While Deutero-Isaiah and Ezekiel both employ *dĕmût*, they do so for different reasons. Deutero-Isaiah denies that God could be legitimately compared

143. Barr, "The Image of God in the Book of Genesis," 11–26.
144. Ibid., 13.
145. Ibid., 13–14.
146. Ibid., 14.
147. One need not accept Barr's entire argument, particularly his discussion of the semantic range of other "image" words that negated their usage by P, in order to appreciate his line of enquiry and his observations regarding Priestly and Deutero-Isaianic affinities.
148. Miller, "In the 'Image' and 'Likeness' of God," esp. pp. 291–92, 289–90, 302–3.
149. Ibid., 291–92.

to any creation—object or human—while Ezekiel applies the term in a way that acknowledges a resemblance between God's glory and the human form. Thus Miller concludes,

> The priestly writer seems to have held a position very similar to that of Ezekiel. Just as Ezekiel, in spite of his realization that God's glory defied adequate description, indicates that it "had the appearance as it were of a human form" (*děmût kěmarʾēh ʾādām*), so the priestly writer, well known for his otherwise anti-anthropomorphic tendencies, contends that man was created in the *děmût* of God.[150]

And while Miller sees a pre-Priestly stage of transmission of the *imago Dei* passage, this is largely a tradition with *děmût*, not *ṣelem*. The word *ṣelem*, Miller argues, entered into P's language only in the exile. Certainly, this observation of the correlative usage of *děmût* in Ezekiel and Genesis is not unique. Gerhard von Rad suggested the same, describing Ezek 1:26 as "the theological prelude to the *locus classicus* for the *imago* doctrine in Gen I.26."[151]

Taken together, the analyses of Barr and Miller have identified one particularly important point, namely, that Ezekiel, Deutero-Isaiah, and the Priestly redactor are all interacting with *imago Dei* ideology, using either *děmût* or *ṣelem* or both. It seems probable that Ezekiel exploits the Mesopotamian concept of *ṣalam ili/ilāni* in a more complex fashion than either Deutero-Isaiah or P, employing it both positively to describe the God-man relationship and negatively to denounce idolatry. An analysis of several texts in Ezekiel will demonstrate this point.

First, consider more closely Ezek 1:26–28. Here the prophet struggles to express the theophany in which the divine presence, seated over the cherubim platform, rises above the Temple.

וְעַל דְּמוּת הַכִּסֵּא דְּמוּת כְּמַרְאֵה אָדָם . . . הוּא מַרְאֵה דְּמוּת כְּבוֹד־יְהוָה

(26) Above the likeness of a throne was the likeness as of the appearance of a man. . . . (28) Such was the appearance of the likeness of the glory of Yahweh.

The passage is highly anthropomorphic.[152] Ezekiel clearly describes God in the appearance of the likeness of a man. In this regard note also the theophany in Ezekiel 8. There the divine form is described in terms identical to 1:26: דְּמוּת כְּמַרְאֵה־אִישׁ (8:2).[153] Finally, compare Ezekiel's anthropomorphic

---

150. Ibid., 302–3.

151. Von Rad, *Old Testament Theology*, 1.146.

152. In chap. 3, I will discuss in detail this aspect of the passage.

153. On the basis of the LXX's ἀνδρός, read אִישׁ for the MT's אֵשׁ. This verse will be discussed in more detail in chap. 3, below.

description of God with P's description of man's creation in the image and likeness of God (Gen 1:26–27).

וַיֹּאמֶר אֱלֹהִים נַעֲשֶׂה אָדָם בְּצַלְמֵנוּ כִּדְמוּתֵנוּ . . . וַיִּבְרָא אֱלֹהִים אֶת־הָאָדָם
בְּצַלְמוֹ בְּצֶלֶם אֱלֹהִים בָּרָא אֹתוֹ זָכָר וּנְקֵבָה בָּרָא אֹתָם:

(26) And God said, "Let us make man in our image, according to our likeness." . . . (27) And God created man in his image, in the image of God he created him; male and female he created them.

On the surface, the similarities are rather striking. For example, both describe a formal relationship between God and man, and both use the term *dĕmût*. Let us see if a more detailed analysis suggests further connections.

The word דְּמוּת occurs in both the Ezekiel and the Priestly passages (Gen 1:26 and 5:1), as well as Deutero-Isaiah, as seen above. Since Paul Humbert, many have argued that *dĕmût* was used alongside *ṣelem* in Gen 1:26 in order to weaken or limit *ṣelem*'s more material sense.[154] On further analysis, however, this qualifying, less material use of *dĕmût* cannot be demonstrated. *Dĕmût* can clearly express concrete, material form. For example, in 2 Kgs 16:10 *dĕmût* describes the physical model of an altar, and in 2 Chr 4:3 it describes the figures of oxen at the base of the molten sea. Moreover, extrabiblical evidence suggests that *ṣelem* and *dĕmût* are used interchangeably.[155] For example, a bilingual Assyrian-Aramaic inscription found at Tell Fekheriyeh (Syria) in 1979 demonstrates that the two words are rather synonymous. The text is inscribed across the skirt of the statue of Hadad-yisʿi (an Assyrian provincial official and, it appears, a local king), who intended it to be set up before the god Hadad. The first word of the text describes Hadad-yisʿi's sculpture as *dmwtʾ* 'the statue', while the beginning of the second part of the text calls it *ṣlm* (Akkadian rendering *ṣalmu*), with *dmwtʾ* recurring three lines later.[156] Based on the clearly parallel usage of these two terms in this text, Douglas Gropp and Theodore Lewis have argued persuasively that *dĕmût* in Gen 1:26 (also Gen 5:1–3 and Ezek 23:14–15) is not a theologically motivated gloss designed to correct the concrete, physical meaning of *ṣelem*.[157]

---

154. P. Humbert, *Études sur le récit du Paradis et de la chute dans la Genèse* (Neuchâtel: Secrétariat de l'Université, 1940), esp. pp. 153–75. The word order is reversed in Gen 5:1.

155. For a discussion of this issue, see Westermann, *Genesis 1–11*, 146–47; H. Wildberger, "צֶלֶם," *TLOT* 3.1080–85; and E. Jenni, "דמה," *TLOT* 1.339–42.

156. See A. R. Millard and P. Bordreuil, "A Statue from Syria with Assyrian and Aramaic Inscriptions," *BA* 45/3 (1982) 135–41.

157. D. Gropp and T. Lewis, "Notes on Some Problems in the Aramaic Text of the Hadd-Yithʿi Bilingual," *BASOR* 259 (1985) 47. But even prior to this archaeological find, Wildberger had argued that *dĕmût* did not appear to dilute a too bold *ṣelem* ("צֶלֶם," *TLOT* 3.1082).

The word מַרְאָה occurs alongside *dĕmût* in Ezek 1:26, 28, and 8:2. It is generally understood that together these two words attempt to describe God in terms as cautious as possible. Thus Zimmerli says, "The restraint in the description can be seen in the succession of phrases denoting the approximate similarity."[158] This observation, however, is not wholly adequate. To the contrary, *mar'eh* often indicates quite concrete objects.[159] For example, in Leviticus 13 *mar'eh* refers to the visible appearance of a skin disease upon a person's body (vv. 3, 12), and 1 Sam 16:7 uses the word for a man's physical stature. In Ezekiel it is often used for the general vision that the prophet sees in the Temple (11:24), as well as more specifically for individual features of that vision (1:13, 14, 16). On the one hand, I would agree with Miller's assessment that the language of Ezek 1:26–28 "is extremely cautious," giving the impression that the *kĕbôd-Yahweh* "defies adequate description."[160] On the other hand I would emphasize that Ezekiel's language gives the additional impression that it is bridling something potentially dangerous because, in fact, *dĕmût* and *mar'eh* imply a concrete representation. We must remember that Ezekiel, even more explicitly than P, is talking about the physical appearance of God.

It appears, then, that Ezekiel chooses the terms *dĕmût* and *mar'eh* with knowledge of the Priestly *ṣelem* and *dĕmût*. Both Priestly terms were available to Ezekiel as expressions of man's creation in God's image. It cannot be proved that *dĕmût* is an earlier term for the *imago Dei* expression, as Miller argues. However, I believe that both terms came into use during the exile as reactions to Mesopotamian ideology.

The reason that Ezekiel chose *dĕmût* and *mar'eh* rather than *dĕmût* and *ṣelem* to describe God's appearance vis-à-vis man can be determined by comparing the contexts of both P and Ezekiel. The Priestly redactor chose *ṣelem*, thereby directly creating a contrast with the Mesopotamian ideology, but he did so in a context that is not otherwise a prima facie idol polemic. *Ṣelem* occurs in the explicit context of God's role as creator, in which no rival gods are present. In this context God is the sole creator, and man is the sole image of God. In contrast, Ezekiel was concerned fundamentally with the implications that *ṣelem* suggested, for the prophet also was aware of the Mesopotamian ideology of cult statues as the *ṣalam ili/ilāni*. For Ezekiel, the use of *ṣelem* would have been utterly inappropriate, since he was concerned above all with giving no credence to idols. As we saw in §1, he adopted terminology (for

---

158. Zimmerli, *Ezekiel 1*, 122; also Miller, "In the 'Image' and 'Likeness' of God," 291.

159. Indeed, Barr claims that the Priestly writer consciously chose words other than *mar'eh* for this very reason: "*mar'e* was unsuitable because it clearly suggested that God might be *seen*" ("Image of God in the Book of Genesis," 19).

160. Miller, "In the 'Image' and 'Likeness' of God," 291.

example, *gillûlîm*) and avoided terminology (that is, *ʾĕlōhîm*) in order to prevent any hackneyed association between idols and gods. Ṣelem was a dirty word, as it were. (It will be shown below that Ezekiel employed *ṣelem* exclusively in polemics against idols.) Admittedly, *marʾeh* is a rather close parallel to *ṣelem*, but it is one that did not carry with it the full weight of idol associations. Thus in Ezek 1:26–28 the prophet ardently struggles to find appropriate language that indicates both human likeness and divine incomparability. Ezekiel's efforts are directed in several directions: he is at once attempting to align himself with Priestly theology, to contradict Mesopotamian ideology, and to refrain from language that would explicitly suggest other gods. Fundamentally, however, P and Ezekiel are dealing with the same answer, approached from different angles: man is like God, and God is like man. In this answer, both P and Ezekiel remove other gods from the equation.

In short, Ezekiel chooses terminology that is associated with the Priestly *imago Dei* passage, which in turn suggests a knowledge of the Mesopotamian concept of idols as the image of a god. The concept of man as the *ṣelem ʾĕlōhîm* is a felicitous one for the prophet because it denies any divine presence in idols. As with P, it is important for him to assert the likeness between God and man. The use of *ṣelem ʾĕlōhîm*, however, would come at too high a price for Ezekiel. It would require Ezekiel to use a word that for him is too closely associated with idols. Moreover, the context of Ezekiel 1 and 8 is that of judgment (and for idolatry, at that). Nevertheless, it is with knowledge and acceptance of the Priestly צֶלֶם אֱלֹהִים that Ezekiel uses such similar language to describe the vision of God as דְּמוּת כְּמַרְאֵה אָדָם.

Section 3 will build on the suggestion that Ezekiel is aware of the Priestly concept that humans are the image of God. Furthermore, though he does not use the expression himself, for the reasons stated above, he endorses it. The proof will come from recognizing that the *imago Dei* concept underlies another consistent indictment, namely, murder. Before we see how *ṣelem ʾĕlōhîm* forms a basis of Ezekiel's theology, we will consider additional texts that suggest that Ezekiel chose expressions implicitly utilizing the expression.

The evidence presented above suggests that Ezekiel expresses the concept that man is the image (*ṣelem*) of God, though he chooses less troublesome terms (namely, *dĕmût* and *marʾeh*). In addition, Ezekiel employs the concept—specifically using *ṣelem*—to denounce idolatry. He does so by asserting that idols are merely the images of man. Three passages support this point. In 7:19–20, Ezekiel describes the use of gold and silver to make idols, which cannot save them in the day of Yahweh's wrath: וְצַלְמֵי תוֹעֲבֹתָם שִׁקּוּצֵיהֶם עָשׂוּ בוֹ 'their abominable images and detestable things they made of it (their precious metal)'. What are for the worshipers images of their gods are for Ezekiel abominations and detestable things. Ezek 16:17 describes the construction of idols using language similar to 7:20. Here, however, the prophet replaces the caustic but ambiguous terms in 7:20 (*tôʿēbôt* and *šiqqûṣîm*) with a description that provides insight into his understanding of *ṣelem ʾĕlōhîm*: וַתַּעֲשִׂי־לָךְ צַלְמֵי זָכָר ‘You made for yourselves images of men’. I previously argued (in §1) that Ezekiel intentionally substitutes *zākār* for *ʾĕlōhîm* in this passage, but now it also appears that he does this on the grounds that an idol is the image of man, and man is the image of God. In other words, Ezekiel knows of the concept that a cult statue is a *ṣalam ili*, but he purposefully omits what is to him an illegitimate and scandalous usage of "god." A third passage, Ezek 23:14–15 (also discussed above), remarkably employs both *imago Dei* terms, *ṣelem* and *dĕmût*, to describe the idolatrous images that Israel had carved upon the wall. As with 16:17, *ʾĕlōhîm* has been replaced in 23:14–15 with other expressions: these carved figures do not represent images of a god, they are merely צַלְמֵי כַשְׂדִּים (*Qere*) ‘the images of Chaldeans’ and דְּמוּת בְּנֵי־בָבֶל ‘the likeness of Babylonians’.

As already seen, Ezekiel employs *ṣelem* solely for idols (Ezek 7:20; 16:17; 23:14). But these objects are not the images of gods, for Ezekiel polemicizes against the Mesopotamian usage in order to present (1) a negative view of idols as the image of humans and (2) a positive view of man as the image of God. Thus while Ezekiel, in contrast to the Priestly tradition, does not directly use *ṣelem ʾĕlōhîm* for humans, the term is implied through both his anthropomorphic descriptions of God in chaps. 1 and 8 and his descriptions of an idol as merely an image of man.

It follows from the above demonstration that the Mesopotamian concept of cult statues as images of gods belongs in the background of the biblical concept. P perhaps accents the protest against Near Eastern royal ideology, extending the status to all humans. But at least for Deutero-Isaiah and Ezekiel it is clear that idol polemics are fundamental to the context and play a key role in the clash with Mesopotamian ideology. Uniquely for Ezekiel, the contrast between the creation of cult statues and the creation of humans is most conspicuous.

Secton 2 of this chapter demonstrated how the Ezekiel tradition and the targumim share the same theological sensitivity regarding the use of *ʾĕlōhîm* for foreign "gods" or idols. It is also interesting to note that the *Sibylline Oracle*, a text from the Second Temple period, picks up the theological premise that this section suggests is intrinsic to Ezekiel; namely, the image of God is not an idol but man. For example, in the context of a polemic against idolatry, *Sibylline Oracle* 8:395 condemns "Godless ones [who] also call their images gods"; and 8:402 affirms, "Man is my image."[161] In another book of the oracle, also a segment denouncing idolatry, it implores (3:8–9), "Men, who

161. Translation from J. J. Collins, "Sibylline Oracles," *OTP* 1.427.

have the form which God molded in his image, why do you wander in vain, and not walk the straight path ever mindful of the immortal creator."[162]

Section 1 of this chapter emphasized Ezekiel's basic argument that idols are not legitimate representations of divine presence. The above discussion suggests that Ezekiel was aware of the concept that man was made in the image of God and that he endorsed it. He refrained from explicitly using the Priestly terminology because *ṣelem* was so intimately connected with worshiping cult statues. While the Priestly expression is never used, certain texts imply that Ezekiel had it in mind (Ezek 1:26–28; 7:19–20; 16:17; 23:14–15). Thus for Ezekiel humans, not idols, are the image of the divine. Ezekiel emphasizes a relationship of Creator (God) and creation (man as God's image).[163]

§3. The Ethics of Idolatry in Ezekiel

The previous discussion leads to another observation that involves Ezekiel's polemic against idolatry and his implied, though unstated, belief that humans are the image of God. This analysis will substantiate a vigorous ethical dynamic in the book of Ezekiel.

An ethical component to Ezekiel's oracles has not always been appreciated. For example, von Rad has suggested that it is hardly present at all: "Even a cursory reading of the text makes one thing plain. Where Ezekiel speaks of sin he thinks in particular of offenses against sacral orders. Complaints about transgression of the social and moral commandments are very much less

162. Ibid., 362.

163. As an aside, I would note that it is not impossible that the use of the address בֶּן־אָדָם is connected with the argument presented here. The translation of this expression, which occurs 93 times as God's designation of the prophet (compare Ps 80:18), comes closest to 'you individual' (Zimmerli, *Ezekiel 1*, 131), or 'human one' (L. C. Allen, *Ezekiel 1–19* [WBC 28; Dallas: Word, 1994] 3), stressing the creatureliness of the prophet. It highlights the theocentric nature of the book and emphasizes the relationship between God and Ezekiel as one of Creator and creature.

Further, consider James M. Kennedy's observation (in "Hebrew *pitḥôn peh* in the Book of Ezekiel," *VT* 41 [1991] 233–35) that the phrase *pitḥôn peh* in Ezek 16:63 and 29:21 is a technical expression alluding to the Akkadian *pīt pî* ritual. While it is questionable whether 16:63 and 29:21 provide a solid basis for this conclusion, one might consider, nevertheless, the muteness motif in Ezekiel and the theme of Yahweh opening or filling the prophet's mouth (Ezek 2:8; 3:26–27; 24:27; 33:22). In this regard, Kennedy's words are perhaps more relevant: "The startling effect is to portray Ezekiel as a kind of living idol. Like the idol, he is deaf and mute until the deity moves to speak through him. Part of the theological witness of the text that is thus expressed is that Yahweh chooses to speak in and through human beings instead of sculptured stone or wood" (p. 235). In short, Ezekiel becomes in a rather concrete way a *ṣelem ʾĕlōhîm*. (For a somewhat related discussion, see Victor Hurowitz, "Isaiah's Impure Lips and Their Purification in Light of Akkadian Sources," *HUCA* 60 [1989] 39–89.)

prominent."[164] This is a serious overstatement. In Ezekiel's decalogue-like list in 18:5–8 (also 22:6–21), for example, idolatry is only one offense among a list of moral duties.[165] Moreover, we will hear the prophet voice a consistent moral indictment.

Ezekiel repeatedly cites the following expressions—nearly always in the same context with idol polemics—as either the reason for or the consequence of the exile: shedding blood, blood in the city, land full of blood (דָּם: 7:23; 9:9; 16:36, 38; 18:10; 22:3, 4, 6, 9, 12, 13, 27; 23:37, 45; 24:7, 8; 33:25; 36:18). The city and land are also full of violence (חָמָס: 7:11, 23; 8:17; 12:19; 22:2; 24:6, 9; 45:9). The expression 'to shed/spill (שָׁפַךְ) blood' is a frequent element of this condemnation and appears to mean 'to commit murder'.[166] Furthermore, this common collocation of bloodshed/violence and idolatry is fundamentally related to the conclusions in §2. The prohibition of bloodshed and the polemic against idolatry both involve the concept of human creation in the image of God. To demonstrate this point, we must return to the Priestly tradition, specifically the so-called Noahide covenant (Gen 9:1–7).

First, consider the context of Genesis 9, the aftermath of the Flood. Tikva Frymer-Kensky has perceptively noted the connection between the Flood narrative and Ezekiel: "The parallelism between the Flood and the destruction is well developed by Ezekiel, and the early chapters of Ezekiel are replete with Flood imagery, particularly with the repetitive statements that the land is full of *ḥāmās* (Ezek 7:23; 8:17; and cf. 12:19; 45:9; for the Flood story, Gen 6:11)."[167] Ezek 8:17b is particularly interesting in that the catalog of offenses in 8:1–16 involves idolatry and the worship of other gods, while v. 17b adds rather unexpectedly that they have filled the land with violence. Furthermore, Frymer-Kensky notes,

164. Von Rad, *Old Testament Theology*, 2.224.

165. See Weinfeld, *Deuteronomy 1–11*, 254–55.

166. As it does elsewhere in the Hebrew Bible (Gen 9:6; 37:22; Num 35:33; Deut 21:7; 1 Sam 25:31; Ps 79:3; Prov 1:16; Ezek 16:38; 18:10; 22:3, 4, 6, 9, 12, 27; 23:45; 33:25; 36:18). See G. Gerleman, "דָּם," *TLOT* 1.337. Jacob Milgrom notes: "The P strand in Genesis also indicts the human race for its Heb *ḥāmās* ('violence,' Gen 6:11). Since the Noachian law of Genesis 9 is the legal remedy for *ḥāmās*. . . , it probably denotes murder (as in Ezek 7:23)" (Milgrom, "Priestly Source," 457). In Lev 17:4, slaughtering animals in a place other than the altar at the entrance of the Tent of Meeting is equated with shedding blood (i.e., murder).

167. T. Frymer-Kensky, "Pollution, Purification, and Purgation in Biblical Israel," in *The Word of the Lord Shall Go Forth: Essays in Honor of David Noel Freedman in Celebration of His Sixtieth Birthday* (ed. Carol L. Meyers and Michael O'Connor; Winona Lake, Ind.: Eisenbrauns, 1983) 411.

The parallelism between the Flood and the Exile does not involve only pollution and destruction, but also additional themes which are an inherent part of
the parallel. The Flood and the Exile were necessary purgations; they are not
ultimate, permanent destructions. Just as mankind was saved from permanent destruction by Noah's survival, so too God will not exterminate the
people, but will rescue a remnant to begin again.[168]

The association between violence in Ezekiel and the Flood narrative is
not limited, however, to 6:11–13, but also encompasses the Noahide covenant. Consider the pronouncement in Gen 9:4–6.

אַךְ־בָּשָׂר בְּנַפְשׁוֹ דָמוֹ לֹא תאכֵלוּ: וְאַךְ אֶת־דִּמְכֶם לְנַפְשֹׁתֵיכֶם אֶדְרֹשׁ מִיַּד
כָּל־חַיָּה אֶדְרְשֶׁנּוּ וּמִיַּד הָאָדָם מִיַּד אִישׁ אָחִיו אֶדְרֹשׁ אֶת־נֶפֶשׁ הָאָדָם:
שֹׁפֵךְ דַּם הָאָדָם בָּאָדָם דָּמוֹ יִשָּׁפֵךְ כִּי בְּצֶלֶם אֱלֹהִים עָשָׂה אֶת־הָאָדָם:

(4) Only flesh within which is its life, that is its blood, you shall not
eat. (5) For your life-blood I will require a reckoning; for every beast
I will require it, and for every man—for every man's brother I will require the life of a man. (6) Any man who sheds the blood of man, by
man shall his blood be shed; for in the image of God, he made man.

Here the Priestly tradition gives the reason for condemning violence and
bloodshed: man is made in the image of God. Violence is one of the causes
for the Flood (6:11–13), and it is violence that the first post-Flood legislation
addresses (9:5–6).

Gen 9:4–6 prompts us to look further into the significance of the general
prohibition of blood. The ban on consuming blood is fundamental to the Le-
vitical legislation (e.g., Lev 3:17; 7:27; 17:10–14 [6×]).[169] Milgrom has argued that this is hardly a purely ritual concern: "The blood prohibition is an
index of P's concern for the welfare of humanity."[170] So it seems, for shedding blood and eating blood appear side by side (Gen 9:4–6). One principle
on which the blood proscription rests is found frequently: blood is life (Gen
9:4; Lev 17:11, 14; Deut 12:23); thus to shed or pour out blood is to commit
homicide. In Gen 9:4–6 we meet a second principle behind P's concern: man
is made in the image of God.[171]

---

168. Ibid.

169. For a close reading of the complicated layers involved in this Priestly prohibition,
see Baruch J. Schwartz, "Prohibitions concerning the 'Eating' of Blood in Leviticus 17," in
Priesthood and Cult in Ancient Israel (ed. Gary A. Anderson and Saul M. Olyan; JSOTSup
125; Sheffield: Almond, 1991) 34–66.

170. Milgrom, "Priestly Source," 456.

171. See J. Milgrom, *Leviticus 1–16* (AB 3; New York: Doubleday, 1991) 705. For the
wider theological meaning of blood in the Hebrew Bible, see J. Bergman and B. Kedar-
Kopfstein, "דָּם, *dām*," *TDOT* 3.234–50; L. Morris, "The Biblical Use of the Term 'Blood,'"

An exact reflection of the Priestly tradition is found in Ezek 33:25. In the context of a list of moral wrongs, the prophet juxtaposes shedding and consuming blood and presents them as significant offenses by Israel.

לָכֵן אֱמֹר אֲלֵיהֶם כֹּה־אָמַר אֲדֹנָי יְהֹוִה עַל־הַדָּם תֹּאכֵלוּ וְעֵינֵכֶם תִּשְׂאוּ
אֶל־גִּלּוּלֵיכֶם וְדָם תִּשְׁפֹּכוּ וְהָאָרֶץ תִּירָשׁוּ׃ [172]

Therefore, say to them, "Thus says the Lord GOD, '(upon/on) the blood you eat (literally),[173] and your eyes you lift up to your *gillûlîm*, and blood you shed; shall you possess the land?'"

Here is a prohibition comparable to the prohibition found in Gen 9:4–6. Milgrom's summary of the blood prohibition is appropriate to both Genesis 9 and Ezekiel 33: "Man must abstain from blood: human blood must not be shed and animal blood must not be ingested."[174] It is notable that the reference to idols is sandwiched between consuming and shedding blood, as if highlighting the mistaken understanding of *ṣelem 'ĕlōhîm*.[175] Nor is this association found only in Genesis and Ezekiel. It is fascinating that the indictment of Manasseh includes both charges: he caused Judah to sin with his idols (*gillûlîm*, 2 Kgs 21:11), and he shed much innocent blood (*dām nāqî šāpak*, v. 16).

JTS 3 (1952) 216–27, and 6 (1955) 77–82; Dennis J. McCarthy, "The Symbolism of Blood and Sacrifice," *JBL* 88 (1969) 166–76; and M. Vervenne, "'The Blood Is the Life and the Life Is the Blood': Blood as Symbol of Life and Death in Biblical Tradition (Gen. 9,4)," in *Ritual and Sacrifice in the Ancient Near East* (ed. J. Quaegebeur; Leuven: Peeters, 1993) 451–70.

172. The reader should note that while Ezek 33:25 does not occur in the LXX, its absence can be attributed to homoioteleuton (cf. vv. 25 and 27).

173. A complicated issue involves the wording of the blood prohibition. Ezek 33:25; Lev 19:26; and 1 Sam 14:32–34 describe the offensive act as אכל עַל־הַדָּם, while Gen 6:4; Lev 3:17; 7:26; 17:10–14 have merely דָּם or כָּל־דָּם (see, e.g., Y. M. Grintz, "Do Not Eat on the Blood," *ASTI* 8 [1970–71] 78–105). I am not inclined to consider this a significant distinction. Consider, for example, that within their present contexts both Leviticus 17 and 1 Samuel 14 establish the practice of sacrificing on an altar as the prescribed remedy (Lev 17:11b; 1 Sam 14:32–35). Thus it seems that the proscribed actions are not necessarily distinct.

174. Milgrom, *Leviticus 1–16*, 705. *Jubilees*, a text from the Second Temple period, also simultaneously condemns shedding and eating blood: O. S. Wintermute, "Jubilees," *OTP* 2.66–67 (6:4–16); 2.70 (7:26–33); 2.78 (11:1–6).

175. Here too observe that Second Temple literature associates idolatry with eating blood; for example, *Jub.* 21:5–6 (Wintermute, *OTP* 2.95): "Do not follow pollutions or graven images or molten images. And do not eat any blood of beasts or cattle or any bird which flies in heaven." Similarly, in a line missing from the important manuscripts and thought to be a Christian interpolation, note *Pseudo-Phocylides*, line 31 (P. W. van der Horst, "The Sentences of Pseudo-Phocylides," *OTP* 2.575): "Do not eat blood; abstain from what is sacrificed to idols."

The possibility follows, then, that Ezekiel's very frequent charge against Israel—that its people shed much blood—is based on the same *imago Dei* rationale as Genesis 9: the shedding of blood is prohibited because humans are the image of God. Admittedly, we have no direct proof of this association in Ezekiel. The evidence is indirect, based primarily on Gen 9:6 with its reflection on the *imago Dei* dictum in its prohibition of murder, and the argument that this Priestly law against bloodshed is tied to Ezekiel's condemnation of idolatry. As we noted above, the frequent charge against Israel shedding blood generally occurs in the same context as the charge against Israel worshiping *gillûlîm*. [176] Despite the lack of certain evidence, this connection neatly draws together two implications that the *imago Dei* concept suggests to Ezekiel. First, idolatry is a heinous offense, for it is an illegitimate representation of the image of God. Second, violence and bloodshed are acts that ultimately involve God's image. [177] It appears that Ezekiel bases human relations on the same fundamental principle as his polemic against idolatry—the proposition that humans are made in the image of God affects both man's relations with God and man's relations with man. [178]

176. The juxtaposition of idolatry and shedding of blood also occurs in Ezek 36:18aβb. While this passage is missing in the Greek witnesses, it furnishes an early interpretive gloss (Zimmerli's *Nachinterpretation*) that, along with a nice play on words, suggests again that this frequent collocation was perceived also by early receivers of the tradition. The Hebrew text reads (with the addition in brackets): עַל־הַדָּם [עֲלֵיהֶם חֲמָתִי וָאֶשְׁפֹּךְ] אֲשֶׁר־שָׁפְכוּ עַל־הָאָרֶץ וּבְגִלּוּלֵיהֶם טִמְּאוּהָ 'So I poured out my wrath upon you [for the blood which they shed upon the land, and for the idols with which they defiled it]'. The interpreter is certainly playing on the imagery of v. 17 (polluting the land כְּטֻמְאַת הַנִּדָּה), reflecting Priestly tradition (for example, Num 35:33), and playing on שׁפך: the uncleanness is a result of גִּלּוּלִים and the shedding (שׁפך) of blood, which will cause God to pour forth (שׁפך) his wrath.

177. As it does for the Priestly tradition. Thus the observations in this excursus also modify Yehezkel Kaufmann's overgeneralized comments that idolatry and cultic misdeeds are the central reasons the Pentateuch and Former Prophets offer for national destruction, while classical prophecy in Israel saw social immorality as the chief cause of the exile (*Religion of Israel*, 157–60).

178. Note the connection made in the New Testament's Epistle of James 3:9, which sets up the rhetorical argument that, if we bless God with our tongue, how can we curse humans who are made in the likeness (ὁμοίωσι) of God? (reflecting Gen 1:26–27). It is also interesting that 1 John 4:7–5:21, which deals with the commandment to love God and neighbor, includes an argument not to hate one's neighbor that is related to, but rhetorically the reverse of, Jas 3:9. The book ends with an association of God-Jesus-believer (1 John 5:20) and concludes with the injunction: Τεκνία, φυλάξατε ἑαυτὰ ἀπὸ τῶν εἰδώλων 'Children, keep yourselves from idols' (5:21). It seems that here also the religious (theological) and the moral (anthropological) dimensions are tightly interwoven.

§4. Conclusion

This chapter has focused on what the prophet considers to be inappropriate and illegitimate representations of God. Section 1 proved Ezekiel's theology to be radically theocentric and monotheistic. The book of Ezekiel contains a sustained polemic against idolatry. Two aspects of that disputation were examined in detail.[179] First, Ezekiel berates idols by labeling them *gillûlîm*, a highly pejorative expression connoting a quite literal grossness; that is, these objects lack any associative value or merit, and they convey uncleanness. Second, Ezekiel's opposition to idols is so intense that he intentionally avoids using the term *ʾĕlōhîm*—the generic term for gods or God throughout the Hebrew Bible—to identify alleged divine powers other than Yahweh. The prophet will not even associate the term with idols. The expression is inappropriate because idols are mere wood and stone, and any connection with a divine potential is wholly improper. What is more, Ezekiel purposefully mocks idolatry in order to offer the exiles a theological proposition: the physical presence of idols indicates their powerlessness, and the absence of Yahweh's presence indicates God's power. Through this proposition the prophet can offer a paradigm that frees the captives from the conclusion that absence means divine abandonment or defeat. Ezekiel condemns the physical representation of divine presence as folly—a message of judgment— but this is fundamental to resuscitating and encouraging exilic expectation.

Section 2 argued that Ezekiel's anthropology is linked to this same concept, for fundamental to his opposition to idols is that humans are made in the image of God. The basis of this proposal is that the prophet contrasts the Hebrew phrase *ṣelem ʾĕlōhîm* 'image of God' with the Babylonian use of the same cognate expression (*ṣalam ili/ilāni*). Ezekiel, like the Priestly creation account, democratizes the meaning; it now refers to all humans. Thus, along with the

---

179. While it lay outside the scope of this study to examine the so-called Recognition Formula (*Erkenntnisformel*), which occurs more than 50 times in Ezekiel, Zimmerli identified its form-critical location in the profane sphere of proving and demonstrating (see "Knowledge of God in the Book of Ezekiel," in *I Am Yahweh*, 29–98). In Ezekiel the formula is one of divine self-evidencing among Israel and the nations: "All Yahweh's action which the prophet proclaims serves as proof of Yahweh among the nations" (Zimmerli, *Ezekiel 1*, 38). Daniel Bodi extends the comparative bounds of Zimmerli's conclusions (*The Book of Ezekiel and the Poem of Erra* [OBO 104; Freiburg: Universitätsverlag / Göttingen: Vandenhoeck & Ruprecht, 1991] 297–301). Following Gunkel, he argues that the origin of the Formula of Self-Introduction (*Selbstvorstellungsformel*, אני יהוה) is a polytheistic setting (ibid., 298). Furthermore, he asserts, the Recognition Formula is particularly associated with the oracles against foreign nations for which the crucial issue is "the recognition of the glory and honor of Yahweh's *name*" (ibid., 300). In other words, this formula aims at demonstrating the power of Yahweh against the claims of the gods of other nations.

book's principal argument that idols are not legitimate representations of divine presence, the prophet also offers a positive assessment: humans, not idols, are the image of the divine. For Ezekiel, idols are a misrepresentation of God's presence and an illegitimate expression for both God and man.

Ezekiel's polemic against idolatry, thus, is complex and consequential. More than merely condemning such practice, the prophet constructively employs the paradox of God's absence and presence. By emphasizing God's absence, that is, his lack of physical representation, Ezekiel enabled his audience to perceive God's presence in exile. By responding to the misguided understanding of God's presence with the argument that *ṣelem ʾĕlōhîm* are humans, not idols, Ezekiel provided the exiles with a theologoumenon in which they, the people of Israel, were indispensable. The following chapters will show how the prophet continues to develop these themes.

Chapter 3

Idolatry and Theophany:
Legitimate Expressions of God's Presence

And the name of the city from that day will be "Yahweh is here."
Ezekiel 48:35

§1. Introduction

Communicating God's Presence

The book of Ezekiel attempts to provide effective expressions of God's presence among the exiles. This objective raises three questions: (1) What are legitimate descriptions of God's presence? (2) What resolution can be offered for the apparent contradiction between the polemic against images and the rather graphic imagery used to portray the visions of God? (3) What is the relationship between the absence of God from the Temple and the presence of God among the exiles?

Moreover, the prophet faced a problem: his emphasis on theodicy stressed the removal of God's presence from the Temple because of the people's profane behavior; but the exile itself necessitated an idiom that could communicate the power of God's presence beyond the control of border and imperial might. How could Ezekiel provide a metaphor of God's presence without jeopardizing the vigor of his theodicy? An effective positive message of theophany had to fill the gap left by Ezekiel's complete condemnation of idolatry.

In this chapter I analyze characteristic language associated with theophany, namely, the *kĕbôd yhwh*. I show that Ezekiel struggles for unique expressions of the few legitimate ways of depicting Yahweh in concrete terms. The *kābôd* tradition, with its relationship to theophany and sanctuary, receives special attention against the context of the loss of Temple and the claim in Ezek 11:16 that Yahweh himself became their sanctuary.

77

The Structure of Ezekiel

The structure of the book exhibits remarkable symmetry and focus on the theme of the presence and absence of God. In chap. 1, I outlined the book as follows:

A — From Divine Presence to Divine Absence (1:1–11:25)
   B — Preparation for Destruction (12:1–24:27)
      C — Oracles against the Nations (25:1–32:32)
   B' — Preparation for Restoration (33:1–39:29)
A' — From Divine Absence to Divine Presence (40:1–48:35)

Section A opens with a vision of the glory of Yahweh preparing for its imminent departure from Jerusalem. The initial vision and the actual departure form an envelope around the catalog of offenses that have precipitated Yahweh's actions (chaps. 1–11). Section B contains allegories and oracles that further elaborate the profane behavior of the people, opening and closing with the prophet performing symbolic actions relating to the impending exile (chaps. 12–24). The oracles in these chapters directly name Babylon as the instrument of God's judgment against Israel (12:3; 17:2, 16, 20; 19:9; 21:19, 22; 24:2). Section C contains oracles against the nations (chaps. 25–32), which consist of prophetic doom directed against Ammon, Moab, Edom, Philistia, Tyre, Sidon, and Egypt. Babylon is excluded from these pronouncements, though here, too, it is the instrument of God's wrath against Tyre and Egypt (26:7; 29:18–19; 30:10, 24–25; 32:11). Section B' announces the future deliverance of the remnant of Israel (chaps. 33–39). It ends with preparation for the restoration of the people (chap. 37) and the final defeat of its enemies from the north, including Babylon (though unnamed;[1] chaps. 38–39). Section A', the program for the restoration of the Temple and its cult, concludes the book (chaps. 40–48): God provides the prophet with a detailed layout of Jerusalem and the Temple, and in the context of this vision, God's divine presence returns.

---

1. The subjects of this oracle, despite many attempts by scholars, remain obscure. The enemies are archetypal, for certain. That the audience would at least see its Babylonian conquerors as included in this great threat from the northern regions is also certain (Ezek 26:7 and 38:15; note also traditions in Jer 1:13–14, 4:5–31, 5:15–17, etc., and compare with Jer 25:9 and 36:29; the deliverance from the northern countries allows association with the Exodus tradition in Jer 16:14–15 = 23:7–8). On this, see W. H. Schmidt, "צָפוֹן," *TLOT* 3.1096–98; M. C. Astour, "Ezekiel's Prophecy of Gog and the Cuthean Legend of Naram-Sin," *JBL* 95 (1976), esp. pp. 568–71; also W. Zimmerli, *Ezekiel 2* (trans. J. D. Martin; Hermeneia; Philadelphia: Fortress, 1983) 299–300; and H. McKeating, *Ezekiel* (Old Testament Guides; Sheffield: Almond, 1993) 114–22.

Sections B and B' involve the judgment and the restoration of God's people, respectively, in preparation for their return. Section A' ends with a reversal of the situation portrayed in section A, moving from abandonment and impending destruction of Jerusalem and the Temple to reestablishment and reinhabitation. David Noel Freedman has commented on the central significance of the Temple in Ezekiel: "The theme of the Temple runs through the entire book, and is the key to its unity. In a sentence, it is the story of the departure of the glory of God from the Temple, and its return."[2] Indeed, the book ends climactically with the renamed Temple-city, which emphasizes this theme: *yhwh šāmmâ* (48:35).

The polar ends of Ezekiel thus involve the Temple. We can now turn to the principal image of divine presence in the Temple, namely, the *kābôd*-theology and how that concept is integrally linked to the Priestly image of the wilderness sanctuary. In so doing, a paradox will emerge: the divine absence is an image of judgment culminating in exile and a symbol of assurance in the midst of exile.

§2. The <u>kābôd</u>-Theology in the Priestly Tradition

In the vision of the Merkabah, observed Samson Levey, Ezekiel provided the exiles with the expectation that, even though Babylon might lay waste the earthly Temple, the heavenly throne of Yahweh lay beyond the reach of human military power.[3] In this chapter I analyze the characteristic language of Ezekiel that functions, on the one hand, to abstract Yahweh from appearing as a deity limited to a physical locale and yet, on the other, to provide legitimate expression of God's presence among his people. The following section will begin with the theophanic tradition of the 'glory of Yahweh' (*kĕbôd yhwh*), an expression particularly associated with the Priestly tradition. Investigations of

---

2. D. N. Freedman, "The Book of Ezekiel," *Int* 8 (1954) 456. See also Martin Schmidt, *Prophet und Tempel: Eine Studie zum Problem der Gottesnähe im Alten Testament* (Zollikon-Zürich: Evangelischer Verlag, 1948) 129–71. R. E. Clements sees the central role of the Temple even in the book's redactional activity. According to Clements, the perspective of the book of Ezekiel is limited to the sixth century, and the agenda of the restoration program would have predated the rebuilding of the Temple in 515 B.C.E. ("The Chronology of Redaction in Ezekiel 1–24," in *Ezekiel and His Book* [ed. J. Lust; BETL 74; Leuven: Leuven University Press, 1986] 283–94; see also idem, "The Ezekiel Tradition: Prophecy in a Time of Crisis," in *Israel's Prophetic Tradition: Essays in Honour of Peter R. Ackroyd* [ed. Richard Coggins, Anthony Phillips, and Michael Knibb; Cambridge: Cambridge University Press, 1982] 119–36). Clements further suggests that "the shape that has been given to it has made it into a charter for the rebuilding of the Jerusalem temple and for the restoration of its cultus after the disaster of 587 B.C." (ibid., 133).

3. S. Levey, *The Targum of Ezekiel* (The Aramaic Bible 13; Wilmington, Del.: Glazier, 1987) 3.

this element of Israelite theology are extensive.[4] A brief review is necessary, however, to lay the foundation for observing how Ezekiel uniquely develops this theological tradition to depict the complementary aspects of God's absence and presence.

The Form of the Presence

The word כָּבוֹד occurs about two hundred times in the Hebrew Bible. With reference to theophanies, it appears to have a restricted technical meaning involving God's self-manifestation, and it is a significant element in Priestly theology. The following Priestly passages employ the term *kābôd* for God's presence: (1) pre–Sinai Desert wandering (Exod 16:7, 10); (2) Sinai (Exod 24:16, 17; 29:43; 40:34, 35; Lev 9:6, 23); and post–Sinai Desert wandering (Num 14:10, 21, 22; 16:19; 17:7; 20:6). The *kābôd* is a public manifestation of God associated with cultic ceremony (Lev 9:6, 23) and with the wilderness Tabernacle (Exod 16:7, 10; 29:43; 40:34–35), and theological reflection on the Jerusalem Temple adopts this usage (1 Kgs 8:11; Ps 26:8).[5] The primary mode of this self-manifestation of God resembles meteorological phenomena, that is, the imagery involves clouds and fire, or fire enveloped in cloud (e.g., Lev 9:23–24). According to von Rad, "In P's view the כבוד יהוה is simply the form of manifestation which Jahweh employed in order to reveal to Israel particular decisions of his will."[6]

Two aspects of the form of the *kābôd* should be noted. First, the appearance is that of fire wrapped or cloaked in cloud (e.g., Exod 24:16–17); it is an apparition whose presence is potentially lethal (see Exod 16:7, 10; 20:18; Num 14:10; 16:19; 17:7; 20:6; compare Deut 5:24–25).[7] God allows only

---

4. For literature on *kābôd*, see J. Morgenstern, "Biblical Theophanies," *ZA* 25 (1911) 139–93; H. G. May, "The Departure of the Glory of Yahweh," *JBL* 56 (1937) 309–21; J. Lindblom, "Theophanies in Holy Places in Hebrew Religion," *HUCA* 32 (1961) 91–106; M. Haran, "The Divine Presence in the Israelite Cult and the Cultic Institutions," *Bib* 50 (1969) 251–67; C. Westermann, "כבד," *TLOT* 2.590–602; T. W. Mann, *The Divine Presence and Guidance in Israelite Traditions: The Typology of Exaltation* (JHNES 9; Baltimore: John Hopkins University Press, 1977). T. N. D. Mettinger, *The Dethronement of Sabaoth: Studies in the Shem and Kabod Theologies* (trans. Frederick H. Cryer; ConBOT 18; Lund: CWK Gleerup, 1982); M. Weinfeld, "כָּבוֹד, *kābôd*," *TDOT* 7.22–38 (Ger. 1982–84; Eng. 1995); U. Struppe, *Die Herrlichkeit Jahwes in der Priesterschrift: Eine semantische Studie zu kĕbôd YHWH* (Österreichische biblische Studien 9; Klosterneuburg: Österreichisches Katholisches Bibelwerk, 1988).

5. In ancient hymnic texts, the word is part of a divine title (*melek hakkābôd*, Ps 24:7, 10; *'ēl hakkābôd*, Ps 29:3).

6. G. von Rad, *Old Testament Theology* (trans. D. M. G. Stalker; 2 vols.; Edinburgh: Oliver and Boyd, 1962–65) 1.240.

7. G. E. Mendenhall describes the theophanic cloud (עָנָן) as the "mask of Yahweh" and emphasizes that its manifestation portends God's sovereignty and power (*The Tenth Generation* [Baltimore: Johns Hopkins University Press, 1973] chap. 2, esp. pp. 56–66).

Moses to view the *kābôd* (Exod 24:17–18), though even for him this is a unique experience (see Exod 40:34–35). The people are granted a benevolent close encounter with the divine presence during the consecration of the Tabernacle (Lev 9:23–24). Still, the sight of God's *kābôd* causes the assembled to fall upon their faces.

Second, the concept represents something of a departure from Yahwistic expressions of God's appearances. In J, particularly in the pre-Mosaic material, Yahweh is less remote and less shrouded in mystery. For example, Yahweh visits Abraham at Mamre, where three men appear (אֲנָשִׁים; Gen 18:1–2), one of whom Abraham addresses as יהוה (18:10, 13). This one remains behind (18:22, 33) while the two others (now מַלְאָכִים; 19:1) continue on to Sodom. Similarly, in Gen 28:13 יהוה stands before Jacob (see also Gen 17:1, 22). Yahwistic accounts also use מַלְאָךְ יהוה for divine manifestations. For example, Hagar converses with a *malʾāk* (Gen 16:7), which she identifies as God (Gen 16:13). In contrast to manifestations in J, the *kābôd* functions in the Priestly tradition in a more remote, less anthropomorphic manner. Barr describes the Priestly theophany as "a veiled appearance, an appearance in a manner in which no precise lineaments of form can be discerned."[8] Similarly, according to Zimmerli, the *kābôd* is the "personal presence of the deity in light," and he notes that "the human form of the כבוד יהוה is never mentioned in the Priestly Document."[9] And while Julian Morgenstern understands the *kĕbôd yhwh* as not an abstract appearance but a quite concrete image—"the material form in which Jahwe was thought to reveal Himself to mortal eyes"[10]—this "definitely visible manifestation" is nevertheless rather equivocally revealed as "'something like fire' enveloped in 'the cloud of Jahwe.'"[11] In other words, though the form was visible according to P, the appearance had neither definite nor anthropomorphic features. The *kābôd* represents Priestly religious reflection expressing both the transcendence and the immanence of God.

Presence in the Sanctuary

The special place in P upon which the *kābôd* descends (except for the pre-Tabernacle texts in Exodus 16 and 24) is the Tabernacle, called אֹהֶל מוֹעֵד (9 times) and מִשְׁכָּן (Exod 40:34, 35).[12] Exod 40:33b–35 announces the

8. J. Barr, "Theophany and Anthropomorphism in the Old Testament," *Congress Volume: Oxford, 1959* (VTSup 7; Leiden: Brill, 1960) 35.

9. W. Zimmerli, *Ezekiel 1* (trans. R. E. Clements; Hermeneia; Philadelphia: Fortress, 1979) 124.

10. Morgenstern, "Biblical Theophanies," 140.

11. Ibid., 151.

12. On the originally distinct traditions represented by *ʾōhel môʿēd* and *miškān*, see von Rad, *Old Testament Theology*, 1.235–38. Only in the narrative that concludes the

completion of the Tabernacle construction and provides important information about the *kābôd*'s relationship to the Tabernacle.

וַיְכַל מֹשֶׁה אֶת־הַמְּלָאכָה: וַיְכַס הֶעָנָן אֶת־אֹהֶל מוֹעֵד וּכְבוֹד יְהוָה מָלֵא
אֶת־הַמִּשְׁכָּן: וְלֹא־יָכֹל מֹשֶׁה לָבוֹא אֶל־אֹהֶל מוֹעֵד כִּי־שָׁכַן עָלָיו הֶעָנָן וּכְבוֹד
יְהוָה מָלֵא אֶת־הַמִּשְׁכָּן:

Thus Moses finished the work. Then the cloud covered the Tent of Meeting, and the *kĕbôd yhwh* filled the Tabernacle. But Moses was not able to enter the Tent of Meeting, because the cloud settled upon it and the *kĕbôd yhwh* filled the Tabernacle.

Following the Sinai experience and the erection of the Tabernacle, the Tabernacle itself becomes a mobile sanctuary, a place of rendezvous for Moses and the *kĕbôd yhwh*.

This Tabernacle tradition is also applied to Solomon's Temple, as Joseph Blenkinsopp notes: "Whatever its origins . . . it inevitably came to be associated with the Jerusalem Temple and its inner sanctuary, the Holy of Holies."[13] Thus when Solomon dedicates the new Temple (1 Kgs 8:10–11), the divine presence appears just as it did in Exodus 40.

וַיְהִי בְּצֵאת הַכֹּהֲנִים מִן־הַקֹּדֶשׁ וְהֶעָנָן מָלֵא אֶת־בֵּית יְהוָה: וְלֹא־יָכְלוּ
הַכֹּהֲנִים לַעֲמֹד לְשָׁרֵת מִפְּנֵי הֶעָנָן כִּי־מָלֵא כְבוֹד־יְהוָה אֶת־בֵּית יְהוָה:[14]

And when the priests came from the holy place, a cloud filled the house of Yahweh. But the priests were not able to stand and minister before the cloud because the *kĕbôd yhwh* filled the house of Yahweh.

However, in spite of the usage of the *kābôd*-theology in texts dealing with the Temple, Mettinger is correct to conclude, "The P-materials diverge from the other traditions in this respect, in that they emphasize that God is present in his Tabernacle, without insisting that this ties him to a special, divinely elected place. The important notion stressed here is God's ability to be present among his people even at a previously unknown campsite."[15]

---

instructions to build the Tabernacle (Exodus 25–31) and the actual construction (Exodus 35–40) do we find the combined usage of *miškān* and *ʾōhel môʿēd* (39:32, 40; 40:2, 6, 22, 24, 29, 34, 35).

13. Joseph Blenkinsopp, *A History of Prophecy in Ancient Israel* (Philadelphia: Westminster, 1983) 195.

14. The LXX renders בית יהוה with τὸν οἶκον (i.e., הבית in both verses; compare v. 6). Otherwise, no serious text-critical concerns occur in these verses.

15. Mettinger, *Dethronement of Sabaoth*, 96. As we will see, Mettinger thinks that the Sitz im Leben of the Priestly Tabernacle theology lay in circles that were devastated by the exile (ibid., 96). While Mettinger may be correct regarding the final narrative form of P,

Permanence of the Presence

The elements of the Priestly *kābôd*-theology just reviewed—namely, its function as a technical expression for God's presence, its appearance with nonanthropomorphic features, and its association with the wilderness Tabernacle—occasion little dispute among scholars. The aspect of the permanence of the presence in the Tabernacle, however, is a matter of some debate.

As noted above, a distinct theology, the so-called Sabaoth-Zion theology, has been observed within monarchic traditions.[16] This ideology is characterized by the divine epithet יֹשֵׁב הַכְּרֻבִים, that is, the God who sits enthroned above the cherubim (1 Sam 4:4; 2 Sam 6:2). Its transferal to the Temple of Solomon thereby championed a theology of God's election of and permanent presence in the Jerusalem Temple (2 Kgs 19:15). In a related expression of this theology, God sits enthroned on Zion (Ps 9:12; 135:13; 146:10).

The Priestly *kābôd* has been reckoned a direct response to the Sabaoth-Zion theology, employing specific terminology that attempted to correct the excessive image of God dwelling in the Temple. For example, von Rad argues that the Tabernacle in P is a coalescing of the Tent and ark traditions. And while the date of the combination of these originally distinct traditions cannot be determined, the compound represents a "revival of the old Tent and manifestation theology" in which "the dwelling-place and throne idea is practically superseded."[17]

---

this does not preclude the existence of earlier Tabernacle and Tent traditions (which he affirms), or of intermediary forms of Priestly theology that may have coexisted with Zion-Sabaoth theology (which he does not). The latter consideration is a consistent objection I have to Mettinger's methodology and argument. For example, Mettinger analyzes the Deuteronomistic Name (*šēm*) theology and argues that it arose as a challenge to the Sabaoth theology of the monarchy, which had asserted that Yahweh "sat" upon the cherubim throne in the Temple (see the following section). He concludes that the external circumstances that demanded a different understanding of God's presence from that of the Sabaoth theology must have been the exile, and he places the *šēm*-theology in the period following 597 B.C.E. (ibid., 78). However, it is equally possible that circumstances in the late eighth and seventh centuries might be just as relevant to this challenge. Indeed, Sabaoth and *šēm* views may have existed side by side for a considerable time. Similarly, regarding the *kābôd*-theology, Mettinger argues that Ezekiel's concept of God's presence in the Temple is closer to the Sabaoth-Zion theology than P's is, and therefore Ezekiel predates P. Again, such responses to external challenges may have existed simultaneously, and one need not resort to explaining these ideas as a singular evolutionary development.

16. See Ibid., 19–37, for a review of the Zion-Sabaoth theology of the Jerusalem cult tradition; also F. Stolz, "צִיּוֹן," *TLOT* 2.1071–76; and M. Görg, "יָשַׁב, *yāšab*," *TDOT* 6.432–38.

17. Von Rad, *Old Testament Theology*, 1.238–39.

Thus, in contrast to the Zion theology, the Priestly *kābôd* has been understood to emphasize the temporary quality of God's presence in the wilderness Tabernacle. The *miškān* and *ʾōhel môʿēd* are not the dwelling places of the divine but transitory points for God's rendezvous with Israel. Fundamental to this opinion is that, in contrast to the verb *yāšab* ('to sit, to dwell'), characterizing the Zion tradition, the common expressions for God's mode of appearance in the Tabernacle and Tent traditions are *yārad* ('to descend') and *sûr* ('to depart'), indicating the impermanence of the appearance (see, e.g., Exod 33:7–11; Num 11:14–17, 24–30; 12). Von Rad notes that other peculiar language suggests impermanence; for instance, the verbs *yāʿad* (*Niphal*), *rāʾāh* (*Niphal*), and *mālēʾ* (*Qal*) indicate the temporary nature of the appearance. The expression that Yahweh will meet with (or present himself to) the people (Exod 25:22; 29:42–43; 30:6, 36; Num 17:19) makes sense according to von Rad only in the context of the special but provisional nature of the Tabernacle.[18] These expressions were part of a theology in P that attempted to correct the image in Temple theology of God dwelling on earth.[19]

A particularly important term for the argument of the *kābôd*'s impermanence is the verb *šākan*. For example, Frank Cross contends that it is a denominative verb from *miškān*; the oldest usages of the verb, he argues, suggest the meaning "to tent, to tabernacle," and P intended this archaic understanding.[20] R. E. Clements follows Cross's position, focusing on the Priestly use of *šākan* and *miškān* as a deliberate substitution for *yāšab*.

> This development, in which a quite special technical theological sense was imparted to the verb "to tabernacle" (Heb. *šākan*), came to a new importance in the Priestly Writing. The authors are perfectly explicit that the manner in which Yahweh's presence abides in Israel is by his glory "tabernacling" there. . . . This seems to be a deliberate attempt to derive a theology out of an old cult-institution.[21]

Clements argues further that P is a late-exilic text whose theology of the *kābôd* was intended to respond to the crisis of the Temple destruction and the exile.

---

18. Idem, "The Tent and the Ark," in *The Problem of the Hexateuch and Other Essays* (trans. E. W. Trueman Dicken; New York: McGraw-Hill, 1966) 105–6.

19. This line of reasoning is extended by A. Kuschke, "Die Lagervorstellung der priesterschriftlichen Erzählung," *ZAW* 63 (1951) 74–105; and esp. by T. E. Fretheim, "The Priestly Document: Anti-Temple?" *VT* 18 (1968) 313–29.

20. F. M. Cross, "The Priestly Tabernacle," *BA* 10 (1947) 45–68; also idem, *Canaanite Myth and Hebrew Epic* (Cambridge: Harvard University Press, 1973) 245–46.

21. R. E. Clements, *God and Temple* (Oxford: Blackwell, 1965) 116–17.

For almost three-quarters of a century the temple of Jerusalem . . . had lain desolate and Yahweh's glory had not "tented" there. To make this intelligible, and to show that the divine glory was not permanently bound to one place, but only settled impermanently on earth, these authors found a very suitable expression in the verb "to tabernacle."[22]

He further describes the Priestly concept of the divine presence as a "permanent concept" of a "semi-permanent phenomenon."[23]

T. N. D. Mettinger proposes a thesis that suggests that the divine *kābôd* in the Priestly Tabernacle was an expression of permanent presence.[24] For example, regarding Exod 40:34–38 Mettinger maintains, "The passage in question does not really deal with a temporary visit, but with how the Lord takes possession of his sanctuary when it is completed."[25] Thus the *kābôd* indicates the permanent presence of God in the sanctuary. Furthermore, the use of incense restricts and regulates the access of the priest; it screens the *kappōret* from view (Lev 16:2, 13) and replicates the protective cloud that covered the fire of the *kĕbôd yhwh*: "It therefore seems probable that the *kābôd* was conceived of as continuously present, and further, as being theoretically visible above the *kappōret*."[26] Mettinger suggests that the various public appearances outside the Tabernacle (e.g., Leviticus 9; Numbers 14; 16; 17) "are not so much temporary descents of the divinity as 'emanations' of the divine *kābôd*, which is constantly present in the interior of the Tabernacle."[27]

The verbs associated with the *kābôd* are also important to Mettinger, for they indicate how the Priestly views transformed earlier traditions. First, P differs from the old Tent tradition by avoiding the verb *yārad*; that is, God does not descend upon the Tabernacle. While the encounters may be temporary in the Tabernacle accounts, this tradition nowhere implies that God does not remain present at the Tabernacle between such encounters.[28] Second, P differs from the Zion-Sabaoth theology by avoiding the verb *yāšab*; that is, God is not described as sitting enthroned above the cherubim. But in contradistinction to Cross and Clements, Mettinger believes that *šākan* as used by P does not indicate temporary presence. Rather, the difference is in the enthronement concept, which P circumvents. Mettinger regards *šākan* and *yāšab* as quite closely related; *šākan* does not have the denominative meaning as argued by Cross. It has durative and ingressive *Aktionsarten*.[29] Essentially,

---

22. Ibid., 117.
23. Ibid., 118.
24. Mettinger, *Dethronement of Sabaoth*, chap. 3, pp. 80–115.
25. Ibid., 88.
26. Ibid., 89.
27. Ibid.
28. Ibid., 86.
29. Ibid., 96.

šākan was favored over *yāšab* as a marker indicating that P discouraged the idea that God was enthroned in the Temple: "The idea of one elected place (Mt. Zion) was abandoned; instead, God is depicted as leading his people from campsite to campsite."[30] In other words, Mettinger's emphasis, relative to the opinions of Cross and Clements, is on the permanent character of God's mobile presence.

Thus, for Mettinger, the Priestly Tabernacle purposefully adapts earlier tradition. It is closely related to the premonarchic Tent tradition, but it does not retain the notion of God's temporary rendezvous (*yārad*) with Israel. Unlike the Deuteronomistic Name (*šēm*) theology, P does not remove God from the Temple.[31] While P breaks with the Zion-Temple tradition of Jerusalem, Mettinger perceives "a straight line leading from the Jerusalem tradition, insofar as the basic notion is that of divine immanence. The divine *kābôd* is depicted as being constantly present in the tabernacle."[32] Mettinger identifies P's developments of earlier theological traditions as the direct result of the historical circumstance of the exile.

In assessing the scholarly views just outlined, I would emphasize that in matters of implication, Clements and Mettinger have complementary elements. For both, first of all, the Priestly tradition underscores the special nature of the Tabernacle as the point of rendezvous for God and Israel. Second, the Tabernacle in the Priestly tradition asserts that the presence of God is mobile; Israel encounters God continually during the wilderness wanderings. When we turn to Ezekiel, we will find that these two aspects are fundamentally important in the prophet's use of *kĕbôd yhwh*. Indeed, even though Clements appears to develop Cross's argument, his conclusions imply the Tabernacle as a continually available symbol of divine presence in the wilderness. For example, regarding the portability of the ark (note 2 Sam 7:6), he comments: "No longer is the presence of Yahweh associated with a particular place at all, but instead it is related to a cultic community."[33] In this Clements and Mettinger agree. The image of the movable ark functioned as a theological expression reminding the exiles that Yahweh accompanied Israel in the wilderness. God's presence was both immanent and transcendent.

Finally, the Priestly tradition was intentionally vague as to the permanence of that presence. Mettinger surely overestimates the permanence, since P's dilemma lay in the question not only of theophany but of theodicy as well. For P it was enough that Yahweh was available to Israel outside the Temple. Through its reuse of older traditions, this is the main theological

---

30. Ibid., 97.
31. For this discussion, see ibid., chap. 2, pp. 38–79.
32. Ibid., 97.
33. Clements, *God and Temple*, 120.

proposition P offered. But this concept still leaves open the function of that presence for both judgment and guidance.

§3. The *kābôd*-Theology in Ezekiel

The expression *kĕbôd yhwh/ʾĕlōhîm* occurs fifteen times in Ezekiel (1:28; 3:12, 23; 8:4; 9:3; 10:4, 18, 19; 11:22, 23; 43:2, 4, 5; 44:4 [see *kābôd* also in 28:22; 39:13, 21]). At a quick glance, it appears to be closely related to the Priestly tradition in its depiction of theophany. For one thing, Ezekiel's vision of God's *kābôd* occasions a reaction similar to that of the people in Leviticus 9 (see Ezek 1:28; 3:23; 44:4). And, as with both the Tabernacle (Exod 40:34–35) and Temple (1 Kgs 8:11) traditions, Yahweh's *kābôd* fills the Temple of Ezekiel's visions (Ezek 10:4; 43:5; 44:4).

But does a more detailed scrutiny confirm this close connection between Ezekiel's vision of the divine presence and the tradition in P? Two features of Ezekiel's visions attract attention and pose questions. First, while the general description of the *kābôd* appears to be similar to that of P (e.g., fire and cloud, Ezek 1:4 and 10:4), Ezekiel's vision moves on to another level altogether, one that is entirely more graphic and anthropomorphic. Why might this be so? Second, as noted already, references to the divine *kābôd* are always in the context of the Jerusalem Temple—the visions of divine abandonment and restoration (sections A and A′). To what extent does this identify the location of the *kābôd*? I will discuss at length both of these questions involving Ezekiel's theology of God's presence.

The Form of the Presence

Having reviewed the characteristic nonanthropomorphic language in the Priestly tradition, I now suggest the way in which Ezekiel effectively provides a message of hope for the exiles in what might initially appear a most incongruous marriage of metaphors. This apparent paradox is the bold anthropomorphic expressions for God in Ezekiel 1 and 8. Recall (chap. 2 above) the general prohibition of physical depictions of the divine (e.g., Exod 20:4; 34:17; Deut 4:15–17; 5:8). The Priestly tradition stresses the incorporeal nature of the deity; through the *kĕbôd yhwh* it avoids the more anthropomorphic descriptions of the Yahwistic source. God makes his presence known through fire and cloud (Exod 13:21–22; 14:24; 40:38; Num 9:15–16; note Isa 4:5). God's glory descends upon the desert sanctuary (Exod 40:35). In the Elohistic source as well, the form of the theophany emphasizes God's remoteness.[34] Thus Exod 33:20 warns: כִּי לֹא־יִרְאַנִי הָאָדָם וָחָי (also Judg 13:22).

---

34. See Otto Eissfeldt, *The Old Testament: An Introduction* (trans. P. R. Ackroyd; New York: Harper & Row, 1965) 184.

Elsewhere in E, Yahweh appears only to community leaders (Exod 24:10–11; Num 12:8), especially to Moses (Exod 33:11a). In Deuteronomistic tradition, the Jerusalem Temple is the place "the Lord your God will choose as a dwelling for his name" (Deut 12:11, etc.; 1 Kgs 8:11).

When the above expressions from P, E, and D prohibiting physical depictions of the divine are combined with a similar aversion in Ezekiel, which we saw in chap. 2, it is remarkable to meet in Ezekiel's visions such astoundingly anthropomorphic descriptions of God's *kābôd*. Indeed, Ezek 1:1–3:15 and 8:1–11:25 contain the most graphic portrayals of the divine presence in the Hebrew Bible.[35]

Chapter 1 begins with a vision that the priest Ezekiel received among the exiles in Babylonia, when the heavens were opened and he saw visions of God (מַרְאוֹת אֱלֹהִים). Reflecting language of the Priestly theophany, the manifestation commences (v. 4) with a great cloud (עָנָן) and fire (אֵשׁ). God's heavenly entourage appears in the likeness of four living creatures (דְּמוּת אַרְבַּע חַיּוֹת) in human form (דְּמוּת אָדָם; v. 5). Most astonishing is the description of God, who also appears in human form (v. 26b): וְעַל דְּמוּת הַכִּסֵּא דְּמוּת כְּמַרְאֵה אָדָם עָלָיו מִלְמָעְלָה 'Upon the likeness of the throne was the likeness of the appearance of a man upon it'.[36] Ezek 1:27 redundantly emphasizes the fiery glow surrounding the divine presence: 'From the appearance of his loins upward (מִמַּרְאֵה מָתְנָיו וּלְמָעְלָה) it was like *ʿên ḥašmal*,[37] like the appearance of fire (כְּעֵין חַשְׁמַל כְּמַרְאֵה־אֵשׁ)'; below his loins, too, was brightness like the appearance of fire.[38] The opening theophany concludes in v. 28a with a description chiastically related to v. 26b: מַרְאֵה דְּמוּת כְּבוֹד־יְהוָה '(This was) the appear-

---

35. Mettinger describes Ezekiel's *kābôd* as "humanoid" (*Dethronement of Sabaoth*, 113).

36. The final עליו מלמעלה presents a problem. The LXX omits עליו and Zimmerli (*Ezekiel 1*, 88) and Leslie Allen (*Ezekiel 1–19* [WBC 28; Dallas: Word, 1994] 9) follow this version when they translate. However, two observations warn against considering the word redundant and secondary: (1) the context of this passage is filled with repetition, so the reiteration here may be stylistic; and (2) the construction מלמעלה + על occurs elsewhere; e.g., Exod 25:21 describes the הַכַּפֹּרֶת resting upon the ark, which in its entirety—ark and mercy seat—is covered by the wings of the cherubim (see also 1 Kgs 7:25). Indeed, the repetition appears deliberate. It is part of the prolix language common to many visions, as human language is stretched, twisted, and nearly broken to make it describe something that is essentially nonhuman.

37. The word השמל is found only in Ezekiel (1:4, 27; 8:2). For a discussion of Assyriological evidence that may lie behind the Hebrew, see Daniel Bodi, *The Book of Ezekiel and the Poem of Erra* (OBO 104; Freiburg: Universitätsverlag / Göttingen: Vandenhoeck & Ruprecht, 1991) 82–94; and S. P. Garfinkel, *Studies in Akkadian Influences in the Book of Ezekiel* (Ph.D. diss., Columbia University, 1983) 81–82.

38. Compare the theophany in Num 9:15. On the synonymous usage of כמראה אש with כבוד יהוה, see Morgenstern, "Biblical Theophanies," 143–44.

ance of the likeness of the glory of Yahweh'. The repetitive use of דְּמוּת (12 times)[39] and כְּמַרְאֵה (12 times) presents the prophetic struggle to describe the divine presence, particularly considering Ezekiel's attempt to sketch God in such graphically anthropomorphic terms.[40]

In chaps. 2 and 3 the divine presence directly addresses Ezekiel and commands him to speak God's words to Israel, a commission that is dramatically carried out (2:8b–3:3). God commands the prophet to open his mouth and eat what he gives him: וָאֶרְאֶה וְהִנֵּה־יָד שְׁלוּחָה אֵלָי וְהִנֵּה־בוֹ מְגִלַּת־סֵפֶר 'And I looked and there was a hand stretched out to me, and there was in it a scroll of writing' (2:9). God feeds the prophet this scroll, and Ezekiel opens his mouth and eats it (3:2–3). The commission ends with an exit as dramatic as God's theophanic entrance: the Spirit lifts the prophet as the presence of Yahweh rises from the Temple (3:12–13; compare 11:23–24), and the hand of Yahweh (יַד־יְהוָה) returns the prophet to his fellow exiles in Babylonia (3:14–15).

Perhaps nowhere in Ezekiel is the paradox of legitimate representation of the divine presence more extraordinary than in chap. 8, which contains a lengthy condemnation of practices that involve idolatrous representations in the Temple (vv. 5–18). God shows Ezekiel these visions of worship in the Temple and calls them תּוֹעֵבוֹת. Yet in spite of this thoroughly aniconic tirade, Ezekiel 8 launches with a graphic description of Yahweh (vv. 1–3a) that recalls the opening vision of chap. 1.

וַיְהִי בַּשָּׁנָה הַשִּׁשִׁית בַּשִּׁשִׁי בַּחֲמִשָּׁה לַחֹדֶשׁ אֲנִי יוֹשֵׁב בְּבֵיתִי וְזִקְנֵי יְהוּדָה
יוֹשְׁבִים לְפָנָי וַתִּפֹּל עָלַי שָׁם יַד אֲדֹנָי יְהוִה: וָאֶרְאֶה וְהִנֵּה דְמוּת
[כְּמַרְאֵה־](אֵשׁ) אִישׁ מִמַּרְאֵה מָתְנָיו וּלְמַטָּה אֵשׁ וּמִמָּתְנָיו וּלְמַעְלָה
כְּמַרְאֵה־זֹהַר כְּעֵין הַחַשְׁמַלָה: וַיִּשְׁלַח תַּבְנִית יָד וַיִּקָּחֵנִי בְּצִיצִת רֹאשִׁי וַתִּשָּׂא
אֹתִי רוּחַ בֵּין־הָאָרֶץ וּבֵין הַשָּׁמַיִם וַתָּבֵא אֹתִי יְרוּשָׁלְַמָה בְּמַרְאוֹת אֱלֹהִים[41]

---

39. Ezek 1:5 (2 times), 10, 13, 16, 26 (2 times), 28; 10:1, 10, 21, 22. On *dĕmût*'s special connection with the theophanic tradition, see Barr, "Theophany and Anthropomorphism in the Old Testament," 31–38; and idem, "The Image of God in the Book of Genesis: A Study in Terminology," *BJRL* 51 (1968) 11–26.

40. As an aside, Dan 8:15–17 clearly appropriates the imagery of Ezek 1:26–28. Consider the expression כְּמַרְאֵה־גָבֶר (v. 15) used for Gabriel, Daniel's designation as בֶּן־אָדָם (v. 17b), and the same awe-struck response to the visions (v. 17a; see Ezek 1:28b).

41. This passage raises several text-critical concerns. See Zimmerli, *Ezekiel 1*, 216–17 for a full evaluation. Many of the problems in 8:1–2 revolve around determining the relation between both the MT and the LXX, and 8:1–2 and 1:26–27. Only the more significant issues will be noted here. In 8:1 the LXX omits אדני; Zimmerli (*Ezekiel 2*, 556) considers this a possible secondary intrusion, being originally the shorter form יד־יהוה (1:3; 3:14, 22; 33:22; 37:1; 40:1), but becoming expanded in the light of Ezekiel's very characteristic אדני יהוה (217 occurrences). In 8:2a the LXX's understanding of אִישׁ for the MT's

(1) In the sixth year, in the sixth month, on the fifth day of the month, as I was sitting in my house, and the elders of Judah were sitting before me, the hand of the Lord Yahweh fell upon me. (2) I looked and there was the likeness of [the appearance of] a man; from the appearance of his loins and below was fire, and from his loins upward was like the appearance of shining, like *ʿên ḥašmal.* (3) He put forth the form of a hand, and he took me by a tuft of my hair; and the Spirit lifted me up between earth and heaven, and brought me to Jerusalem, in visions of God.

It would seem that for Ezekiel highly graphic portrayals of the divine presence did not constitute idolatry.[42]

The question of the form of God's anthropomorphic appearance is a complex one and no doubt also involves the issue of Israelite self-conception. That there is a strong tradition of anthropomorphic representation of God in the Hebrew Bible, both as a man and as a *malʾāk*, James Barr notes,[43] but he suggests that "the central truth in this is the ability of God to assume a form and to let this form be seen by men."[44] In other words, such theophanies have a purpose in the divine-human encounter that eclipses the form of the appearance. The signficance of the form is derived from its function. The essential issue is not whether God is conceived of in human form but why such anthropomorphic theophanies occur and how they function in that context.

אֶשׁ (set in angle brackets) is clearly preferable, corresponding as it would with 1:26. The corruption to אֵשׁ may have entered either as an error through contact with אֵשׁ in v. 2b or from an intentional association with כמראה אשׁ in 1:27 (2×). The first כמראה (set in square brackets) is difficult; it may be original reflecting 1:26 (with אִישׁ) or it may be secondary, reflecting 1:27 (with אֵשׁ). ממראה is not attested in the LXX, though it is not necessarily a secondary gloss reflecting 1:27. If it is, it merely indicates that a later hand was emphasizing the clear relationship between this passage and the vision in chap. 1.

42. Note too that in this vision it is a form of a hand תַּבְנִית יָד that reaches out to take Ezekiel by his hair (8:3), while the room of idolatrous pictures is described as כָּל־תַּבְנִית רֶמֶשׂ וּבְהֵמָה . . . מְחֻקֶּה עַל־הַקִּיר (8:10). This observation raises an issue that M. Halbertal and A. Margalit address in chaps. 2 and 3 of *Idolatry* (trans. Naomi Goldblum; Cambridge: Harvard University Press, 1992), namely, what are the boundaries of *legitimate* representations of God? The prophet's answer appears to be twofold: idolatry, that is, a physical image, is an illegitimate depiction of a deity, while a linguistic description of God's presence is permissible.

43. Barr, "Theophany and Anthropomorphism in the Old Testament," 37. On מלאך יהוה, see Johannes Lindblom, "Theophanies in Holy Places in Hebrew Religion," *HUCA* 32 (1961), esp. pp. 101–6. Note the sharp distinction in Exod 33:1–6 between the presence of God and the use of a surrogate *malʾak*. In this Elohistic narrative, it indicates God's presence one step removed.

44. Barr, "Theophany and Anthropomorphism in the Old Testament," 32.

Ezekiel's attempt to mediate between God's boundlessness and God's real presence among the exiles is the theological dilemma that motivates the striking nature of the *kābôd*-visions. The struggle for an effective medium produces such vividly graphic portrayals of the otherwise abstract theology of the *kĕbôd yhwh*. It is a testament to Ezekiel's theological imagination that he employs the Priestly technical expression of God's transcendence and formless immanence.

Here again is a permutation of the paradox of God's absence and presence. An effective exilic theology must do two things: (1) it must maintain God's transcendence in order to provide the vehicle for God to trespass borders; and (2) it must employ an image of God's proximity whose sentient quality the prophet can communicate to those who have no vision. Through such concrete portrayals of God presence, Ezekiel's vision functions in a way that is similar to the *kĕbôd yhwh* that brings an end to the wilderness murmurings (Num 14:10; 16:19; 20:16): the appearance of God's glory introduces divine judgment (theodicy), guarantees the presence of God in their midst, and affirms the divinely appointed leadership (Moses and Aaron in Numbers, the prophet himself in Ezekiel). These observations understand the purpose of the *kābôd* in Ezekiel as stressing the reality of God's presence in the people's midst and the role of the prophet who mediates that presence.

The Location of the Presence

It is clear from the above review of the P tradition that the incorporation of the *kābôd*-theology was essential to Ezekiel, accomplishing significant conceptual objectives—on the one hand, as we have just seen it endorsed, the notion of a real presence located in Jerusalem. Through this notion of divine presence, Ezekiel could then fashion an utterly effective image of God's absence through the vision of God's removing the *kābôd* from the Temple, thereby accenting the message of judgment. On the other hand, the image of God's absence, that is, his removal from the Temple, allowed the potential for an effective message of his theophanic presence in exile. The *kābôd*-theology in Ezekiel thus served dual purposes: it provided an effective image of God's absence from Jerusalem and an effective image of God's presence in exile.[45]

Both functions of the *kābôd* are especially manifest through the image of the wheels, emphasizing God's mobility (1:15–21; 10:9–17). Indeed, this appears to be a governing concept. While the Temple is the initial site of God's presence, the accent is on the mobility of the *kābôd* as a means of expressing judgment (God's absence) and stressing God's presence in exile. Thus while Ezekiel may retain the concept of cherubim and throne (which may also be

---

45. Interestingly, in Hos 10:5–6 the *kābôd* is inseparable from Samaria's idol that is taken into exile, carried to Assyria as tribute.

in the deep background of P), the controlling image is the same: God's presence has no boundaries. The Temple, too, in Ezekiel is only a temporary residence. It is implicit that the same vision of God's glory that appeared to rise from the Temple (Ezekiel 1) and depart from Jerusalem (Ezek 11:22–23) is the same divine presence that Ezekiel sees in exile during the sixth year (8:1–4; compare 1:2).

In this matter, Mettinger's reconstruction of the theological lineages of P and Ezekiel is inadequate. He argues that the *kābôd* concept in Ezekiel represents an earlier phase than the concept represented in P.[46] According to him, the *kābôd*-theology in Ezekiel exhibits a close relationship to the Sabaoth-Zion theology because the Jerusalem Temple is the usual dwelling place for the *kābôd*.

> Thus our general conclusion is necessarily that the presence of God in the sanctuary is in Ezekiel the same nature as that expressed in the Zion-Sabaoth theology: The Temple on Zion is envisioned as the site of the continuous presence of God; it is there he sits enthroned above the cherubim.[47]

Mettinger attempts systematically to arrive at a relative dating of the various theologies of God's presence, moving from the Sabaoth-Zion theology to Ezekiel's *kābôd*-theology to the Priestly *kābôd*-theology: "Ezekiel and P are both exponents of a common Priestly tradition, though P's *kābôd* theology appears to be a more advanced development than that propounded by Ezekiel."[48] Again, the basis of this conclusion is primarily the emphasis on the throne motif, which Mettinger argues is absent from P; in Ezekiel the primary presence of God is the Zion Temple, whereas P's *kābôd* is located in the wilderness ark.

This relative dating, however, is not certain. Instead, Ezekiel and P are more likely interacting with the same theological stream, dipping into the same well of tradition.[49] Indeed, here Ezekiel is drawing on a central aspect of the Priestly Tabernacle theology: the mobility of the ark as it moves through the wilderness from campsite to campsite.[50]

---

46. Mettinger, *Dethronement of Sabaoth*, 116.

47. Ibid., 119. Mettinger, of course, adds that Ezekiel differs from the Sabaoth theology in that the *kābôd* becomes mobile and abandons the Jerusalem Temple (p. 117).

48. Ibid., 113.

49. Incidentally, I suggested in chap. 2 that Ezekiel and the Priestly writer adopted and adapted the Mesopotamian tradition of the "image of (a) god." The redactor P and the prophet Ezekiel are exilic responses to the sixth-century crisis, drawing both on earlier Israelite material (priestly and nonpriestly) and on concepts encountered in exile.

50. In §4 below we will see how this motif of the wilderness ark explicitly operates in Ezekiel.

Mettinger suggests that the *kābôd*-theology was used by Ezekiel in order to emphasize the conditional nature of God's presence in the face of the people's sin: "The Lord surrenders the Temple and delivers Jerusalem to judgment. But towards the end of his prophetic career, Ezekiel also found occasion to proclaim the hope that the Lord would return to his sanctuary."[51] Thus, the Temple is the locale of the divine *kābôd* in Ezekiel.[52] Though Jerusalem and the Temple are razed, God is secure, for the *kābôd*-theology saw fit to replace the image of God's dwelling on a throne with the more transcendent image of the divine presence.

This view, however, is only partially correct. Ezekiel drew upon a tradition that answered a related question: Was God's presence available outside of the Temple, outside of Jerusalem, even in exile? Barr has rightly observed, "In Ezekiel there is the special interest in the mobility of the *kabod* which was no doubt already attached to the tradition of the migration in the desert and which was of value to Ezekiel for its relation to the exile."[53] Zimmerli has expressed precisely this understanding of the opening vision.

> It is at least clear from Ezek[iel] 1 that the prophet, in his encounter with the glory of Yahweh in the land to which he had been exiled, experienced something which shattered all his expectations and which also, of necessity, decisively determined his subsequent preaching. No vague presence of deity passed him by, but Yahweh, the God of Israel, in the glory of the כבוד יהוה met him as he had met with Israel in the great events of the wilderness period, as recalled in the related Priestly view of the nation's past history.[54]

It is to this function of Ezekiel's *kābôd*, its association with the wilderness wanderings, that we now turn.[55]

---

51. Mettinger, *Dethronement of Sabaoth*, 111–12.

52. It appears that Clements agrees with this point (*God and Temple*, 120).

53. Barr, "Theophany and Anthropomorphism in the Old Testament," p. 37.

54. Zimmerli, *Ezekiel 1*, 124.

55. An analysis of the possible relationship between Ezekiel's use of *kābôd* and the various Mesopotamian concepts associated with divine presence lies outside the present scope of this study. For example, Mesopotamian terminology expressing divine presence—*melammu, puluḫtu, rašubbatu,* and *namurratu*—might be considered in context of Ezekiel's use of *kĕbôd yhwh/ʾĕlōhîm*. For discussion of these concepts, see CAD M/2 9–12 (on *melammu*); CAD N/1 253–54 (on *namurratu*); A. Leo Oppenheim, "Akkadian *pul(u)ḫ(t)u* and *melammu,*" *JAOS* 63 (1943) 31–34; E. Cassin, *La splendeur divine* (Civilisations et societiés 8; Paris: Mouton, 1968); M. Weinfeld, "The Creator God in Genesis 1 and in the Prophecies of Deutero-Isaiah," *Tarbiz* 37/2 (1968) 131–32; idem, "כָּבוֹד, *kābôd,*" *TDOT* 6.29–31; Mendenhall, *The Tenth Generation,* chap. 2; P. Machinist, "Assyria and Its Image in the First Isaiah," *JAOS* 103 (1983) 727; also idem, *The Epic of Tukulti-Ninurta I: A Study in Middle Assyrian Literature* (Ph.D. diss., Yale University, 1978) 67 and 177 (for a discussion of its use in the epic, col. I.A obv. line 12′); and M. Haran, "The Shining of Moses'

§4. Yahweh's Presence in Exile

Ezekiel contains striking associations between the exile and the wilderness wanderings. In this section, I outline several areas in which the book of Ezekiel reflects the post-Exodus tradition of Moses and Israel in the מִדְבָּר. The subsequent analysis suggests that this reflection was intended to stress the nature and purpose of the *kābôd*. Specifically, the function of these associations continue the theme already seen: exile is both a means of punishment and an opportunity for divine presence.

Exile and Wilderness

As noted above, it is implicit in Ezekiel that the divine *kābôd* that appeared to abandon the Temple (Ezekiel 1) and leave Jerusalem (Ezek 11:22–23) is the same divine presence that Ezekiel sees in exile during the sixth year (8:1–4; compare 1:2). While in Ezek 8:3b and 11:24 it is the רוּחַ that transports the prophet between Jerusalem and Babylonia, Ezek 8:2–3a, 4 (cited above) describe an identical figure associated with the *kĕbôd yhwh* in chap. 1. In other words, while it is not clear what the *kābôd* does after it reaches the mountain on the east side of the city (11:23), it is implied in 8:2 that Ezekiel encountered this same presence in exile. The mobility of the *kābôd* in the wilderness sanctuary is paralleled by Ezekiel's vision of the same mobile presence and its availability for Ezekiel to experience in exile. No doubt, too, the characteristic expression of the prophetic role, namely, וַיְהִי דְבַר־יְהוָה אֵלַי לֵאמֹר, which occurs nearly fifty times in Ezekiel, emphasizes the exilic encounter with God.[56]

When we turn to Ezekiel 20, we find a direct connection between the exile and the wilderness tradition. The chapter is Ezekiel's abstract of Israel's history. Like a refrain, the wilderness experience is rehearsed 9 times (20:10, 13, 15, 17, 18, 21, 23, 35, 36). Two elements in this usage are particularly striking. First, Ezekiel emphasizes a tradition that Israel had turned to idols in Egypt (*gillûlê miṣrayim*; 20:7, 8). The Exodus, according to Ezekiel, was the result of God's growing wrath.

Face: A Case Study in Biblical and Ancient Near Eastern Iconography," in *In the Shelter of Elyon* (ed. W. B. Barrick and J. R. Spencer; JSOTSup 31; Sheffield: JSOT Press, 1984), esp. pp. 167–68 nn. 18–21. For the iconography associated with such concepts, see Mettinger, *Dethronement of Sabaoth*, 103–6; and Othmar Keel, *Jahwe-Visionen und Siegelkunst* (SBS 84/85; Stuttgart: Katholisches Bibelwerk, 1977).

56. Ezek 1:3; 3:16; 6:1; 7:1; 11:14; 12:1, 8, 17, 21, 26; 13:1; 14:2, 12; 15:1; 16:1; 17:1, 11; 18:1; 20:2; 21:1, 6, 13, 23; 22:1, 17, 23; 23:1; 24:1, 15, 20; 25:1; 27:1; 28:1, 11, 20; 29:1, 17; 30:1, 20; 31:1; 32:1, 17; 33:1, 23; 34:1; 35:1; 36:1; 37:15; 38:1.

וַיַּמְרוּ־בִי וְלֹא אָבוּ לִשְׁמֹעַ אֵלַי אִישׁ אֶת־שִׁקּוּצֵי עֵינֵיהֶם לֹא הִשְׁלִיכוּ
וְאֶת־גִּלּוּלֵי מִצְרַיִם לֹא עָזָבוּ וָאֹמַר לִשְׁפֹּךְ חֲמָתִי עֲלֵיהֶם לְכַלּוֹת אַפִּי בָּהֶם
בְּתוֹךְ אֶרֶץ מִצְרָיִם: וָאַעַשׂ לְמַעַן שְׁמִי לְבִלְתִּי הֵחֵל לְעֵינֵי הַגּוֹיִם אֲשֶׁר־הֵמָּה
בְתוֹכָם אֲשֶׁר נוֹדַעְתִּי אֲלֵיהֶם לְעֵינֵיהֶם לְהוֹצִיאָם מֵאֶרֶץ מִצְרָיִם: וָאוֹצִיאֵם
מֵאֶרֶץ מִצְרַיִם וָאֲבִאֵם אֶל־הַמִּדְבָּר: [57]

(8) But they rebelled against me, and they would not listen to me. No
one threw away the detestable things that were before their eyes, and
the idols of Egypt they did not abandon. So I determined that I
would pour forth my wrath against them, sate my anger against them,
in the midst of the land of Egypt. (9) But I acted for the sake of my
name—so that it might not be profaned in the sight of the nations in
whose midst they were, in whose sight I made known myself to
them—by bringing them from Egypt. (10) So I led them forth from
the land of Egypt and I brought them to the wilderness.

Thus while Ezekiel says that God had promised to bring them to a land flow-
ing with milk and honey (20:6), their idolatries in Egypt led them first to the
wilderness. But even in the wilderness they followed idols.

Moreover, the wilderness is the focus of Ezekiel's history of Israel (20:10–
26). The postwilderness experience in the land that God gives them is but an
interlude, again marked by idolatry (20:27–34). The exile is the wilderness
revisited (20:35–36).

וְהֵבֵאתִי אֶתְכֶם אֶל־מִדְבַּר הָעַמִּים וְנִשְׁפַּטְתִּי אִתְּכֶם שָׁם פָּנִים אֶל־פָּנִים:
כַּאֲשֶׁר נִשְׁפַּטְתִּי אֶת־אֲבוֹתֵיכֶם בְּמִדְבַּר אֶרֶץ מִצְרָיִם כֵּן אִשָּׁפֵט אִתְּכֶם נְאֻם
אֲדֹנָי יְהוִה:

(35) And I will bring you into the wilderness of the peoples, and I will
judge you there face to face. (36) As I judged your fathers in the wilderness of the land of Egypt, so I will judge you, says the Lord Yahweh.

Clearly, the image of the wilderness tradition is key to Ezekiel and to his interpretation of the exile. Allen is partially correct when he says that Ezekiel
"associated the wilderness not with a high level of human commitment, as in
Hos 2:17 (15) and Jer 2:2, but with sin and judgment, as in Exodus 16 and
32 and Numbers 14 and 16. The present had to be interpreted in terms of
this theological past. Ezekiel had no positive reply from God to give to the
exilic leaders."[58] The former point is accurate, but the latter is not.

The positive element of Ezekiel's wilderness imagery becomes apparent
when we consider Ezekiel's role. Regarding the reality of Ezekiel's setting in

57. No text-critical concerns are present here.
58. L. C. Allen, *Ezekiel 20–48* (WBC 29; Dallas: Word, 1990) 15.

Babylonia, recall Orlinsky's comment that if the prophet had received his call
in Jerusalem, instead of in a foreign land, this would have been clearly mentioned: "There is only one difference between Ezekiel's call and theirs (i.e.,
previous prophets), namely, the Lord came from Judah to Babylonia, and
with His holy presence on foreign soil commissioned Ezekiel as His prophet."[59] Yet tradition does attribute a call on foreign soil to another prophet—namely, Moses. Nor is this the only association between Moses and
Ezekiel. For example, Jon Levenson has discussed the "new Exodus" traditions in Ezekiel 40–48 and suggested (in reference to Ezek 20:32–44), "This
idea of a 'new Moses,' already apparent in Deuteronomic thinking (Dt.
18:15), is not alien to Ezekiel's theology, where the concept of a 'new Exodus'
is explicit."[60] And more recently, Henry McKeating has taken Levenson's
statement as a starting point, elaborating the literary and theological relationship between Ezekiel and Moses. McKeating focuses on chaps. 20 and 40–48
but also notes that the active role of Ezekiel in the vision of the dry bones
(chap. 37) depends on Mosaic tradition.[61]

In other words, Israel is not bereft of leadership. Though they have entered a wilderness for judgment, they have prophetic presence before whom
the elders continually come (Ezek 8:1; 14:1; 20:1). The next section will
develop this point, suggesting how more than mere prophetic presence is
granted to Israel in exile. The Exodus traditions, particularly the traditions
involving the sanctuary and the *kābôd*, are essential elements of Ezekiel's theology of God's absence and presence.

Yahweh as Sanctuary

The association between the Exodus and the wilderness, between Moses
and Ezekiel, has an ultimately positive function in the prophet's theology.
Consider, for example, Ezekiel 1–11 in the context of Exod 40:34–38.[62] The

---

59. H. M. Orlinsky, "Where Did Ezekiel Receive the Call to Prophesy?" *BASOR* 122
(1951) 35. On rabbinic tradition that Ezekiel must have received his initial call in Israel because God did not reveal himself outside the land, see §3 in S. Spiegel, "Ezekiel or Pseudo-
Ezekiel?" *HTR* 24 (1931) 244–321 (repr. in *Pseudo-Ezekiel and the Original Prophecy and
Critical Articles by Shalom Spiegel and C. C. Torrey* [ed. M. Greenberg; New York: KTAV,
1970] 123–99).

60. J. Levenson, *Theology of the Program of Restoration of Ezekiel 40–48* (HSM 10;
Missoula, Mont.: Scholars Press, 1976) 38.

61. H. McKeating, "Ezekiel the 'Prophet Like Moses'?" *JSOT* 61 (1994) 97–109.

62. Though it is outside the immediate scope of this study, I believe that a relationship
that deserves further attention exists between the Exodus narrative of the ark construction
and the book of Ezekiel. In particular, it appears significant that the ark construction (Exodus 25–31, 35–40) is split, as it were, by the incident of the idol-calf (chap. 32), Moses'
appeal to God's continued presence (chap. 33), and the renewal of the covenant (chap. 34),

focus of the opening chapters is the rising of the divine *kābôd* above the Temple. It departs from the Temple and dramatically leaves the city, settling rather suspensefully on the mount east of the city. Exod 40:34–38 provides a tradition of the *kābôd* that Ezekiel drew upon for his theology of God's presence in exile. In the Exodus account, as already seen, the Tabernacle is complete, and Yahweh fills the Tabernacle with his presence. The passage concludes with the function of God's presence in the Tabernacle; that is, the *kābôd* is poised to lead Israel through the wilderness (40:36–38).

וּבְהֵעָלוֹת הֶעָנָן מֵעַל הַמִּשְׁכָּן יִסְעוּ בְּנֵי יִשְׂרָאֵל בְּכֹל מַסְעֵיהֶם: וְאִם־לֹא
יֵעָלֶה הֶעָנָן וְלֹא יִסְעוּ עַד־יוֹם הֵעָלֹתוֹ: כִּי עֲנַן יְהֹוָה עַל־הַמִּשְׁכָּן יוֹמָם וְאֵשׁ
תִּהְיֶה לַיְלָה בּוֹ לְעֵינֵי כָל־בֵּית־יִשְׂרָאֵל בְּכָל־מַסְעֵיהֶם:

(36) When the cloud went up from the Tabernacle, the children of Israel journeyed onward during all their journeys. (37) And if the cloud did not rise up, they did not journey onward until the day it went up. (38) For the cloud of Yahweh was upon the Tabernacle daily, and the fire was in it every night, in the sight of all the house of Israel during all their journeys.

It appears, too, that the *kĕbôd yhwh* in Ezekiel 11 is poised on the mountain just outside the Temple. And while we hear no explicit mention of what happens next, the direction of the withdrawal from the Temple implicitly reveals its function. Recall that Ezekiel 11 describes the departure of the divine *kābôd* out of the city toward the east (11:23). This direction is then reversed in Ezek 43:1–5, when the divine *kābôd* returns to the Temple: "And behold, the *kĕbôd ʾĕlōhê yiśrāʾēl* came from the east" (v. 2). This is the same form that Ezekiel saw when God came to destroy the Temple and that he saw by the River Kebar (v. 3). The *kĕbôd yhwh* then enters the Temple through the east gate (v. 4) with the same finale as Exodus 40: וְהִנֵּה מָלֵא כְבוֹד־יהוה הַבָּיִת (v. 5). In the interim between God's departure from the Temple and God's expected return, the divine *kābôd* would be available to Israel in exile, as it was available to Israel in the wilderness.

Ezek 11:16 adds one more vital clue about the function of this departure eastward. In this passage, the prophet responds to the inhabitants of Jerusalem, who claim that the exiles have gone far from Yahweh and assert that they themselves are the rightful possessors of the land (11:15). The prophet censures this boast with a response that identifies Yahweh's presence among the exiles as a type of sanctuary (v. 16).

---

while the structure of Ezekiel moves from God's presence in the Temple to his absence because of idolatrous sin to a restoration of God's presence in a newly constructed Temple.

לָכֵן אֱמֹר כֹּה־אָמַר אֲדֹנָי יְהוָה כִּי הִרְחַקְתִּים בַּגּוֹיִם וְכִי הֲפִיצוֹתִים בָּאֲרָצוֹת
וָאֱהִי לָהֶם לְמִקְדָּשׁ מְעַט בָּאֲרָצוֹת אֲשֶׁר־בָּאוּ שָׁם: [63]

Though I removed them far among the nations, and though I have
scattered them in the lands, yet I have been to them a little sanctuary
(or a sanctuary for a little while) in the lands where they have gone.

The meaning of מִקְדָּשׁ מְעַט is only slightly difficult. While Zimmerli may be
correct to view this a "counterpart of the covenant formulation אהיה להם
לאלהים, which follows in v. 20,"[64] his translation ('I have been a sanctuary to
them [only] a little in the countries to which they have come'[65]) misses the
point. The expression is better rendered as one of the following: 'small sanctuary' or 'a sanctuary for a little while'. Greenberg translates it with the
former sense, noting Dan 11:34, עֵזֶר מְעַט 'little help'.[66] Accordingly, the distinction between Yahweh's presence in Jerusalem and in exile is one of relative degree. Alternately, the latter translation, 'a sanctuary for a little while',
underscores the nature of God's presence as one of duration. Perhaps 11:17
better supports this understanding, since it emphasizes that the exile will be
temporary, for Yahweh will restore the scattered Israel. Both translations re-

63. Ezek 11:14–21 is often regarded a secondary addition. To be sure, the entire chapter has inconsistent qualities: (1) Ezek 11:1–13 describes events in Jerusalem, particularly
the counsel of Jaazaniah and Pelatiah, leaders of the people. The passage contains an oracle
of judgment (vv. 5–12). (2) Ezek 11:14–21 directs a message of hope and restoration to the
exiles. (3) Ezek 11:22–25 appears to resume the action of chap. 10, namely, the departure
of the *kĕbôd yhwh*. While chap. 11 certainly has undergone editorial transformation, 11:1–
13 and 11:14–21 appear to be self-contained units. These have been joined and inserted
between the action of 10:22 and 11:22. However, both 11:1–13 and 11:14–21 are likely
early material from the hand of Ezekiel himself. Two points support this. First, judgment
and restoration need not be considered incongruous and therefore marks of different authorship (contra S. Herrmann, *Die prophetischen Heilserwartungen im Alten Testament*
[BWANT 85; Stuttgart: Kohlhammer, 1965], esp. p. 290). Indeed, Thomas Raitt has explained the structural and verbal tension between the oracles of judgment and the oracles
of restoration as an essential element in Ezekiel's theology (*A Theology of Exile: Judgment/
Deliverance in Jeremiah and Ezekiel* [Philadelphia: Fortress, 1977], esp. pp. 181–82 on
Ezek 11:17–21). Second, it is evident that both passages were written before the destruc-
tion of the Temple in 587 B.C.E. (see Zimmerli, *Ezekiel 1*, 263; and also Paul Joyce, *Divine
Initiative and Human Response in Ezekiel* [JSOTSup 51; Sheffield: Sheffield Academic
Press, 1989] 115). Ezek 11:16 is a response to the inhabitants of Jerusalem (11:15), whose
claim to the land rests on a claim to the Temple, which is still standing (as it also is in 11:1).

64. Zimmerli, *Ezekiel 1*, 262.

65. Ibid., 230.

66. M. Greenberg, *Ezekiel 1–20* (AB 22; Garden City, N.Y.: Doubleday, 1983) 186,
190. Note also Ezek 5:3. Compare B. Waltke and M. O'Connor's "I have been to *some extent* a sanctuary for them" (*An Introduction to Biblical Hebrew Syntax* [Winona Lake, Ind.:
Eisenbrauns, 1990] 663), in which מעט is an adverbial disjunct.

flect the syntax and context of the passage: the clause is set off disjunctively from the two clauses introduced by *kî*; and the verses that follow reveal the ultimately positive role that Yahweh will have in exile, as he had in the wilderness (11:17–21; compare also 20:34–44).

The imagery in Ezek 11:16 is a direct outgrowth of the Priestly tradition's portrait of God's presence in the Tabernacle.[67] Yahweh will be present among Israel *as* a sanctuary. Ezek 11:23 indicates the direction of the *kābôd*—the *miqdāš mĕʿāṭ*—will take: God is moving eastward to accompany his people in exile.[68] The absence of God from the Temple (the removal of the divine *kābôd*) is both theodicy and theophany: it allows the presence of God to be associated with Israel in exile. And the Tabernacle, as so often in the Priestly accounts, serves a dual role: assurance of God's presence and judgment. The manifestation of the *kābôd* to Ezekiel among the exiles marks the relocation of God's presence from the Jerusalem to Babylonia.[69]

§5. *Conclusion*

As the earlier outline showed, the Temple is a structuring device in the book of Ezekiel. In part A, the *kĕbôd yhwh* abandons the Temple. In part A′, the divine presence returns to a renewed people in a restored Temple. Notwithstanding, the Temple is not the exclusive location for God's presence in Ezekiel. Rather, the prophet adapts Priestly traditions involving the wilderness sanctuary in order to emphasize two prophetic points: judgment and guidance. The Temple is a stage on which the prophet dramatizes both the presence and absence of God. Presence and absence, like a polar field, exist as opposites and as complements.

In the face of Israel's sin, idolatry, the prophet constructed a theology of God's presence that transcended the physical representation of God but

---

67. The term *miqdāš* is used in the Priestly source as an equivalent to both *miškān* and *ʾōhel môʿēd* (Exod 25:8; Lev 12:4; 16:33; 19:30; 20:3; 21:12; 26:2; Num 3:38; 10:21; 18:1; 19:20), and in Ezekiel it is used synonymously for the Temple (5:11; 8:6; 23:38, 29; 24:21 [!]; 25:3; 37:26, 28; 43:21; 44:1, 5, 9, 15, 16; 45:3, 4, 18; 47:12; 48:8, 10, 21).

68. As an aside, note the aggadic interpretation of מָקוֹם for God. Josephus appears to have known this tradition (*Ant.* 11.6.7 §227, on Esth 4:14), as did Philo (τόπος; e.g., *De Somniis* 1.11). Additional texts that reflect this tradition can be found in Louis Ginzberg, *The Legends of the Jews* (7 vols.; Philadelphia: Jewish Publication Society, 1909–38; repr. Johns Hopkins University Press, 1998) 5.289 n. 130, and 6.470 n. 139.

69. I arrived at this point independently of Paul Joyce's recent study of Ezek 11:16 ("Dislocation and Adaption in the Exilic Age and After," in *After the Exile: Essays in Honour of Rex Mason* [ed. John Barton and David J. Reimer; Macon, Ga.: Mercer University Press, 1996] 45–58). He expresses his assessment of this phrase thus: "Ezekiel affirmed nothing less than the presence of the God of Israel in alien Babylonia, far from the Temple site" (p. 57).

nevertheless effectively communicated the objective reality of God's presence. In Ezekiel's description of theophany, the *kābôd*-tradition delivered both messages. On the one hand, God's abandonment of the Temple emphasized the argument against idolatry: the absence of the Temple was not equal to the absence of the deity. On the other hand, the wilderness motif asserted God's continued presence. God *was* a sanctuary in exile, in spite of his apparent absence and the loss of the Temple. Such a determined emphasis on God's presence was an absolute necessity, considering Ezekiel's ubiquitous denial of the physical representation of divinity. Theophany had to stand up to the challenges of idolatry.

The twin problems of idolatry and exile become joined in the mind of Ezekiel; the theological paradox of God's absence and presence becomes a prophetic response to both dilemmas. As seen in chap. 2, God's absence was an argument for his presence and power, while the presence of idols indicated their absence and impotence. Chapter 3 shows that Ezekiel extends this proposition into a corollary: God's presence is not consigned to sanctuary, for God *is* a sanctuary. In this regard, absence from the Temple is a message of judgment and the precursor to a message of restoration. If God can become a sanctuary, his presence in exile becomes a message of victory even over imperial powers.

God was a *miqdāš mě'āṭ* in exile. The return of the *kābôd* to the Temple was merely the finale of a long experience of God's presence. Thus it is significant that Ezekiel's preferred term for the restored Temple in chaps. 40–48 is *miqdāš*. That the prophet could foresee such a restoration in Jerusalem, that the people could accept such an expectation, was due to the already proclaimed presence in the second wilderness—the exile. It is interesting that when 2 Kgs 23:27 announces that God has rejected Jerusalem, the Deuteronomist describes the Temple as "the house of which I (Yahweh) had said, יִהְיֶה שְׁמִי שָׁם." As if to reverse the effects of the exile, Ezek 48:35 promises the return of God's presence to Jerusalem, which God now renames וְשֵׁם־הָעִיר מִיּוֹם יְהוָה שָׁמָּה.

Chapter 4

Idolatry and Theonomy:
The Power of God's Presence

And they will say, "This land that was desolate
has become like the Garden of Eden."
Ezekiel 36:35

§1. Introduction

Chapter 3 outlined the significance of the structure of the book of Ezekiel. The divine presence abandons his sanctuary, which faces destruction, and the people are deported to Babylonia, where Israel is cleansed of its sins, revivified, and promised return from exile. Ezekiel is shown a vision of the restored Jerusalem Temple, to which the divine presence returns. It should also be obvious from the structure described in chap. 3 that the historical context of Ezekiel is intrinsic to the polemic against idolatry. The very consequence of the exile is instructive: the loss of the Temple confronted the exiles with a God present in his absence, who *was* a 'little sanctuary' (*miqdāš mĕ'aṭ*, 11:16), not a deity residing *in* a sanctuary—a God not limited by boundary or building. The exile was an object lesson of God's continued presence and activity outside of the identity of the Jerusalem Temple.

In this chapter I will pursue Ezekiel's argument further, focusing on the contrast with Mesopotamian religiopolitical concepts that he establishes, especially as these concepts relate to the departure of the divine presence and the restoration of the Temple. The discussion will suggest a particularly subtle and sophisticated argument that the prophet derives from circumstances in exile in Babylonia. Furthermore, the "case study" developed here incorporates my analysis from the previous chapters by (1) relating the overall structure of the book described in chap. 3 and (2) extending the prophet's polemic against cult statues presented in chap. 2.

Specifically, I will demonstrate that elements of the structure of Ezekiel suggest an association with stereotypical features in Mesopotamian accounts of destruction. In these accounts, the defeated nation is destroyed, persons and deities (divine statues) are exiled and, following appeasement of the

101

conqueror, the exiled gods are reconstituted and restored to their homeland. This discussion will draw upon several studies that have investigated biblical texts against the background of Mesopotamian religious ideology.[1] For example, the motif of divine abandonment has been collected and commented on by Cogan and Bodi,[2] the latter scholar interpreting the theme specifically in the context of Ezekiel. Cogan, McKay, Spieckermann, and most recently Holloway[3] have also discussed the Assyrian imperial policy of deporting and returning divine images. While I have clearly benefited from these studies, my emphasis here will be to show that Ezekiel adapts these common themes both as a backdrop for his message of return and as further instruction on the futility of idolatry. Instead of an earthly conqueror restoring and returning exiled deities, the deity restores and returns his own people.

What we will see is that Ezekiel constructively employs sets of imagery that demonstrate Yahweh's special relationship with Israel, his complete distinction from other gods, and his ability to restore—indeed, recreate—the exilic community. This message that I will identify in Ezekiel 36–37 is achieved by the prophet through inverting Mesopotamian imagery associated with the treatment of divine images captured in war. In §§2 and 3 below, I will present in detail the thesis that Ezekiel (1) integrates his polemic against idolatry with imagery of restoring God's people and (2) furthers his argument that Yahweh is effectively present in exile—indeed, the only divine presence.

This argument, then, is based, first, on recognizing a pattern in Mesopotamian imperial policy and, second, on identifying a reflection of that pattern in the book of Ezekiel. Ezekiel, like any effective rhetorician, relies on a common body of knowledge from a shared experience without necessarily explicitly referring to it. This knowledge is the subtext from which the communicator allows the recipient to evoke meaning and significance. From the historical and cultural distance at which we now stand, after all the evidence is assessed, interpretation of that ancient rhetoric still ends with arguing for what is probable. This is particularly true in the argument presented here for,

---

1. See also chap. 1, which provides evidence for the geographical setting of Ezekiel's ministry in Babylonia, as well as the accessibility of Mesopotamian concepts outside of the specific scribal and priestly circles that composed or preserved them.

2. M. Cogan, *Imperialism and Religion: Assyria, Judah and Israel in the Eighth and Seventh Centuries B.C.E.* (Missoula, Mont.: Scholars Press, 1974) 9–21; Daniel Bodi, *The Book of Ezekiel and the Poem of Erra* (OBO 104; Freiburg: Universitätsverlag / Göttingen: Vandenhoeck & Ruprecht, 1991) 183–218.

3. John W. McKay, *Religion in Judah under the Assyrians, 732–609 BC* (SBT n.s. 26; Naperville, Ill.: Allenson, 1973) 60–66; Hermann Spieckermann, *Juda unter Assur in der Sargonidenzeit* (FRLANT 129; Göttingen: Vandenhoeck & Ruprecht, 1982), esp. pp. 344–62; Steven W. Holloway, *The Case for Assyrian Religious Influence in Israel and Judah: Inference and Evidence* (Ph.D. diss., The University of Chicago, 1992) 547–57, table 7.

in order to understand the warp of the rhetorical strategies that the prophet wove into the woof of his community's experience, the interpreter must also reconstruct that experience.

§2. Status and Treatment of Divine Images Captured in War

While the royal inscriptions of Mesopotamia mention the fate of a conquered people, a significant amount of textual evidence from that region involves the treatment of cult statues in imperial warfare and the religiopolitical concepts that underlie this practice for both conqueror and conquered alike. However, before we turn to an examination of this evidence, it is necessary first to discuss its application in the context of Ezekiel.

The Nature and Admissibility of the Evidence

The evidence that will be assembled primarily derives from Mesopotamian imperial practices. The discussion of the administration of the Assyrian empire, for example, has received great attention. This is also true specifically regarding the question of Assyrian cultic influence and policy in Palestine during the Israelite monarchy. Within the span of two decades, detailed studies of this particular question have been made by McKay, Cogan, Spieckermann, and, recently, a magisterial and comprehensive work by Holloway.[4]

A central issue in assessing the evidence involves the distinctions between imperial management of provinces and imperial control of vassals. Of course, economic and logistical constraints are key. This aspect of the evidence would be a prime concern for this study if I were discussing the particular historical workings of the imperial policy that Israel and Judah experienced.

Certainly, the data that can be compiled do include examples of imperial control of areas in Palestine and neighboring territories that specifically involve treatment of divine statues. But, admittedly, the majority of the evidence that follows involves areas just outside of the Assyro-Babylonian heartland. The reader should keep in mind, first, that I do not wish to focus on the actual facts of Assyro-Babylonian imperial practice but on the ancient rhetoric of imperial goals and governance, for it is this rhetoric that would have influenced various Israelite and Judean thinkers and writers as they looked at the world.[5] Imperial communication included oral, written, and

---

4. See n. 3. See also the recent monograph by B. Oded, *War, Peace, and Empire: Justifications for War in Assyrian Royal Inscriptions* (Wiesbaden: Reichert, 1992).

5. The reader is directed to the discussion in chap. 1 that considers the availability of Assyrian and Babylonian royal and religious traditions both within non-scribal Mesopotamian circles and outside of Mesopotamia altogether. The evidence that Mesopotamian traditions directly had an effect on Ezekiel was also reviewed there.

iconographic media, and certainly elements of imperial policy would have reached its victims. No doubt such communication was itself an effective tool for maintaining control. The literary motifs available to us, then, would have been part of a historical experience of the exiles. And in this discussion it is clear that history makes literature and literature makes history. Second, while the evidence for imperial policy will be drawn widely from both Assyrian and Babylonian sources (from the first millennium B.C.E. and earlier), the Neo-Babylonian rhetoric, which Ezekiel and his audience would have faced, was a continuation of these earlier traditions.

Divine Displeasure: Motif of Divine Abandonment

The classic study on the association of the divine sphere of activity with historical events in ancient Israelite and other ancient Near Eastern ideologies is by Bertil Albrektson.[6] The material he surveyed portrays the pious king who may ask the gods to bestow divine favor on his pursuits. Conversely, the offender suffers divine retribution. Among such offenders, the gods may number even their own people, toward whom they could display displeasure by permitting martial or natural disaster. In the military context the conquered people, it is understood, were destroyed and exiled because their own gods were angry and so commanded it. The conquered deities in some formulations even allowed themselves to be exiled.

It is not necessary to restate comprehensively this evidence, although a summary suggests the extensiveness of the theme.[7] Efforts to explain disaster with theological interpretation by the nation suffering destruction occur in Mesopotamian literature from the third millennium to the first millennium B.C.E. "The Lamentation over the Destruction of Sumer and Ur" is an early example.[8] Ur's destruction through natural catastrophe and invasion is attributed to the unalterable decree of the Sumerian gods.

---

6. B. Albrektson, *History and the Gods* (Lund: CWK Gleerup, 1967).

7. For fuller discussions of pertinent texts, see Albrektson, *History and the Gods*, esp. pp. 16–41, 98–114; Peter Machinist, *The Epic of Tukulti-Ninurta I: A Study in Middle Assyrian Literature* (Ph.D. diss., Yale University, 1978) 149–56; E. A. Speiser, "Ancient Mesopotamia," in *The Idea of History in the Ancient Near East* (ed. R. C. Dentan; New Haven: American Oriental Society, 1983) 55–60; Cogan, *Imperialism*, 9–21; D. I. Block, *The Gods of the Nations* (Jackson, Miss.: Evangelical Theological Society, 1988) 125–48; and Bodi, *Ezekiel*, 183–218; and idem, "The Absence of God in the Book of Ezekiel" (paper presented at the annual meeting of the Society of Biblical Literature, San Francisco, 23 November 1997).

8. See the collation, transliteration, and translation of this text by Piotr Michalowski, *The Lamentation over the Destruction of Sumer and Ur* (Mesopotamian Civilizations 1; Winona Lake, Ind.: Eisenbrauns, 1989). The destruction of Ur by the Elamites and Subarians, again with the consent of Enlil, is presented in "The Lamentation over the Destruction

After An had frowned upon all the lands,
After Enlil had looked favorably on an enemy land,
After Nintu had scattered the creatures that she had created,
After Enki had altered (the course of) the Tigris and Euphrates,
After Utu had cast his curse on the roads and highways,
In order to forsake the divine decrees of Sumer, to change its (preordained) plans.[9]

A reconstructed text from the reign of Nebuchadnezzar I of Babylon (1125–1104 B.C.E.),[10] the so-called "Marduk Prophecy," describes Marduk abandoning Babylon on three occasions.[11] He subsequently sojourns in the land of each conqueror: Hatti, Assyria, and Elam. Marduk voluntarily undertakes these journeys, though the reason for each departure is uncertain. For example, column II, lines 2–6 describes social chaos: "The corpses of the people block the doorways. Brothers consume one another. Friends beat each other up with weapons. The nobles against the poor stretch out their hands."[12] But it is difficult to determine whether this is the cause or the effect of Marduk's traveling to Elam.

The Poem of Erra narrates a situation in Babylon similar to this description. Composed sometime during the early first millennium B.C.E., the

---

of Ur" (Samuel Noah Kramer, *ANET*, 455–63; text in idem, *Lamentation over the Destruction of Ur* [Chicago: University of Chicago Press, 1940]; also by Thorkild Jacobsen in *The Harps That Once . . . Sumerian Poetry in Translation* [New Haven: Yale University Press, 1987] 447–74); and most recently by Jacob Klein in *COS* 1.535–39. For other texts of the so-called "city laments" genre, see discussion in Michalowski, *Lamentation*, 4–8.

9. Lines 22–27; translation from Michalowski, *Lamentation*, 36–37.

10. For the sake of consistency, hereafter the dates for Mesopotamian rulers follow the appendix by John A. Brinkman, "Mesopotamian Chronology of the Historical Period," in A. L. Oppenheim, *Ancient Mesopotamia: Portrait of a Dead Civilization* (rev. and completed E. Reiner; Chicago: University of Chicago Press, 1977) 335–48.

11. For the text, transcription, and transliteration, see R. Borger, "Gott Marduk und Gott-König Šulgi als Propheten: Zwei prophetische Texte," *BiOr* 28 (1971) 3–24; for English translations, see Benjamin Foster, *Before the Muses: An Anthology of Akkadian Literature* (Bethesda, Md.: CDL, 1993) 1.304–7; Block, *Gods of the Nations*, 169–76; and Tremper Longman III, "The Adad-Guppi Autobiography," in *COS* 1.480–81. Additional discussion can be found in W. G. Lambert, "The Reign of Nebuchadnezzar I: A Turning Point in the History of Ancient Mesopotamian Religion," in *The Seeds of Wisdom: Essays in Honor of T. J. Meek* (ed. W. S. McCullough; Toronto: University of Toronto Press, 1964) 3–13; and W. W. Hallo, "Cult Statue and Divine Image: A Preliminary Study," in *Scripture in Context II* (ed. W. W. Hallo, J. C. Moyer, and L. G. Perdue; Winona Lake, Ind.: Eisenbrauns, 1983) 12. The return of Marduk is also noted in the text in L. W. King, *Babylonian Boundary Stones and Memorial Tablets in the British Museum* (London: British Museum, 1912), no. 24, 11–12; and see also text cited by T. Jacobsen, "The Graven Image," in *Ancient Israelite Religion* (ed. Patrick D. Miller Jr. et al.; Philadelphia: Fortress, 1987) 17 n. 3.

12. Translation from Block, *Gods of the Nations*, 171.

historical motivation for the text appears to be the Sutu invasions.[13] The text itself describes the heavenly causes. Erra persuades Marduk to leave Babylon because his statue has fallen into disrepair, apparently signifying cultic neglect: "What happened to your statue (*šukuttu*), to the insignia of your lordship, magnificent as the stars in the sk[y]? It has been [d]irtied! Your lordly crown, which used to light up Ehalanki like Etemenanki is dimmed!"[14] Consequently, Marduk's abandonment of his throne permits Erra to carry out cosmic catastrophe.

Peter Machinist has demonstrated that in the Tukulti-Ninurta Epic this motif of the victim is adopted from its southern Babylonian neighbors and adapted by the victor for new political purposes.[15] Here the conquering monarch could use this ideological explanation against his enemy for rationalization and justification. The epic has the Babylonian gods express their anger against the Babylonian leader, Kaštiliaš, by abandoning their sanctuaries.[16] The Assyrian ruler, Tukulti-Ninurta I (1243–1207), is thus the instrument of the will of the Babylonian gods.

This adaption becomes a familiar motif in later Neo-Assyrian annals. For instance, Sennacherib (704–681) credits the gods of foreign foes for his victories against cities in the Upper Euphrates, describing the cities as being abandoned (Akk. *ezēbu*) by their own gods.[17] Sennacherib's son, Esarhaddon (680–669), describes Sanduarri, king of Kundu and Sissu, as one "whom the gods had forsaken (Akk. *wašāru*)."[18]

Striking texts with this motif come from the reign of Esarhaddon. The city of Babylon and Marduk's Temple, the Esagila, constituted an ancient sacred religious and cultural center throughout Mesopotamia. Thus when Babylon became a political problem for the Assyrian Empire, Assyrian policy

---

13. See Bodi, *Ezekiel*, 54–56.

14. Erra i 127–28 (translation from ibid., 192; also pp. 196–97, for this interpretation). For text in transliteration, see L. Cagni, *L'epopea di Erra* (Studi Semitici 34; Rome: Istituto di Studi del Vicino Oriente, University of Rome, 1969). For English translations, see Luigi Cagni, *The Poem of Erra* (Studies in the Ancient Near East 1/3; Malibu: Undena, 1973); Stephanie Dalley, "Erra and Ishum," in *Myths from Mesopotamia* (Oxford: Oxford University Press, 1991) 282–315; idem, "Erra and Ishum," in *COS* 1.404–16; and Foster, *Before the Muses*, 2.771–805.

15. Peter Machinist, "Literature as Politics: The Tukulti-Ninurta Epic and the Bible," *CBQ* 38 (1976) 462.

16. For the list of divine abandonments, see column I B 32′–47′ (transliteration and translation in Machinist, *The Epic of Tukulti-Ninurta I*, 62–67, with discussion of these lines on pp. 149ff.; also Foster, *Before the Muses*, 1.212).

17. OIP 2 64.22–24; see Cogan, *Imperialism*, 11.

18. *Nin* rec. A, §27, ep. 6, line 22 (R. Borger, *Die Inschriften Asarhaddons, Königs von Assyrien* [AfO Beiheft 9; Graz: Weidner, 1956] 49); see also Cogan, *Imperialism*, 13.

toward Babylon needed to balance control and custom.[19] Consequently, the infamous destruction of Marduk's Temple by Sennacherib, Esarhaddon's father, required apologetic. The text designated *Babylon* (recensions A, B, D, and G) provides such a response.[20] It describes how Marduk himself grew angry at his people and planned to wipe out the land and its inhabitants. The situation portrayed is analogous to Ezekiel's indictment of Israel and the rationale provided for Yahweh's self-exile. For example, the following section describes cultic offenses:

> At that time, in the reign of a former king, there were evil signs in the land of Sumer and Akkad. The people who lived in (the city) answered "yes" and "no" to one another. They spoke lies. They pushed away and neglected their gods. Their goddesses forsook their ordained practices and rode (away). . . . On the possessions of (the temple) Esagila—a place where entry is forbidden—they laid their hands, and gold and silver and precious stones they give to the land of Elam as a purchase price.[21]

But also, moral turpitude is cited.

> [When] in the reign of a form[er king, there were] evil [omens, all the shr]ines. . . . Violence (and) murder was inflicted upon their bodies, and they oppressed the weak—they give them to the strong. Within the city there was oppression (and) accepting of bribes, and daily without ceasing they stole one another's goods. The son in the marketplace has cursed his father, the slave [has disobeyed?] his master, [the female slave] does not listen to her mistress.[22]

In summary, we can readily observe this theological explanation for historical events in the rationale of the defeated to understand personal trauma, as well as the apologia of the conqueror to justify military exercise.

---

19. Barbara Porter (*Images, Power, and Politics: Figurative Aspects of Esarhaddon's Babylonian Policy* [Philadelphia: American Philosophical Society, 1993]) has exhaustively studied Esarhaddon's "Babylonian Policy." See also J. A. Brinkman, "Sennacherib's Babylonian Problem: An Interpretation," *JCS* 25 (1973) 89–95; and idem, "Through a Glass Darkly: Esarhaddon's Retrospects on the Downfall of Babylon," *JAOS* 103 (1983) 35–42. Peter Machinist ("The Assyrians and Their Babylonian Problem: Some Reflections," *Wissenschaftskolleg zu Berlin Jahrbuch* [1984–85] 353–64) discusses this as a recurring dilemma in Assyrian-Babylonian relations.

20. Titles of texts from Esarhaddon's reign follow titles in Borger, *Die Inschriften Asarhaddons.*

21. See ibid., 12–13, §11, recs. A, B, D, eps. 2–3; translation from Porter, *Images*, 101 (see also *ARAB*, 2.245, §649; Cogan, *Imperialism*, 12).

22. See Borger, *Die Inschriften Asarhaddons*, 12, §11, recs. B and G, ep. 3; translation from Porter, *Images*, 101–2.

Divine Self-Exile

The book of Ezekiel opens with the absence of Yahweh from Jerusalem and the presence of his *kābôd* in exile (Ezek 1:1). The first eleven chapters describe this departure, summarizing the situation and the reason for his evacuation. Clearly, this event is an example of the theme of divine self-exile, which is a subtheme of divine abandonment.[23] The local deity willingly abandons his people by abandoning the place of his presence—the sanctuary—and taking up residence in other lands, often in the land of the conqueror, where members of the population have also been deported. The divine departure is seen to be directly related to the disaster that follows.

The amount of Mesopotamian evidence suggests that this motif is also quite common.[24] Some of these texts have been mentioned above, such as the Marduk Prophecy describing the self-imposed exiles of Marduk to Hittite, Assyrian, and Elamite lands. It is not necessary to review all of the associated material; what follows is evidence relatively contemporaneous with the prophet's time and milieu.

The conquest of Babylon by Sennacherib mentioned above included the removal of the statue of Marduk from the Esagila to Assur. In addition to the references to this event by Esarhaddon, an inscription from Nabonidus of Babylon (555–539) portrays the Assyrian king as an aide-de-camp during the self-exile of Marduk: "He (Sennacherib) took Marduk by the hand and led him to Assur. He dealt with the country (i.e., Babylon) consonantly with the divine anger, and the prince Marduk did not cease from his anger. For twenty-one years he made his residence in Assur."[25]

The reign of Ashurbanipal (668–627) offers examples from the annalistic accounts. In one case the Assyrian monarch refers to an incident when a local patron deity abandoned her people. During his eighth campaign against Elam, Ashurbanipal reports the opportunity for the goddess Nanâ finally to return home to Uruk. Her ancient self-exile is noted first: "The goddess Nanâ, who had been angry for 1,635 years, and who had gone and dwelt in Elam, a place not suitable for her."[26] A second example describes similar ac-

---

23. The theme of divine abandonment occurs in the story of Israel's defeat at Shiloh (1 Sam 4:21–22; Ps 78:59–61).

24. Textual evidence is collected in Bodi, *Ezekiel,* 183–218; and Block, *Gods of the Nations,* 125–48.

25. Nabonid no. 8 i 14–25. Transcription in S. Langdon, *Die neubabylonische Königsinschriften* (Leipzig, 1912) 271. Translation from Jacobsen, "Graven Image," 17.

26. *Rassam Cylinder* VI 107–12 (M. Streck, *Assurbanipal und die letzten assyrischen Könige bis zum Untergange Nineveh's,* vol. 2: *Texte* [VAB 7; Leipzig: Hinrichs, 1916] 58–59; translation from *ARAB,* 2.311, §812). The incident is mentioned several times in Ashurbanipal's inscriptions, as well as in Esarhaddon's inscriptions (see *Uruk* rec. B, Borger, *Die*

tion taken by patron deities of his enemy, the rebel brother Shamash-shum-ukin: because of his evil deeds, the gods grew angry and left for other lands.[27]

The anger of the gods at their own people and the abandonment of their sanctuaries continues as a theological explanation into the Neo-Babylonian and Persian periods. A text reconstructed from stelae found in Harran, apparently by Adad-guppi, mother of Nabonidus, provides the reason for the destruction of Harran and the Ehulhul, the Temple of Sin: the gods grew angry at the city and departed.[28] Similarly, the Cyrus Cylinder claims that Nabonidus incurred the wrath of the gods by bringing them to Babylon, and for this they departed their sanctuaries.[29]

Forcible Removal of Divine Images

While Yahweh deliberately abandons the Temple in the book of Ezekiel, annalistic accounts from Mesopotamia often refer to the imperial military policy of forcibly removing divine images from conquered lands.[30] Conceptually, however, this category is also a subtheme of divine abandonment; for here, too, the fate of the people is closely associated with the fate of the gods. Using conventionalized language, the conqueror describes the cult images as being taken as spoil to the victorious nation.[31] Thorkild Jacobsen summarizes

---

Inschriften Asarhaddons, 76, §48). Note that the duration is different in K3101a+K2664+ 2628; see *ARAB*, 2.365, §941.

27. K4457; see translation in *ARAB*, 2.403, §1104. This motif is also used against Arab tribes, when it is reported that these gods abandoned their own people and relocated to Assyria (K3405; *ARAB*, 2.365–66, §943).

28. Text and translation in C. J. Gadd, "The Harran Inscriptions of Nabonidus," *Anatolian Studies* 7 (1957) 35–92; see also, conveniently, translation by A. Leo Oppenheim, "The Mother of Nabonidus," *ANET*, 560–62; and by Longman, *COS* 1.477–78.

29. A. Leo Oppenheim, "Babylonian and Assyrian Historical Texts," *ANET*, 315.

30. Both willing and unwilling departure of the local deity at the hands of the conquering foreign king could exist side by side; for example, compare 2 Kgs 18:25 with 33–35. Both elements exist together in the Poem of Erra (e.g., Erra iv 69 and v 40), as Bodi has commented: "On the one hand, an allusion is made to the removal or spoliation of divine statues from their shrines, and on the other hand to the anger of the gods. The motif of the divine wrath against humans appears several times in the Poem. The gods are angered as a consequence of the improper worship. By negligence in the matters of cult and morals, the humans provoked the gods who left their shrines and caused the destruction of the country" (Bodi, *Ezekiel*, 196–97).

31. See also the biblical references to this practice against Moab (Chemosh, Jer 48:7), Ammon (Milcom, Jer 49:3; on Amos 1:15, see E. Puech, "Milkom, le dieu Ammonite, en Amos I 15," *VT* 27 [1977] 117–25, though this conjecture lacks support other than the possible blending of Jer 49:3 [30:3] and Amos 1:15 in the LXX), and Babylon (Marduk and Nabu, Isa 46:1–2). The characteristic vocabulary used is listed by Cogan, *Imperialism*, 23; see also Hallo, "Cult Statue and Divine Image," 14. The most common term for the capture of divine images, the verb *šalālu* ('to despoil'), is also the most frequent expression

this strategy, which was developed particularly in the first millennium B.C.E.: "Since the gods were in large measure identified with their main places of worship as local and national gods, they became, of course, unavoidably drawn into political conflicts as partisans; and they and their statues and their temples were felt to be at the mercy of the conqueror."[32]

Mordechai Cogan has collected examples of this motif, which he labeled the "spoliation of divine images,"[33] as has Steven Holloway.[34] The reader should also consult the appendix (pp. 157–69), which includes a list of occurrences of the motif of the removal of divine images (from annalistic accounts, dedicatory inscriptions, and chronicles), along with other elements related to this motif.[35] The following discussion incorporates representative examples.

As already seen, the "Marduk Prophecy" describes the "wandering" of the god to Hittite lands, presumably referring to the attack on Babylon by the Hittite king Mursilis I (ca. 1595).[36] Though clearly the statue was abducted, the prophecy presents it as self-imposed exile. The text also indicates Marduk's wandering (self-imposed exile) to Assyria during the reign of Tukulti-Ninurta I (1243–1207). Regarding this incident, however, Chronicle P reports that Tukulti-Ninurta I abducted the statue, "He took out the property of Esagil and Babylon amid the booty. He removed the great lord Marduk [from] his [dais] and sent (him) to Assyria."[37]

A consistent policy of spoliation is noted as early as the reign of Tiglath-pileser I (1114–1076). For example, against the land of Sugu, the monarch boasts, "I brought out 25 of their gods, their booty, their possessions, (and)

---

in royal inscriptions for denoting the deportation of human beings (B. Oded, *Mass Deportations in the Neo-Assyrian Empire* [Wiesbaden: Reichert, 1979] 7). Amos 5:26–27 describes Israel going into exile, carrying its own gods with it.

32. Thorkild Jacobsen, *The Treasures of Darkness: A History of Mesopotamian Religion* (New Haven: Yale University Press, 1976) 232. On the theological significance attached to divine statues, see W. G. Lambert, "Review of *Das Era-Epos*," *AfO* 18 (1957–58) 398–99.

33. Cogan, *Imperialism*, 22–34, and 119–21, table 1.

34. Holloway, *The Case for Assyrian Religious Influence in Israel and Judah*, 547–57, table 7; and see discussion on pp. 319–23.

35. The second column in the appendix combines both self-imposed exile and forceful removal of divine images. Frequently, the account depends simply on the frame of reference. The goddess Nanâ, for example, was pillaged by the Elamites, although she is described in Neo-Assyrian accounts as willingly taking residence in the foreign land (likewise, Marduk in the "Marduk Prophecy"). An incident may also be given a different spin, such as when a ruler gathers the deities from local shrines into a central sanctuary for safekeeping, but the opposition describes this in terms of abduction against their will (e.g., Sargon II versus Merodach-Baladan II; Cyrus versus Nabonidus).

36. Borger, "Gott Marduk," 21.

37. *ABC* 22 iv 5–6, p. 176.

their property."[38] Indeed, Tiglath-pileser I reported employing this practice with a relatively high frequency.[39]

During the classical period of Neo-Assyrian imperial might, deporting foreign gods from resistant peoples was regularly used as a military strategy. As Hallo has observed, "So far from imposing her cults on subjugated peoples, Assyria symbolized her victory by carrying the cult and the cult-statue of the defeated people back to Assyria."[40] Indeed, the frequency of this tactic is noted by Holloway, who calls it "a staple *topos* in the self-conscious historiography of Assyrian imperialism."[41] In addition to the records listed in the appendix, several reliefs of deportations of gods also survive.[42]

Sennacherib's reign provides numerous examples of this activity, including the taking of gods from Uruk, Arabia, and Dêr.[43] Great concern also attends the fate of Marduk's statue, which was removed from the Esagila by Sennacherib. As discussed above, Sennacherib sacked Babylon in 689 and carried the statue of Marduk off to Assur, where it remained until restored to Babylon by Ashurbanipal in 668.[44] The texts, however, interpret this event as willful abandonment by Marduk, who took up residence in Assur.[45]

Furthermore, as evidence in the appendix indicates, the policy of spoliation was continued extensively by Sennacherib's successors, Esarhaddon and

---

38. RIMA 2 20.

39. See examples in the appendix.

40. Hallo, "Cult Statue and Divine Image," 13. This is the focus of chap. 2, "Assyrian Spoliation of Divine Images," in Cogan, *Imperialism*.

41. Holloway, *The Case for Assyrian Religious Influence in Israel and Judah*, 319; see also p. 343. Note also that an Amarna text (55:42, a letter from Qatna) records that 'the king of Hatti carried off the images and the men of Qatna' (DINGIR.MEŠ-*šu u* LÚ.MEŠ *mutēšu* U[RU *Qatn*]*a šar Ḫatte ilteqīšunu*; see CAD I–J 102).

42. For a relief from Nimrud (British Museum 118934) from the reign of Tiglath-pileser III, see A. H. Layard, *Monuments of Nineveh* (London: J. Murray, 1849) 1.65; and Richard D. Barnett and Margarete Falkner, *Sculptures of Tiglath-Pileser III* (London: British Museum, 1962) 29–30. For reliefs from the reign of Sennacherib, see A. Paterson, *Assyrian Sculptures: The Palace of Sinacherib* (The Hague: Nijhoff, 1915) plates 38, 80, 91.

43. Ur: Babylonian Chronicle, *ABC* 1 iii 1, p. 79; Arabia: *Nin* rec. A, ep. 14 (Borger, *Die Inschriften Asarhaddons*, 53, §27; *ARAB*, 2.214, §536, Prism A [also Prism S, p. 207, §518a]); Dêr: Babylonian Chronicle, *ABC* 1 iii 44–46, p. 82 (see also *ABC* 14 3–4, p. 125, and *AsBb* rec. A, lines 40–44 [Borger, *Die Inschriften Asarhaddons*, 84; *ARAB*, 2.262, §674]).

44. See, e.g., Esarhaddon Chronicle: *ABC* 14 31–37, p. 127 = Akitu Chronicle: *ABC* 16 1–8, p. 131. For a discussion of this event, see Brinkman, "Through a Glass Darkly."

45. *Bab* recs. B and G, ep. 3 (Borger, *Die Inschriften Asarhaddons*, 12; *ARAB*, 2.245, §649). Also *Bab* rec. E (Borger, *Die Inschriften Asarhaddons*, 14; *ARAB*, 2.255, §662). Also see the text called by scholars "The Sin of Sargon," which will be discussed below (published by H. Tadmor, B. Landsberger, and S. Parpola, "The Sin of Sargon and Sennacherib's Last Will," *SAAB* 3 [1989] 3–52).

Ashurbanipal. Accounts report the practice administered against Syria, Egypt, Elam, and the Arab tribes. Forced travels of the gods are mentioned often in the Babylonian Chronicle, including frequent references to the exercise of this policy under the Neo-Babylonain ruler, Nabopolassar (625–605), and continuing to the end of the Chaldean dynasty under Nabonidus.

Finally, the so-called Akitu Chronicle may provide some additional evidence that this practice was quite common.[46] The chronicle highlights the severity of the insurrections in Assyria and Babylon during the seventeenth through the twentieth years of Shamash-shum-ukin, as well as during the accession year of Nabopolassar, using the refrain, "Nabu did not come from Borsippa for the procession of Bel (and) Bel did not come out."[47] The situation indicates not only that the general social chaos caused the Akitu festival to be suspended but also that the warfare created the potential danger of their gods' being captured and held for ransom.[48]

Treatment and Condition of Captured Divine Images

The comments above from both Jacobsen and Hallo indicate the ideological value that deportation of divine images implied to the conqueror and conquered alike. In this regard the destination of the gods is often recorded, and the purpose of their removal is occasionally noted, as in an inscription from the reign of Tiglath-pileser I.

> At that time I donated the 25 gods of those lands, my own booty which I had taken, to adorn the temple of the goddess Ninlil, beloved chief spouse of the god Ashur, my lord, (the temple of) the gods An (and) Adad, (the temple of) the Assyrian Ishtar, the temples of my city, Ashur, and the goddesses of my land.[49]

The deported images of gods are dedicated to victorious patron gods. Such examples can be multiplied by the frequent short mention by the ruler that "I gave their gods as gifts to X, my lord."[50]

---

46. *ABC* 16.

47. *ABC* 16 18–19, 20–21, 23, 27, p. 132.

48. The Akitu festival is also suspended during the reign of Nabu-mukin-apli (977–942) because of hostility from the Aramaeans (Chronicle 17:4–10).

49. *AKA* iv 32–39 (RIMA 2 20). In the narrative in 1 Samuel 5, the ark is treated as booty by the Philistines, who set it up before the statue of Dagon (vv. 1–2). So also the אראל דודה of the Moabite inscription of Mesha (*KAI* no. 181, line 12), which he brings before Chemosh.

50. Adad-nirari II against the Land of Qumanu, quoted from *ARAB*, 2.83, §403. This feature of the motif of spoliation is discussed, with examples, in Cogan, *Imperialism*, 27–30. See also Hos 10:6.

As with the human counterpart, during the execution of a seige, the divine images might also be destroyed. For example, a relief from Khorsabad depicts the smashing of a divine image during the battle of Muṣaṣir.[51] And there are, of course, numerous examples of the destruction of temples and sanctuaries, which certainly would have included smashing statues of deities in many instances.[52] In some cases the evidence indicates several fates of the images, as in Ashurbanipal's eighth campaign against Elam.

> I struck down the people living therein. I smashed their gods, and pacified the divine heart of the lord of lords (Assur). His (Ummanaldasi, king of Elam) gods, his goddesses, his property, his goods, his people, great and small, I carried off to Assyria.[53]

In the same campaign against Elam still another fate is described: "The sanctuaries of Elam I destroyed totally. Its gods (and) goddesses I scattered to the wind(s)."[54]

In general, the texts provide little detail about the treatment of gods brought to Assyria. But we can infer some information about the condition of the statues from texts that describe the end of their exile. Following the conquest of a people, when circumstances permitted a more beneficent policy, a monarch might return the divine images captured in war. These texts also frequently indicate that prior to repatriation, the statues needed repair and reconstruction, indicating tangentially the hospitality (or lack thereof) that they received as expatriates. It is to this evidence that we now turn.

Return of Divine Images Captured in War

While Mesopotamian royal inscriptions mention instances of the restoration of a dispersed people following the appeasement of its conqueror,[55] a significant amount of documentary evidence involves the cult statues of the gods taken as booty by a conquering king. When the political climate allowed, cult images might be returned to their homeland. Furthermore, preceding the

---

51. P. E. Botta, *Monument de Ninive* (Paris: Imprimerie nationale, 1849) vol. 2, plate 140, panel 3. See also Cogan, *Imperialism*, 24–25.

52. See Holloway, *The Case for Assyrian Religious Influence in Israel and Judah*, 54, table 5 ("Aggression against Foreign Cults: Foreign Temples Destroyed by the Assyrians"); on the inferred routine nature of this action, despite the sparsity in the written record, see ibid., 317. Regarding destruction of foreign idols, Assyrian royal inscriptions, e.g., are particularly silent (ibid., 318).

53. *Rassam Cylinder* V 119–20 (Streck, *Assurbanipal und die letzten assyrischen Könige*, 50–51; translation from *ARAB*, 2.308, §808).

54. *Rassam Cylinder* VI 62–64 (Streck, *Assurbanipal und die letzten assyrischen Könige*, 54–55; translation from *ARAB*, 2.310, §810). See also Jer 51:18.

55. Bodi, *Ezekiel*, 285–86.

repatriation of cult statues taken as spoil, the ruler might refashion the deities that had fallen into disrepair.

In the discussion that follows, I will reverse the order of these elements— that is, I will first describe the return of images; then I will consider the act of refashioning the gods that took place before their return. This is done for the sake of emphasis. My intention is to highlight the elements and motifs involved in the treatment of divine images captured in war—divine abandonment, exile from the sanctuary, repair, and return to the sanctuary—and the way these elements may provide background to an aspect of the message in the book of Ezekiel. The Near Eastern elements of divine abandonment, self-exile, and the return of the divine presence to the sanctuary are features that have been examined for their relation to biblical texts,[56] and specifically Ezekiel.[57] But it is the motif involving the repair of divine images that has a particularly striking correspondence in the prophet's polemic against idolatry and his understanding of the power of Yahweh's presence.

The rebuilding of the sanctuaries of local patron deities is a ubiquitous theme in Near Eastern texts.[58] Such public policy attracted the favor of gods, priests, and the common folk. During these public works, the gods might be temporarily housed until the project was completed, after which they would be returned to new quarters.[59] For example, the accession year of Tiglath-pileser I witnessed this effort: "The gods An and Adad, the great gods my lords who love my priesthood, commanded me to rebuild their shrines," and following a description of the care taken in this enterprise, the text concludes, "I brought the gods An and Adad, great gods, inside."[60]

Such domestic public works projects have a counterpart in imperial policy.[61] As noted above, the spoliation of divine images had political and theological value. The loss of the statue involved, in Hallo's words, "the inexorable disruption of the cult and implied the withdrawal of divine favors."[62] Consequently, the restoration of statues also had ideological value, whether it

56. E.g., Cogan, *Imperialism.*

57. Bodi, *Ezekiel.*

58. Royal inscriptions dedicating the building and renovation of temples are legion, as any collection of such inscriptions will confirm. See also V. Hurowitz, *I Have Built You an Exalted House: Temple Building in the Bible in Light of Mesopotamian and Northwest Semitic Writings* (JSOTSup 115; Sheffield: Sheffield Academic Press, 1992).

59. See V. Hurowitz, "Temporary Temples," in *Kinattūtu ša dārâti: Raphael Kutscher Memorial Volume* (ed. A. F. Rainey; Tel Aviv: Tel Aviv University, Institute of Archaeology, 1993) 37–50.

60. RIMA 2, I vii 71–75, 109–112, pp. 28–29.

61. See Holloway, *The Case for Assyrian Religious Influence in Israel and Judah,* 563–67, table 9 ("Assyrian involvement in local cults: [Re]construction of the cult centers outside of Assyria"); and discussion on pp. 325ff.

62. Hallo, "Cult Statue and Divine Image," 13.

was accomplished as an act of political independence or, in due course, as a benevolently persuasive feature of imperial policy.

As with the evidence in the discussion on the removal of divine images, the appendix also indicates the frequent occurrence of the motif of repatriation.[63] At least as early as the sixteenth century B.C.E., we have textual evidence of these claims. An inscription from the reign of King Agum II (Agumkakrime) of Babylon mentions a period when the statue of Marduk and his consort, Sarpanitum, were removed from the Esagila and taken to the land of Hana. Agum II records the blessings bestowed by the gods in granting to his reign the return of the gods.

> When in Babylon the great gods by their holy pronouncement had decreed the return to Babylon of Marduk, Lord of Esagila and Babylon. . . . By means of the (sacrificial) lamb of the diviner I made enquiry of Shamash (the sungod) the king, and so sent to a faraway land, the land of the Haneans and so they (i.e. the Haneans) verily led hither by the hand Marduk and Sarpanitum (Marduk's divine consort), who loves my reign. To Esagila and Babylon I verily returned them. To a house which Shamash had confirmed for me (as suitable) in the enquiry (by divination) I verily took them back.[64]

Appendix A reveals that the most concentrated evidence for both the deportation and the return of the divine images comes from the late Neo-Assyrian period.[65] For example, Sargon II returned gods to their shrines in Ur, Uruk, Eridu, Larsa, Kullab, Kisik, and Dur-Yakin. Esarhaddon returned to Uruk gods previously taken to Elam. And, once more, an event already discussed furnishes the backdrop for an extensive application of this policy: the sack of Babylon in 689 by Sennacherib of Assyria, who carried off the statue of Marduk and of other gods to Assur.

Barbara Porter details the extensive and ambitious efforts of Esaharhaddon to rebuild Babylonia, which included the restoration of destroyed and dilapidated temples.[66] Marduk's Temple, Esagila, received special attention.[67]

---

63. Steven Holloway has collected instances of Neo-Assyrian repair and return of divine images (*The Case for the Assyrian Religious Influence in Israel and Judah*, 576–79, table 12).

64. Agum II inscription i 44–ii 17 (see P. Jensen, "Inschrift Agum-Kakrimi's," in *Keilinschriftliche Bibliothek 3/1* [ed. Eberhard Schrader; Berlin: H. Reuther's, 1892] 138–41); translation by Jacobsen, "The Graven Image," 16.

65. See the work of Cogan, *Imperialism*, 35–41; Porter *Images*, 58, 60–62, 65–66, 69, 98, 122–25; and Holloway, *The Case for Assyrian Religious Influence in Israel and Judah*, esp. tables 7 and 12 (pp. 547–57 and 576–79, respectively), and discussion on pp. 309–76.

66. See chap. 4, "Gifts and Public Works Projects in Babylonia and Assyria," in Porter, *Images*, 41–76.

67. See the appendix for the extensive reference to this project. Interestingly, in a letter from Nippur (CT 54 212) a diviner admonishes Esarhaddon to pay as much attention to

When the work was completed, the gods were returned to their sanctuaries. In a statement of a policy remedying the acts of Sennacherib, Esar-haddon calls himself,

> The restorer of Esagila and Babylon, who restored (the images of) the gods and goddesses (dwelling) therein, who returned the pillaged gods of the lands from Assyria to their places and let them stay in comfortable quarters until he completed temples (for them), and could set the gods upon daises as a lasting abode.[68]

Hence, an oft-repeated epithet of Esarhaddon is "Restorer of Esagila and Babylon."[69]

Esarhaddon's revitalization project in the south was not limited to Babylon. As Porter has shown, "Esarhaddon nevertheless took pains to extend the tangible benefits of Assyrian rule to other Babylonian cities, as well. His first gesture in this direction was the return of statues of Babylonian gods that had been captured in wars and were being kept in Assyria."[70] Several accounts ex-

---

Nippur (the home of Enlil) as he is paying to Babylon. The diviner quotes from the "Advice to a Prince," a text from the ninth or eighth century composed to warn kings, governors, and princes not to conscript or tax the inhabitants of the sacred cult centers of Sippar, Babylon, and Nippur (see W. G. Lambert, *Babylonian Wisdom Literature* [Oxford: Clarendon, 1960; repr., Winona Lake, Ind.: Eisenbrauns, 1997] 114–15, lines 55–59). See J. A. Brinkman in "Babylonia under the Assyrian Empire, 745–627 B.C.," in *Power and Propaganda* (ed. M. T. Larsen; Mesopotamia 7; Copenhagen: Akademisk, 1979), esp. p. 228, on the special status of Babylonian cities; also Hayim Tadmor, "Temple City and Royal City in Babylon and in Assyria," in *The City and the Community* (Jerusalem: Israel Historical Society, 1968) 189–96 [Heb.]; and A. Kuhrt, "The Cyrus Cylinder and Achaemenid Imperial Policy," *JSOT* 25 (1983) 89–90. Esarhaddon did, of course, attend to his own city, Assur, where he renovated the Temple of Assur and the places of Ninurta and Nusku, among other gods (see *Assur* rec. A., VI 28–36 [see Borger, *Die Inschriften Asarhaddons*, 5, §2]).

68. *Nin* rec. A, ep. 3 (ibid., 45, §27; *ARAB*, 2.203, §507). See also Cogan, *Imperialism*, 29 and 39.

69. E.g., *Uruk* rec. A, line 16 (Borger, *Die Inschriften Asarhaddons*, 74, §47); also *AsBb* rec. A, obv. lines 36–37 (ibid., 80, §53). In actuality, the return of the Marduk statue to the Esagila is less than clear. Esarhaddon claims to have accomplished both the rebuilding and the return of Marduk and other gods. But while the inscriptions assume it is a fait accompli, it appears that the return was stalled in media res due to an ominous event. See Parpola, *LAS*, vol. 2, p. 32; also W. G. Lambert, "Esarhaddon's Attempt to Return Marduk to Babylon," in *Ad bene et fideliter seminandum* (ed. G. Mauer and U. Magen; AOAT 220; Kevelaer: Butzon & Bercker / Neukirchen-Vluyn: Neukirchener Verlag, 1988) 158–59. It is his son, Ashurbanipal, who claims to have completed his father's work and heralds the final return of the statue of Marduk to Babylon (see, e.g., Babylonian Chronicle: *ABC* 1 iv 34–36, p. 86; and Esarhaddon Chronicle: *ABC* 14 31–37, p. 127).

70. Porter, *Images*, 60; see map on p. 42.

ist of these efforts, indicating the political effectiveness of this policy. The *Ashur-Babylon* text of Esarhaddon, recension A, lists quite extensive return of statues to Nineveh, Der, Erech, Larsa, and Sippar-Arur.[71] In the context of renovating the Esagila, Esarhaddon's magnanimity is indicated by the general amnesty granted this area: "The plundered gods of the land, from Assur and Elam, I returned them to their places, and in every cult-city I established the proper (rites)."[72] Outside this southern sphere Esarhaddon also allegedly applied this policy to Arab kings and to the land of Bazu.[73] In each case the defeated kings petitioned Esarhaddon, who granted their request.

Indeed, the evidence in the appendix indicates that the repatriation of divine statues was an oft-repeated practice in Assyria's dealings with the Arabs. The record of this interaction includes the reigns of Sennacherib, Esarhaddon, and Ashurbanipal, and in many cases they recollect previous exchanges. For example, after defeating the Arabs, Sennacherib brought Hazael and his goddess to Assur; in due course he returned both king and statue.[74] Esarhaddon, too, claims to have returned the gods of Hazael.

> Hazael, king of the Arabs, came to Nineveh, my royal city, with his rich (heavy) gifts, and kissed my feet, imploring me to give (back) his gods. I had mercy upon him and repaired the injuries done to (the images of) those gods.[75]

Evidence for the practice of repatriation continues for more than a century afterward. Concerning Nabopolasar the Babylonian Chronicle states that he "returned to Susa the gods of Susa whom the Assyrians had carried off and settled in Uruk."[76] And, of course, the famous cylinder of Cyrus incorporates this motif in order to present Cyrus as an ideal king in the Assyro-Babylonian tradition.[77]

---

71. Borger, *Die Inschriften Asarhaddons*, 78–91, §53. This can be supplemented by references to gods being returned to Der and Dur-Sharukin (Khorsabad) in *ABC* 1 iii 44–46 and *ABC* 14 3–4. On the identification of Sippar-Aruru in line 44 of *AsBb* rec. A with Dur-Sharukin in *ABC* 1 iii 46, see discussion in Porter, *Images*, 60 n. 127.

72. *Bab* rec. C, ep. 36 (Borger, *Die Inschriften Asarhaddons*, 25, §11; also *ARAB*, 2.253, §659D).

73. See the appendix. The location of Bazu (various spellings and also listed in the inscriptions of Esarhaddon as a city [URU] and as a land [KUR]) is not certain. It has been identified both with the Kewir Desert in Iran and with an area in North Arabia. See literature in *ABC*, p. 252, appendix C.

74. See K3405, lines 1–8. Text and translation in Cogan, *Imperialism*, 16–17.

75. *Nin* rec. A, ep. 14 (Borger, *Die Inschriften Asarhaddons*, 53, §27; *ARAB*, 2.214, §536, prism A).

76. Babylonian Chronicle: *ABC* 2 16–17, p. 88.

77. See Oppenheim in *ANET*, 316.

Repair of Divine Images Captured in War

What we have seen is the frequency with which Assyro-Babylonian rulers attended to the return of cult statues. What remains to review is the motif of the repair of divine images captured in war, that is, the preparatory step to the policy of repatriation, which together form part of a larger pattern of the exile of divine statues to a foreign land. After examining this last part of the pattern, I will return to Ezekiel, where the elements of this pattern provide the framework with which Ezekiel constructs his continuing polemic against idolatry and the foundation that informs his understanding of Yahweh's relationship to Israel in exile. Ezekiel represents Yahweh through this pattern and its motifs and in contrast to them.

The evidence for repairing statues and temples of local patron deities occurs often and is part of the responsibilities of the king, of which he frequently makes mention.[78] For example, dedicatory inscriptions from temples at Assur frequently laud this activity: "Sennacherib, king of the universe, king of Assyria, maker of images of Assur (and) the great gods, am I."[79] The significance of the physical appearance of the divine statue may be inferred from the Poem of Erra. The poor condition of the statue of Markuk does not seem to be in question. Erra's disingenuous proposal to clean and repair Marduk's soiled image finds no objection from Marduk. Coincidentally, the chief deity of Babylon appears, in Landsberger's description, as "the senile Marduk."[80] Perhaps more accurately, the fact that Marduk is dupable may be a consequence of the damaged condition of the divine image. Thus appearance reflects potency; it is not enough merely to be present.

The evidence for the repair of divine images captured in war is concentrated in the late Neo-Assyrian period. The ideological value of such efforts provided important messages, as noted by Porter: "Benefits conferred upon the gods of a city or upon their statues and temples were understood as fun-

---

78. For a review of the theological ideas involved in the renovation and adornment of divine statues, see the brief discussion in chap. 2 above, as well as Lambert, "Review of *Das Era-Epos*," 389–99; A. Leo Oppenheim, "The Golden Garments of the Gods," *JNES* 8 (1949) 172–93; and E. Douglas Van Buren, "The *ṣalmê* in Mesopotamian Art and Religion," *Or* 10 (1941) 66–70.

79. *ARAB*, 2.191, §459 (*VS* 1, no. 75). Other occurrences of this epithet are *ARAB*, 2.192, §460 (*KAH* 1, no. 48); p. 192, §461 (Meissner-Rost, *Die Bauinschriften Sanheribs*, plate 14); p. 192, §462 (*KAH* 1, no. 73); p. 193, §463 (*KAH* 1, no. 74); p. 193, §464 (*KAH* 1, no. 72); p. 193, §466 (*KAH* 1, no. 43); p. 193, §468 (*KAH* 1, no. 45); p. 194, §471 (*KAH* 1, no. 49).

80. B. Landsberger, "Akkadische-Hebräische Wortgleichungen," *Hebräische Wortforschung: Festschrift zum 80. Geburtstag von Walter Baumgartner* (VTSup 16; Leiden: Brill, 1967) 198.

damental favors to the city as a whole."[81] This was a central aspect of Esar-haddon's imperial policy.

A fascinating and complex text from this period is the so-called "Sin of Sargon."[82] It purports to be written by Sennacherib to explain prima facie why Sargon II, his father, died uninterred on the battlefield. Sennacherib concludes through divination that Sargon had not paid adequate attention to the gods of Babylon, and he is warned through the same divine means not to repeat this mistake. Despite his known destruction of Babylon and deporta-tion of the gods to Assur, this document claims that he had actually intended to repair the statue of Marduk, apparently the real reason for taking the gods from Babylon. In this case, however, the road to good intentions was paved with bad advice: "As for me, after I had made the statue of Aššur my lord, As-syrian scribes wrongfully prevented me from working [on the statue of Mar-duk] and did not let me make [the statue of Marduk, the great lord]."[83] While the text may date to the end of Sennacherib's reign, it may also be a fictive account from Esarhaddon's reign, presenting Sennacherib as an an-cient Jacob Marley, redeeming himself, defending his changed policy, and admonishing his successor to complete it.[84]

This is certainly the outcome. Marduk and the statues from Babylon are not only returned, as we have seen, but they are repaired with great care. Evi-dence of these efforts is found in many of Esarhaddon's inscriptions.[85] *Assur-Babylon* recension A, cited above, describes the restoration of sanctuaries, and the repair of statues of gods removed by Sennacherib, particularly, but not exclusively, from Babylon. The text begins with divine appointment to this task and concludes with the refabrication of the damaged gods prior to their return: "At the beginning of my rule . . . there occurred, in heaven and earth, favorable signs, commanding the restoration of the (images) of the gods, the rebuilding of sanctuaries."[86] Esarhaddon prays to the gods, who are themselves called 'creators of gods and goddesses' (*ba-nu-u ilâni* ^{meš} *u* ^{d}*iš-tar*), for insight in naming skilled craftsmen to carry out this work. The king re-ceives an answer in a vision: the work should take place in the *bît mu-um-me* ('temple workshop') in the city of Assur, 'the home of the god Assur, the

81. Porter, *Images*, 66.

82. See A. Livingston, *Court Poetry and Literary Miscellanea* (SAA 3; Helsinki: Hel-sinki University Press, 1989) 77–79; and the primary publication of this text by Tadmor, Landsberger, and Parpola, "The Sin of Sargon and Sennacherib's Last Will."

83. Livingston, *Court Poetry*, 79.

84. For these appraisals of this text, see Tadmor, Landsberger, and Parpola, "The Sin of Sargon and Sennacherib's Last Will."

85. See the appendix for a full list.

86. *AsBb* obv. line 52 to rev. line 2 (Borger, *Die Inschriften Asarhaddons*, 81; *ARAB*, 2.259, §669).

father of the gods' (*šu-bat ab*[AD] *ilâni*^meš *Aššur*). The gods also name craftsmen (*mârê*^meš *um-ma-ni*). No expense should be spared. For this favorable
answer, the king offers sacrifices.[87] And Esarhaddon proceeds faithfully to
carry out the commands.

> I entered the Bit-mummu, the place of renewal (*tēdištu*), which was pleasing
> to them (the gods), and carpenters, masons, metalworkers, engravers, skilled
> artisans, learned in secret lore (divine mysteries), I caused to enter that
> house.[88]

The final products, restored images of the gods, are described.

> [Bēl], Bēltiya, Bēlet-Babili, Ea, and Mandānu, the great gods, in Esharra
> (temple of Assur), the temple of their begetter (*zārû*), were truly born (*ma-
> lādu*) and grew in stature. Out of ruddy *z/ṣariru*, the product of Arallu, the
> dust of its mountain, I made their forms magnificent, with ornaments of
> rank, I adorned their necks. . . . The images of their great divinities (*ṣa-al-me
> ilu-ti-šú-nu rabî-ti*) I made more beautiful than they were before. I made
> them exceedingly splendid, I made (their) magnificence awe-inspiring.[89]

The reconstruction is portrayed as rebirth in the house of their father (*abu*)
and begetter (*zārû*), Assur, in the land of their captivity. The text concludes
with a further list of images of gods repaired and returned to their sanctuaries: Tashmetu to Babylon; Ile-Amurru to Babylon; Abshushu and Abtagigi to
Nineveh; Aia, Siru, Durrunitum, and Asharid to Der; Usur-amatsa to Uruk,
Shamash to Larsa; and Humhumumia, Shuqamuna, and Shimalia to Sippar-
Aruru. Line 41b states that the king restored the statues of "whatever gods

---

87. Rev. lines 14–26 (Borger, *Die Inschriften Asarhaddons*, 82–83; *ARAB*, 2.260,
§671).

88. Rev. lines 28–30 (Borger, *Die Inschriften Asarhaddons*, 83; translation from *ARAB*,
2.261, §672). In the larger context of this preparatory work, note a similar description in
the polemic of Isa 40:19–20, "The idol: a craftsman casts it, a goldsmith plates it with gold,
and a silversmith forms silver chains. (Or) *Mskn*-wood fit for tribute, wood that will not
rot, he chooses. He seeks for himself a skilled craftsman, (in order) to set up an idol that
will not be shaken." C. Westermann (*Isaiah 40–66* [OTL; Philadelphia: Westminster,
1969] 66; also p. 54) calls 40:19–20 a "fugitive text" and reconstructs the context of these
two verses as a prelude to 41:6–7 (see also 44:9–17).

In this passage from Isaiah, המסכן is difficult. H. G. M. Williamson assesses the range
of possibilities that have been offered in "Isaiah 40,20: A Case of Not Seeing the Wood for
the Trees," *Bib* 67 (1986) 1–19. Williamson considers עץ לא־ירקב to be a gloss on the difficult תרומה המסכן, and his translation is adopted here, along with the comparison of
המסכן with Akkadian *musukkannu*, a type of tree (specifically on this, see I. Ephʿal, "On
the Linguistic and Cultural Background of Deutero-Isaiah," *Shnaton* 10 [1986/1989] 31–
35 [Heb.], xi–xii [Eng.]).

89. Rev. lines 35–38 (Borger, *Die Inschriften Asarhaddons*, 83–84; translation from
ARAB, 2.261–62, §§673–674).

and goddesses Assur and Marduk commanded." And lest the role of the king be missed, an epithet describes Esarhaddon as

> *mu-ub-bi-ib ṣa-lam ilâni*[meš] *rabûti*[meš] . . . *e-piš É-sag-íl u Bâbili*[ki] *ša* [*ilâni*][meš]
> *mâtâti*(KUR.KUR) *šal-lu-u-ti a-na áš-ri-šú-nu ú-ter-ru-ma*

> Cleaner of the images of the great gods . . . maker of the Esagila and Babylon who returned the plundered gods of the lands to their places.[90]

Recension E describes more than two hundred gods "truly born" in the Temple of Assur, and concludes with their trip to Babylon and a reference to the *pīt pî* ceremony.[91]

The circumstances that damaged the statues exiled in Assur are also explained. The text published as *Babylon* by Borger relates these conditions in the context of the return to the Esagila.

> The gods and goddesses dwelling therein, whom the unchecked floods and rains had carried off and defaced their images,—the damage and harm they (had suffered, I repaired) and their disfigured (lit., darkened) features I renovated (lit. caused to shine). Their garments I cleansed. In their [holy] shrines I caused them to dwell.[92]

This policy was also observed beyond the borders of Assyria-Babylonia. The ongoing imperial problem with Arab tribes included this form of reprisal. The text cited above, which rehearses the Arab-Assyrian relations from

---

90. Obv. lines 36–37 (Borger, *Die Inschriften Asarhaddons*, 80).

91. Rev. lines 9–24 (Borger, *Die Inschriften Asarhaddons*, 88–89, §57; *ARAB*, 2.275–76, §712). In a broken context, the creation of a royal tiara, which appears to be a part of Marduk's attire, is mentioned (see Lambert, "Esarrhaddon's Attempt to Return Marduk to Babylon," 157–74, on K6048+8323, obv. i 2). Contrast the reference to Assur's tiara in *AsBb* rec. A, rev. lines 32–34 (Borger, *Die Inschriften Asarhaddons*, 83; *ARAB*, 2.261, §672). Mesopotamian texts record the processes and rituals involved in the final stage of creating divine images: the so-called *mīs pî/pīt pî* ('washing/opening of the mouth' ritual). The literature on the subject is extensive. Descriptions of this ritual, with references to the primary material and further literature, can be found in Oppenheim, *Ancient Mesopotamia*, 183–98; Jacobsen, "The Graven Image," 23–28. A full treatment appears in C. B. F. Walker and Michael B. Dick, "The Induction of the Cult Image in Ancient Mesopotamia: The Mesopotamian *Mīs Pî* Ritual," in *Born in Heaven, Made on Earth: The Making of the Cult Image in the Ancient Near East* (ed. M. B. Dick; Winona Lake, Ind.: Eisenbrauns, 1999) 55–121. Also note Ann Macy Roth's comments on the "opening of the mouth ritual" in Egypt: "This ritual could also be extended to a newly-carved cult statue, since the verb for making such a statue is *ms*, 'to give birth'" ("The *psš-kf* and the 'Opening of the Mouth' Ceremony: A Ritual of Birth and Rebirth," *JEA* 78 [1992] 146). It is not my purpose here, however, to engage in a full description or analysis of these rituals.

92. *Bab* rec. A, esp. ep. 32 (Borger, *Die Inschriften Asarhaddons*, 23; translation from *ARAB*, 2.247, §653). Also *Bab* rec. D (*ṣa-lam ilâni*[meš]), ep. 32 ("Black Stone" in *ARAB*, 2.244, §646).

Sennacherib to Ashurbanipal, refers to a star emblem of gold and precious stones that Esarhaddon had made and that presumably was to adorn the Arab goddess upon her return.[93] In addition to the fortunes of this goddess, others are mentioned in Borger's *Nineveh* recension A. The text, cited above, reports that Hazael, king of the Arabs, came to Nineveh beseeching Esarhaddon to return the gods pillaged during the capture of Adumu, an Arab fortress. Esarhaddon says he took pity, repaired (*edēšu*) their decay (*anḫūtu*), and returned the gods of the Arabs.[94]

Accessibility and Duration of Motifs

What we have seen thus far is the significant role that cult statues played in Mesopotamian ideology, specifically imperial policy. The images of gods suffered the fortunes of war and disaster. The pattern presented in the preceding pages involves their removal to foreign lands, their repair, and their return. Not all situations are identical, but the value placed on these motifs is consistent. What is more, the provenance of the evidence suggests that it was quite a common practice throughout Assyrian and Babylonian history. To be sure, detailed evidence is concentrated within the Neo-Assyrian period. But this should not be unexpected, considering the imperial ambitions of the Assyrians. Indeed, these imperial practices continue, as we have seen, during the Neo-Babylonian and early Persian periods. Thus the policy of exile, revivification, and return is centered particularly well, both in time and in place, within the context of Ezekiel. Before turning to Ezekiel, however, we will consider the accessibility and duration of the motifs in this pattern.

A methodologically similar study by Hurowitz was undertaken to consider temple-building accounts in the Hebrew Bible in the light of such texts in Syria and Mesopotamia.[95] Hurowitz's conclusions are noteworthy. Concentrating on 1 Kings 5–9, he observed that the building account in these chapters shows closest, if indirect, signs of influence from Assyrian literary practices, influence that seemed apparent even in the Deuteronomic elements (glosses, orations, blessings, and curses). He suggests two explanations for this relationship. On the one hand, the Deuteronomic elements of the story might be coterminous with the historical period of the Assyrian literature, namely, pointing to a preexilic Deuteronomic redaction. On the other hand, one could conclude that Assyrian literary influence remained in the

---

93. K3405, obv. lines 15–17; see text and transliteration in Cogan, *Imperialism*, 16–17. Ashurbanipal refers to this emblem during his own relations with Uaiteʾ, king of Arabia (rev. lines 13–15 [Cogan, *Imperialism*, 18–19]).

94. *Nin* rec. A, ep. 14, lines 6–16 (Borger, *Die Inschriften Asarhaddons*, 53, §27; prism A in *ARAB*, 2.214, §536).

95. Hurowitz, *I Have Built You an Exalted House*.

west well after the fall of Assyria: "It is possible that certain specifically Assyrian literary practices took root in the west and lived on in the periphery, even after their extinction in the Mesopotamian homeland."[96]

A case in point: Amélie Kuhrt has drawn similar conclusions regarding the traditions employed in the Cyrus Cylinder.[97] Kuhrt's thesis is based on Harmatta's previous study[98] and is an elaboration of the notice by Walker concerning the recently identified Yale fragment of the Cyrus Cylinder. Walker notes that the Cyrus Cylinder is hardly a *sui generis* declaration of religious toleration but is simply a "building inscription, in the Babylonian and Assyrian tradition, commemorating Cyrus's restoration of the city of Babylon and the worship of Marduk previously neglected by Nabonidus."[99] The genre of the Cylinder is that of a typical royal foundation deposit, going back two millennia. Indeed, the new fragment from the Yale collection has Cyrus saying, "In it (i.e., the gateway) I saw inscribed the name of my predecessor King Ashurbanipal," thereby linking the Persian monarch with the type of inscription that the Assyrian king had left. Thus Cyrus presents himself not as a destroyer but as a restorer of correct practice as established by his predecessors. Kuhrt is no doubt correct when she observes, "The main significance of the [Cyrus] text lies in the insight it provides into the mechanism used by Cyrus to legitimize his conquest of Babylon by manipulating local traditions."[100]

This is an especially pertinent observation for the argument that such motifs were available to Ezekiel and his audience. Cyrus made effective use of Neo-Assyrian literary conventions, such as the motif of divine assistance from the gods, the motif of divine abandonment of the conquered peoples, and the forceful removal and return of divine images. Not only had these Assyrian literary practices survived, they had obtained a standard by which a monarch could measure himself and seek political approval.[101] It seems clear, as Kuhrt has shown, that much of the ideological success of Cyrus came from the attention paid to the application of standard literary motifs.

---

96. Ibid., 126, 315.

97. Kuhrt, "The Cyrus Cylinder and Achaemenid Imperial Policy," 83–97.

98. J. Harmatta, "The Rise of the Old Persian Empire," *Acta Antiqua* 19 (1971) 3–15.

99. C. B. F. Walker, "A Recently Identified Fragment of the Cyrus Cylinder," *Iran* 10 (1972) 159.

100. Kuhrt, "The Cyrus Cylinder and Achaemenid Imperial Policy," 92.

101. Of course, Nabonidus claimed that his intention was to gather into Babylon the neighboring gods for protection (see the so-called Nabonidus Chronicle, col. III; *ANET,* 306), a claim directly countered by Cyrus in order to secure the loyalty of these communities and to obtain divine blessing (Cyrus Cylinder, *ANET,* 315).

§3. Ezekiel 36–37: Renewal, Re-creation, and Return

What was said above about Cyrus is no less true of Ezekiel. He relies on the same standard literary motifs for their conceptual framework (which his audience would also share), but he denies their theological credibility. Instead, he fills the old pattern with new content, thereby establishing both a critique and a counterclaim through his use of these traditions.

Prefatory Remarks

The first section of this chapter reviewed the structural elements of the book of Ezekiel. The movement of this structure accents the close relationship between Yahweh and the exiles. As seen in chap. 3, Yahweh abandons the Temple and appears to exiled Israel. In Babylonia the eventual cleansing and revivification of the people are foretold, and the defeat of their great foe and their return from exile are anticipated. Israel's return to the land will be followed by Yahweh's arrival: Ezekiel is shown the Temple, reconstructed according to divine plan, and it is to this restored sanctuary and city that the presence of God returns.

The second section of this chapter examined the Assyro-Babylonian pattern of the removal, cleaning and repair, and return of divine statues. I suggest that this pattern informs elements of the structure in the book of Ezekiel. The Near Eastern motifs of divine abandonment and return already have been described as analogues to Ezekiel: Yahweh abandons his Temple and Yahweh returns to his Temple. But this parallel may be more extensive. In Ezekiel 36–37, prior to the return of the people to a restored land (described in chap. 36) and Yahweh to a reconstructed Temple, another reconstruction takes place, which also has an analogue in the Near Eastern pattern described in §2: just as the images of the gods were repaired by the earthly king, Yahweh "repairs" his people.

In chap. 2 I argued that the concept of the "image of God" was implied in the book of Ezekiel. The prophet contrasts the Mesopotamian concept of an idol as the image of god (*ṣalam ilī/ilāni*) with the Priestly tradition that man is made in the image of God (*ṣelem ʾĕlōhîm*). This contrast also informs Ezekiel 36–37. It appears, for example, that 37:1–14 does not use imagery of either human resuscitation or resurrection per se; rather, the imagery in this chapter should first and foremost be understood in the light of Mesopotamian imagery of the repair of cult statues that occurred prior to their return from a foreign land.

Cleansing of Israel

As discussed in chap. 2, the sin of idolatry is a primary focus of Ezekiel's condemnation of Israel and his justification for the people's exile and Yahweh's abandonment of the Temple. Routine terminology for Israel's sins include the following: גִּלּוּלִים, שִׁקּוּצִים, and תּוֹעֵבוֹת. The result leaves Israel unclean and polluted, expressed by the verb טמא (in *Qal, Niphal, Piel, Pual,* and *Hithpael*), the noun טֻמְאָה, and the adjective טָמֵא. This terminology is common to P and H and to the book of Ezekiel.[102] Of the 160 occurrences of the verb טמא in the Hebrew Bible, over 85% are in Leviticus (85 times), Numbers (P; 23 times), and Ezekiel (30 times).[103] The main cause of defilement is idolatry (specifically גִּלּוּלִים): 20:7, 18, 30–31, 43; 22:3–4; 23:7, 13, 17, 30; LXX 36:18aβb;[104] 37:23; also metaphorically adultery, 18:6, 11, 15; 22:11; 33:26). The result of this activity, says Ezekiel in 36:16–22, is that they polluted (טמא) the land. The exile of the עַם־יהוה, in turn, causes God's name to be profaned (חלל).

In chap. 36 the oracles of Ezekiel begin describing the restoration of the polluted and profaned land using images that recollect language from chap. 6. In both passages the prophet directs the oracles אֶל הָרֵי יִשְׂרָאֵל (6:2; 36:1) and לֶהָרִים וְלַגְּבָעוֹת לָאֲפִיקִים וְלַגֵּאָיֹת (6:3; 36:4). Execration shifts to restoration. Furthermore, this restoration unfolds into the realm of human renewal, drawing upon metaphors and images from sections A (especially chap. 6) and B (especially chap. 20) of the book of Ezekiel.

For example, before the final withdrawal of the divine presence, Yahweh offers a message of hope in 11:18–20.[105] This text is repeated nearly verbatim in 36:25–27, where it functions as a preface to the vision and oracle in chap. 37.[106] In 36:25–27 the text includes a promise of restoration and cleansing from idolatry.

---

102. Ezekiel describes the role of the priests, who execute the law, as distinguishing between holy and profane, clean and unclean (22:26).

103. Statistics from F. Maass, "טמא," *TLOT* 2.495–96.

104. On this passage, see note below.

105. See chap. 3 for a discussion of Ezek 11:14–21, a passage often considered secondary.

106. Two text-critical issues are involved in determining the status of 36:16–38. The first issue involves the relationship among the subunits vv. 16–32, 33–36, and 37–38. For example, W. Zimmerli (*Ezekiel 2* [trans. J. D. Martin; Hermeneia; Philadelphia: Fortress, 1983] 244–45, 246) considers 36:16–38 to be a unit, of which vv. 33–36 and 37–38 are secondary additions of the Ezekiel school. The second text-critical issue involves the omission of Ezek 36:23bβ–38 in Greek papyrus 967 (see summaries of this discussion in Zimmerli, *Ezekiel 2,* 242 and 245; and L. Allen, *Ezekiel 20–48* [WBC 29; Dallas: Word, 1990] 177–78, with bibliography). Regarding the first issue, it seems that the material is too tightly integrated to conclude that vv. 33–36 and 37–38 do not belong integrally to vv. 16–32. While these two subunits (vv. 33–36 and 37–38) include bipartite proof-sayings and begin with the messenger formula (as does v. 22), they flow smoothly together and function as further exposition on the preceding promise of cleansing. The promise of cleansing (vv. 22–32) is well framed by the assertion regarding God's act (vv. 22 and 32). The matter

וְזָרַקְתִּי עֲלֵיכֶם מַיִם טְהוֹרִים וּטְהַרְתֶּם מִכֹּל טֻמְאוֹתֵיכֶם וּמִכָּל־גִּלּוּלֵיכֶם
אֲטַהֵר אֶתְכֶם: וְנָתַתִּי לָכֶם לֵב חָדָשׁ וְרוּחַ חֲדָשָׁה אֶתֵּן בְּקִרְבְּכֶם וַהֲסִרֹתִי
אֶת־לֵב הָאֶבֶן מִבְּשַׂרְכֶם וְנָתַתִּי לָכֶם לֵב בָּשָׂר: וְאֶת־רוּחִי אֶתֵּן בְּקִרְבְּכֶם
וְעָשִׂיתִי אֵת אֲשֶׁר־בְּחֻקַּי תֵּלֵכוּ וּמִשְׁפָּטַי תִּשְׁמְרוּ וַעֲשִׂיתֶם: [107]

(25) I will sprinkle upon you clean water, and you shall be clean from
all your uncleannesses—*from all your idols I will clean you.* (26) I will
give you a new heart, and I will put a new spirit within you; *I will take
away the heart of stone from your flesh,* and I will give you a heart of
flesh. (27) My spirit I will put within you. I will cause you to walk in
my laws, and my justice I will cause you to keep.

According to Ezekiel the uncleanness of Israel, the result of idolatry, will
be removed prior to their return. In the Hebrew Bible, טהר includes physical,
moral, and cultic cleanness, and purity and impurity are expressed by the
roots טהר and טמא, respectively.[108] Israel is not fit to be returned from exile
until this religious state is restored. The act of purifying is not carried out by
priestly personnel.[109] The metaphor of washing portrays God as the acting
subject and the people as the receiving object (also 37:23).[110]

---

of the textual witness, Codex 967, raises the consideration that vv. 23bβ–38 are a separate
later composition, not present in the original Hebrew. For example, Zimmerli argues that
it is an "original (later) unit" (p. 245), that vv. 22–32 should not be broken up. Two compelling criteria should be underscored, however, that suggest that they were not even relatively later: (1) vv. 16–23bα would end on an incomplete note, without supplying an
exposition on the holiness of Yahweh's name, and (2) the framework created by repetition
in vv. 22 and 32. Allen (p. 177) notes the argument that the omission is a result of para-
blepsis, specifically homoioteleuton, simultaneously admitting that the amount of over-
sight of so much material would be unusual. He does speculate on the state of Codex 967,
whose extant form is not all in order. He also notes that v. 27 has structural importance,
since v. 27a is repeated in 37:14a, and v. 27b is repeated in 37:24b (incidentally, an argument for evaluating the text of Ezekiel 37, as well). (See also L. J. McGregor, *The Greek Text
of Ezekiel* [Atlanta: Scholars Press, 1985] 12.) Based on these observations, then, vv. 16–38
are all of a piece and an original composition.

107. These verses present no text-critical concern.

108. H.-J. Hermisson, *Sprachen und Ritus im altisraelitischen Kult* (Neukirchen-
Vluyn: Neukirchener Verlag, 1965) 84–99. Note also the Akkadian verbs *ebēbu, elēlu,* and
zakû 'to be pure' include both physical and cultic cleanness (AHw 180–81, 197–98; CAD
Z 23–32). As seen above, an epithet of Esarhaddon describes him as "cleaner (*ebēbu*) of the
images of the great gods" (*AsBb* rec. A, obv. line 36). See also F. Maass, "טהר," *TLOT*
2.482–86.

109. The altar is cleansed by human hands in Ezek 43:18–27.

110. Note the theological distinctions between P and H as demonstrated by J. Milgrom, *Leviticus 1–16* (AB 3; New York: Doubleday, 1991), esp. pp. 1–63; and I. Knohl,
The Sanctuary of Silence: The Priestly Torah and the Holiness Code School (Minneapolis:

Moreover, in describing this cleansing it appears that Ezekiel is playing on the cause of the impurity, namely, idolatry. In other words, Ezekiel describes Israel in terms that recollect idols themselves.

To understand this, first consider Ezekiel 20, an extended discourse against Israel's sin that catalogs its history of apostasy, specifically the worship of גִּלּוּלִים. The chapter concludes with a promise of restoration, implying Yahweh's superiority over the wood and stone of idols in vv. 32–34.

וְהָעֹלָה עַל־רוּחֲכֶם הָיוֹ לֹא תִהְיֶה אֲשֶׁר אַתֶּם אֹמְרִים נִהְיֶה כַגּוֹיִם כְּמִשְׁפְּחוֹת
הָאֲרָצוֹת לְשָׁרֵת עֵץ וָאָבֶן: חַי־אָנִי נְאֻם אֲדֹנָי יְהוִה אִם־לֹא בְּיָד חֲזָקָה וּבִזְרוֹעַ
נְטוּיָה וּבְחֵמָה שְׁפוּכָה אֶמְלוֹךְ עֲלֵיכֶם: וְהוֹצֵאתִי אֶתְכֶם מִן־הָעַמִּים וְקִבַּצְתִּי
אֶתְכֶם מִן־הָאֲרָצוֹת אֲשֶׁר נְפוֹצֹתֶם בָּם בְּיָד חֲזָקָה וּבִזְרוֹעַ נְטוּיָה וּבְחֵמָה
שְׁפוּכָה: 111

(32) What is on your mind shall never be, "Let us be like the nations, like the clans of the land, and serve *wood and stone*." (33) I swear, says the Lord-Yahweh, with a mighty hand and an outstretched arm, and with *wrath poured out*, I will be king over you. (34) I will bring you forth from the peoples, and I will gather you from the *lands in which you are scattered*—with a mighty hand and an outstretched arm.

The initiation of the oracle of 36:16–38 recollects this theme from chap. 20. The reconstructed Hebrew text of 36:18–19a reads,

וָאֶשְׁפֹּךְ חֲמָתִי עֲלֵיהֶם [עַל־הַדָּם אֲשֶׁר־שָׁפְכוּ עַל־הָאָרֶץ וּבְגִלּוּלֵיהֶם טִמְּאוּהָ]
וָאָפִיץ אֹתָם בַּגּוֹיִם וַיִּזָּרוּ בָּאֲרָצוֹת

I will pour out my wrath upon them [for the blood that they shed in the land and for the idols with which they polluted it], and I will scatter them among the nations; they shall be dispersed among the lands.112

Fortress, 1995). P restricts the concept of holiness to priets and Levites, while H extends it to all of Israel. Thus, in P's perspective, Israel's moral and ritual violations pollute the sanctuary, and purification is attained through the high priest's ritual. For H, however, polluting forces (especially covenant violation, incest, idolatry, and sabbath profanation) violate the entire land. And in marked contrast to P, "Pollution for H is nonritualistic, as shown by the metaphoric use of Heb *ṭāmēʾ* (e.g., Lev 18:21, 24; 19:31) and by the fact that the polluted land cannot be expiated by ritual, and, hence, the expulsion of its inhabitants is inexorable (Lev 18:24–28; 20:2)" (Milgrom, *Leviticus*, 49). Here, too, may be another association between H and Ezekiel. The recovery of the land is affected by Yahweh, with no apparent prescriptive mediation or ritual.

111. In v. 33 the LXX adds διὰ τοῦτο, thereby regarding it as the conclusion to v. 32. Also in v. 33, אדני is lacking in the LXX and the targum (on this, see Zimmerli, *Ezekiel 2*, 556–62, appendix 1).

112. It appears that the Greek versions, which omit v. 18aβb (set in square brackets), preserve the best reading of v. 18. The reference to *gillûlîm* in v. 18aβb in the Hebrew was

The association of these two verbs, שׁפך and פוץ, is unique to Ezek 20:33–34 and 36:18–19. Furthermore, in both pericopes the punishment for Israel's sins is described in identical words (Ezek 36:19a and 20:23b): Yahweh will scatter (*Hiphal*) them among the nations, and they shall be dispersed (*Niphal*) among the lands. It seems defendable, then, to identify the language of Ezekiel 20 and 36 as interrelated expressions of punishment and subsequent restoration.

Second, consider another interplay of terminology between Ezekiel 20 and the previously discussed 36:25–27. Viewed in its own context, but especially in its association with chap. 20, it is possible that Ezek 36:26 is interacting with the description of idols as wood and stone (20:32).

Ezek 20:32:

וְהָעֹלָה עַל־רוּחֲכֶם הָיוֹ לֹא תִהְיֶה אֲשֶׁר אַתֶּם אֹמְרִים נִהְיֶה כַגּוֹיִם . . . לְשָׁרֵת
עֵץ וָאָבֶן׃

What is on your mind (lit. spirit) shall never be, namely, your saying, "Let us be like the nations . . . and serve wood and stone."

Ezek 36:26:

וְנָתַתִּי לָכֶם לֵב חָדָשׁ וְרוּחַ חֲדָשָׁה אֶתֵּן בְּקִרְבְּכֶם וַהֲסִרֹתִי אֶת־לֵב הָאֶבֶן
מִבְּשַׂרְכֶם וְנָתַתִּי לָכֶם לֵב בָּשָׂר׃

I will give you a new heart, and I will put a new spirit within you; I will take away the heart of stone from your flesh, and I will give you a heart of flesh.

Israel's attraction to the idols of the nations is expressed figuratively in the metaphor of a 'stone heart' (לֵב הָאֶבֶן), which Yahweh will transplant with a 'living heart' (לֵב בָּשָׂר, parallel in 36:27a to רוּחִי).[113] In other words, Israel's identity with idols is made explicit. Moreover, this association between idols and the heart is not alone in the metaphors of Ezekiel.[114] Consider Ezek

---

added on the basis of v. 25. This actually strengthens the point being made here, since the tradition that inserted *gillûlîm* into the text made the association that is reflected in chap. 20: God is pouring out his wrath because of idolatry.

113. See also the descriptions of Israel having a 'hard heart' (*ḥzq*, 2:4; *qšh*, 3:7). On the use of *lēb* in the Deuteronomic and Priestly sources, as well as Jeremiah and Ezekiel, see F. Stolz, "לֵב," *TLOT* 2.640–42. Interestingly, *Jubilees*, a Second Temple pseudepigraphical text, describes the idol worshiper as having no heart (22:18; see translation of O. S. Wintermute, "Jubilees," *OTP* 2.98). This discussion necessarily raises the concern of distinguishing when, on the one hand, phraseology is part of a common stock of expression, and when, on the other hand, the relationship between distinct texts is intentional. Certainty is difficult to establish. But with due circumspection, the possibilities can be introduced. On an innerbiblical level, M. Fishbane discusses the caveats involved in such interpretation (*Biblical Interpretation in Ancient Israel* [Oxford: Clarendon, 1985], esp. pp. 525–43).

114. Interestingly, the LXX exhibits considerable variation with this metaphor, employing several terms to translate *gillûlîm* in Ezekiel (as seen in chap. 2): ἐνθυμήματα

20:16, again in the context of Ezekiel 36: the catalog of Israel's sins in the wilderness includes the figure כִּי אַחֲרֵי גִלּוּלֵיהֶם לִבָּם הֹלֵךְ 'For after other idols their heart(s) went'.[115] This metaphor is even more boldly drawn in Ezek 14:4 (also vv. 3 and 7), where an oracle of Yahweh warns anyone in Israel אֲשֶׁר יַעֲלֶה אֶת־גִּלּוּלָיו אֶל־לִבּוֹ וּמִכְשׁוֹל עֲוֹנוֹ יָשִׂים נֹכַח פָּנָיו 'who sets (up) his idols in his heart and puts the stumbling block of his iniquity before his face'.[116]

Thus it appears that Ezekiel 36 begins to describe the restoration of Israel as cleansing from sin, specifically, idolatry. Furthermore, Ezekiel portrays Israel in terminology associated with that very sin, namely, idols: Israel has taken idols into its heart.

Re-creation and Repatriation of the People Israel

This analysis of the motif of cleansing Israel from idolatry has encountered the notion of God's giving Israel a new heart, suggesting in turn the language of (re)creation. It is clear that Ezekiel 36–37 uses language associated with building and creating: 36:33 describes the waste places being rebuilt, and 37:1–14 simultaneously portrays dry bones re-forming into humans and graves opening with revivified life. This section will describe this imagery in detail and trace its origin.

In this regard, Zimmerli remarks that the specific theological concepts in the historical arrangement of P, including creation with humans being made in God's image, are nowhere present in Ezekiel.[117] That this is not the case has been suggested in chap. 2, where I claimed that the concept of man as the image of God (in P) is present in Ezekiel. It will be further argued here that the imagery of Ezekiel 36–37 likely draws on creation traditions known from Genesis 2 (J).

Prior to the stark imagery of re-creation in Ezekiel 37, Ezekiel 36 shifts from cleansing to creation, closing with a significant comparison.

'thoughts' (Ezek 14:7; 20:16); διανοήματα 'thoughts, ideas' (Ezek 14:3, 4); διάνοια 'thoughts, intelligence' (Ezek 14:5); and ἐπιτηδεύματα 'practices, habits' (Ezek 14:6).

115. This clearly awkward verse has been treated in chap. 2, where we saw the intentional omission of the term *ʾĕlōhîm*.

116. Incidentally, it is possible that the metaphor of a worshiper taking the idol into his heart is operating in the distich of Isa 19:1: וְנָעוּ אֱלִילֵי מִצְרַיִם מִפָּנָיו וּלְבַב מִצְרַיִם יִמַּס בְּקִרְבּוֹ 'The idols of Egypt will tremble before him / And the heart of the Egyptians will melt within them'. Among the sectarians at Qumran, the heart was a battle ground (1QS 4:23; 10:21), the nonhardened heart was a description of its members (1QS 1:6; 2:14, 26; passim), and evil power in the world could enter the heart as idolatry ("idols of the heart," 1QS 2:11).

117. W. Zimmerli, *Ezekiel 1* (trans. R. E. Clements; Hermeneia; Philadelphia: Fortress, 1979) 52.

כֹּה אָמַר אֲדֹנָי יְהוִה בְּיוֹם טַהֲרִי אֶתְכֶם מִכֹּל עֲוֹנוֹתֵיכֶם וְהוֹשַׁבְתִּי אֶת־הֶעָרִים
וְנִבְנוּ הֶחֳרָבוֹת: וְהָאָרֶץ הַנְּשַׁמָּה תֵּעָבֵד תַּחַת אֲשֶׁר הָיְתָה שְׁמָמָה לְעֵינֵי
כָּל־עוֹבֵר: וְאָמְרוּ הָאָרֶץ הַלֵּזוּ הַנְּשַׁמָּה הָיְתָה כְּגַן־עֵדֶן וְהֶעָרִים הֶחֳרֵבוֹת
וְהַנְשַׁמּוֹת וְהַנֶּהֱרָסוֹת בְּצוּרוֹת יָשָׁבוּ:[118]

(33) Thus says the Lord-Yahweh: On the day that I cleanse you from
all your iniquities, I will make your cities inhabited, and your ruins
will be rebuilt. (34) The desolate land *shall be cultivated*, instead of
being the horror that it was in the sight of all who passed by. (35) And
they will say, "This land that was desolate has become like the *Garden
of Eden*; and the cities, ruined and desolate and destroyed, they are inhabited and fortified."

Recollection of the Garden of Eden motif is used elsewhere in Ezekiel.[119]
Clearly, in this context the imagery reflects the creation tradition found in
Gen 2:15.

וַיִּקַּח יְהוָה אֱלֹהִים אֶת־הָאָדָם וַיַּנִּחֵהוּ בְגַן־עֵדֶן לְעָבְדָהּ וּלְשָׁמְרָהּ

And Yahweh-God took the man and put him in the *Garden of Eden*,
to cultivate it and to keep it.[120]

What is more, for the exilic community the language reverberates with images from the Israelite creation traditions. The ideological map of the גַּן־עֵדֶן
in Gen 2:10–14 portrays it at the headwaters of both the river Gihon (Jerusalem) and the rivers Tigris and Euphrates (Mesopotamia), the past and
present residences of the audience of Ezekiel.[121]

Early readers of Ezekiel confirm that this association with creation traditions was conspicuous. For example, the Hebrew text of Ezek 36:11aβ (וְרָבוּ
וּפָרוּ 'They shall multiply and be fruitful'), missing in the Greek witnesses,
appears to be a later insertion.[122] Its absence in the Greek cannot be plainly

---

118. אדני is lacking in v. 33 (as already seen in 20:33).

119. Ezek 28:13; 31:9, 16, 18. Deutero-Isaiah 51:3 uses this imagery in a restoration
oracle (see also Joel 4:18 and Zech 14:8). Note the geographical tradition of Gen 13:10 and
its appearance in Ezekiel 47 (see M. Fishbane, "The 'Eden' Motif / The Landscape of Spatial
Renewal," *Text and Texture: Close Readings of Selected Biblical Texts* [New York: Schocken,
1979] 111–20).

120. For עבד as 'to cultivate', see Theodore Hiebert, "Re-imaging Nature," *Int* 50
(1996) 42.

121. No positive identification can be offered for Pishon, the first river named in Gen
2:11.

122. Zimmerli calls it a "secondary interpretive element" (*Ezekiel 2*, 230). Allen calls
it a "loose comparative annotation" and omits it altogether from his translation (*Ezekiel
20–48*, 167 and 169).

explained other than by concluding that it is an interpretive gloss, following quite closely, however, the imagery of the text. Its presence here, clearly echoing a well-known Priestly phrase (Gen 1:22, 28; 8:17; 9:1, 7; 17:20; 28:3; 35:11; 48:4; Lev 26:9 H; note Jer 23:3 in a similar context), may indicate that the constellation of imagery suggested to an early interpreter the very connection with the creation motifs documented here. It should be noted that this addition reverses the order of the verbs in the Priestly occurrences.[123] Moreover, the expression also indicates the intermingling of imagery from the two Genesis creation accounts (Gen 1:1–2:4a [P] and 2:4b–3:24 [J]). Consider the motifs in Ezek 36:9–11.

כִּי הִנְנִי אֲלֵיכֶם וּפָנִיתִי אֲלֵיכֶם וְנֶעֱבַדְתֶּם וְנִזְרַעְתֶּם: וְהִרְבֵּיתִי עֲלֵיכֶם אָדָם
כָּל־בֵּית יִשְׂרָאֵל כֻּלֹּה וְנֹשְׁבוּ הֶעָרִים וְהֶחֱרָבוֹת תִּבָּנֶינָה: וְהִרְבֵּיתִי עֲלֵיכֶם
אָדָם וּבְהֵמָה וְרָבוּ וּפָרוּ וְהוֹשַׁבְתִּי אֶתְכֶם כְּקַדְמוֹתֵיכֶם וְהֵטִבֹתִי מֵרָאשֹׁתֵיכֶם
וִידַעְתֶּם כִּי־אֲנִי יְהֹוָה:

(9) For behold, I am with you. I will turn unto you, and you shall be cultivated and sown. (10) I will multiply upon you man, the whole house of Israel, all of it. The cities shall be inhabited and the wastelands rebuild. (11) I will multiply upon you man and beast, *and they shall multiply and be fruitful.* I will make you dwell as in your former times, and I will make things better than in your beginning. Then you will know that I am Yahweh.

Allen is partially correct in his suggestion that the "multiply and be fruitful" phrase may have been added as an annotation to פריכם (v. 8) and הרביתי (vv. 10, 11).[124] In addition, however, it appears that the larger setting and the immediate context recall creation concepts from both Genesis 1 and 2: compare עבד in Ezek 36:34 with Gen 2:5, 15; compare יטב in Ezek 36:11

---

123. This is the only place in the Hebrew Bible that the phrase occurs in reverse. I can offer no explanation for this inversion beyond the observation that the use of chiasm (or introversion) characterizes both P and H (see especially Milgrom, *Leviticus 1–16*, 39–42); for example, consider Gen 1:26 (בצלם כדמות) and Gen 5:3 (בדמות כצלם). Chiastic construction is also a frequent literary feature throughout Ezekiel, identified many times by L. Allen in *Ezekiel 1–19* [WBC 28; Dallas: Word, 1994]; and *Ezekiel 20–48*). While I cannot prove that this phrase in 36:11 directly reflects the Priestly tradition, the following definition of a *topos* is relevant to determining such a possible relationship: "A *topos*, whether it occurs in an oral narrative or a written one, is a traditional image. It is not identifiable or even analyzable on the basis of either the formulas or the uniquely arranged words a poet might use to construct it, but rather on the basis of the image to which the words refer" (R. Scholes and R. Kellogg, *The Nature of Narrative* [London: Oxford University Press, 1978] 26–27). Considering this definition and considering the distinctive image of the phrase, v. 11's relationship with Priestly tradition seems likely.

124. Allen, *Ezekiel 20–48*, 169.

with Gen 1:4, 10, 12, 18, 21, 25, 31; and compare ראשׁת in Ezek 36:11 with Gen 1:1). These numerous associations account for this early interpretive annotation.[125]

Since mankind was formerly created and placed in Eden, Ezekiel employs language whose concepts and mythic location recollect this origin and reflect these traditions. This imagery, particularly as it is used in chap. 36, prepares the landscape, as it were, for the next scene.

The scene of revivification in 37:1–14 contains both a vision proper (vv. 1–10) and an oracle interpreting the vision (vv. 12–14), with v. 11 connecting the two subunits. The overall unit achieves a heightened effect by escalating the imagery from a scene of unburied corpses in the first subunit to one of buried corpses in the second.[126] Yahweh restores life in both cases. As for the first subunit, 37:1–10, it too should be analyzed in two parts (vv. 1–8a, vv. 8b–10), with the prophet himself in the second part an active participant in the outcome of the vision.[127]

---

125. There may be another indication from an early interpretive tradition that confirms the argument in this section. Ezek 36:17–18 contains a similar exegetical expanse that may suggest that Ezekiel 36–37 is analogizing the function of the image of G/god in Israel and Mesopotamia. Recall the earlier discussion of a connection between shedding blood and idolatry (note especially Ezekiel 33, but also 22) and their relation to the "image of God" theology (see chap. 2, §3, above). The Hebrew text of 36:18αβb (missing in the Greek witnesses) furnishes an early interpretive expanse that suggests that this comparison was perceived in the context of Israel's re-creation on the analogy of idols. The Hebrew text reads (with the addition in brackets):

וָאֶשְׁפֹּךְ חֲמָתִי עֲלֵיהֶם [עַל־הַדָּם אֲשֶׁר־שָׁפְכוּ עַל־הָאָרֶץ וּבְגִלּוּלֵיהֶם טִמְּאוּהָ]

So I poured out my wrath upon you [for the blood which they shed upon the land, and for the idols with which they defiled it]'.

The interpreter is certainly playing on the imagery of v. 17 (polluting the land כְּטֻמְאַת הַנִּדָּה), playing on שׁפך, and reflecting Priestly tradition (for example, Num 35:33), besides echoing material from elsewhere in the book (for example, Ezekiel 22). Thus on the one hand, v. 18αβb may be an inconsequential insertion, motivated by these elements. But on the other hand, it is quite possible that the imagery in Ezek 36:22–37:14 raised for the ancient reader a recognition of the contrast being laid out here: for Israel the image of God is human creation. Therefore, the re-creation motif extends further Ezekiel's demonstration against idolatry.

126. The unit as a whole has precipitated much discussion concerning its redactional history. Clearly the imagery is related but distinct. Attempts at determining what elements, if any, of vv. 11–14 may be redactional remain inconclusive and without consensus. The debate raises the obvious observation that it is quite difficult to remove any substantive elements. A close look at symmetries in language and structure in the unit at least warns against considering much material intrusive, even if redactional. For perceptive comments on language repetition in this unit, see Allen, *Ezekiel 20–48*, 183–84.

127. H. McKeating ("Ezekiel the 'Prophet like Moses'?" *JSOT* 61 [1994] 105–6) has also noted this uniquely participatory role of the prophet in a vision.

The first subunit is a very graphic vision of a valley strewn with brittle bones. The prophet confirms their condition (v. 2) and is told to prophesy to them (vv. 5–6). The content of the prophecy is then carried out: bone joins bone, sinew joins bone, flesh covers sinew, and skin covers flesh (vv. 7–8a). The action is halted, though, ending the first part of the subunit, and then in the second part the prophet observes: וְרוּחַ אֵין בָּהֶם 'But there was no breath/ spirit in them' (v. 8b). Ezekiel is told again to prophesy the final stage of re-creation (vv. 9–10). In v. 10 when the breath/spirit enters into the bodies, they come to life and stand upon their feet: וַתָּבוֹא בָהֶם הָרוּחַ וַיִּחְיוּ וַיַּעַמְדוּ עַל־רַגְלֵיהֶם.[128] Later in the second subunit the רוּחַ reappears and is associated with the work and spirit of God (v. 14): וְנָתַתִּי רוּחִי בָכֶם וִחְיִיתֶם וְהִנַּחְתִּי אֶתְכֶם עַל־אַדְמַתְכֶם 'I will put my spirit in you, and I will set you in your land'. Interestingly, on two other occasions a very similar expression is used to de-scribe Ezekiel's divine transportation: וַתָּבֹא־בִי רוּחַ וַתַּעֲמִדֵנִי עַל־רַגְלָי (3:24;[129] also 2:2). In each case, it is clear that the רוּחַ originates from Yahweh.

Ezek 37:1–8 thus clearly describes the process of revivification using im-agery of human creation. The point becomes even clearer when we compare vv. 6 and 8 with Job 10:8, 9, 11.

יָדֶיךָ עִצְּבוּנִי וַיַּעֲשׂוּנִי . . . זְכָר־נָא כִּי־כַחֹמֶר עֲשִׂיתָנִי . . . עוֹר וּבָשָׂר תַּלְבִּישֵׁנִי
וּבַעֲצָמוֹת וְגִידִים תְּסֹכְכֵנִי

Your hands fashioned me and made me. . . . Remember now that you made me like clay. . . . With skin and flesh you clothed me, and with bones and sinews you wove me.

What is more, the imagery of 37:1–8 appears directly to reflect and develop the scene of the creation of man in Genesis 2, using a constellation of imag-ery that relates re-creation with creation. For example, the description of this valley of very dry bones suggests imagery of the parched earth, which no man has yet cultivated. Second, man is formed but becomes a living being only after God breathes life into him (Gen 2:5–7).[130] Third, God plants a garden in Eden and sets (נוח) the man there (Gen 2:15), just as God promises to set

---

128. Note the reflection of this imagery (vv. 8–10) in the Rev 11:11: πνεῦμα ζωῆς ἐκ τοῦ θεοῦ εἰσῆλθεν ἐν αὐτοῖς (the two witnesses), καὶ ἔστησαν ἐπὶ τοὺς πόδας αὐτῶν.

129. This also takes place in הַבִּקְעָה (3:22; note 37:1).

130. So also Zimmerli, *Ezekiel 2*, 257–58. The specific language is different: Gen 2:7 describes it as נשמת חיים ('breath of life'), while Ezek 37:5 uses רוּחַ. But the LXX, in appar-ent reflection on the similarity to Genesis 2, appends to the end of 37:5 πνεῦμα ζωῆς. Even more significantly, Deutero-Isaiah pairs this terminology, using both words to describe God's act of creating humans (42:5): כֹּה־אָמַר הָאֵל יְהוָה בּוֹרֵא הַשָּׁמַיִם וְנוֹטֵיהֶם רֹקַע הָאָרֶץ וְצֶאֱצָאֶיהָ נֹתֵן נְשָׁמָה לָעָם עָלֶיהָ וְרוּחַ לַהֹלְכִים בָּהּ 'Thus says God, Yahweh, who created the heavens and spread them out, who spread out the earth and its produce, who gives *breath* to people upon it and *spirit* to those who walk on it'. Similar terminology for the creation

(נוח) the reformed people back in their land (Ezek 37:14). This last association is markedly apparent in the MT, which vocalizes the *Hiphil* of נוח as
form II both in Ezek 37:14 (וְהִנַּחְתִּי) and in Gen 2:15 (וַיַּנִּחֵהוּ), while Ezek
37:1 and 40:2 are in form I.

Having thus far analyzed imagery of human (re)creation in Ezekiel 36–
37, we have seen how Ezekiel's imagery reflects other Israelite creation traditions and how it is subtly infused with language associated with idolatry. The
previous section suggested that Ezekiel 36–37 develops an argument that
parodies the Mesopotamian pattern of re-creation of *cult images* prior to their
repatriation. Confirmation to this effect—namely, that Ezekiel is intentionally contrasting creating humans with imagery involving cult statues—comes
from two points.

The first line of evidence indicates that Ezekiel intends his audience to associate the vision of the dry bones with a vision recorded in Ezekiel 6. Chapter 37 opens with the following description of the scene that Yahweh shows
Ezekiel (v. 2):

וְהֶעֱבִירַנִי עֲלֵיהֶם סָבִיב סָבִיב וְהִנֵּה רַבּוֹת מְאֹד עַל־פְּנֵי הַבִּקְעָה וְהִנֵּה יְבֵשׁוֹת
מְאֹד:

And he (Yahweh) led me round and round about them (the bones in
the valley); and behold, there were very many upon the valley, and
they were very dry.

These bones are, of course, the subject of the vision and oracle, the people of
Israel who will be restored. This scene closely reflects the oracle condemning
the people (Ezek 6:4–6; imagery resumed in v. 13), immediately preceding
Yahweh's abandonment of the land.

וְנָשַׁמּוּ מִזְבְּחוֹתֵיכֶם וְנִשְׁבְּרוּ חַמָּנֵיכֶם וְהִפַּלְתִּי הַלְלֵיכֶם לִפְנֵי גִּלּוּלֵיכֶם:
[וְנָתַתִּי אֶת־פִּגְרֵי בְּנֵי יִשְׂרָאֵל לִפְנֵי גִּלּוּלֵיהֶם] וְזֵרִיתִי אֶת־עַצְמוֹתֵיכֶם סְבִיבוֹת
מִזְבְּחוֹתֵיכֶם: בְּכֹל מוֹשְׁבוֹתֵיכֶם הֶעָרִים תֶּחֱרַבְנָה וְהַבָּמוֹת תִּישָׁמְנָה לְמַעַן
יֶחֶרְבוּ וְיֶאְשְׁמוּ מִזְבְּחוֹתֵיכֶם וְנִשְׁבְּרוּ וְנִשְׁבְּתוּ גִּלּוּלֵיכֶם וְנִגְדְעוּ חַמָּנֵיכֶם
וְנִמְחוּ מַעֲשֵׂיכֶם: [131]

---

of humans from God's spirit/breath is expressed in Ps 104:29–30 (רוח); Job 34:15–16 (רוח
and נשמה); and Qoh 12:7 (רוח).

131. In v. 4a, the LXX does not render the verb שבר, apparently reducing the action
of both verbs to the single שמם.

I have bracketed both the Hebrew and the translation of v. 5a, since evidence of this
text is not found in the LXX. However, I am not compelled to consider it secondary, as
do Zimmerli and Allen, who assume it arose as a later interpretation based on Lev 26:30.
It has been noted already that Ezekiel has many affinities to the language of Leviticus 26.

(4) Your altars will be desolate, and your incense altars will be broken; I will cast your slain before/upon your idols; (5) [I will lay the corpses of the sons of Israel before/upon your idols,] and I will scatter your bones round about your altars. [132] (6) In all your habitations, the cities will be ruined and your high places desolate, so that your altars will be ruined and desolate, your idols will be broken and smashed, your incense altars overturned, and your works wiped out.

Ezek 6:4–6 describes the land that is to be restored, the cities that are to be rebuilt, and the people that are to be reformed. Ezekiel 37 then comes along, it appears, to reverse this scene depicting scattered idol pieces and human bones. [133] Israel's initial fate was analogous to that of idols (chap. 6), but the final outcome (chap. 37) is distinct: Yahweh sifts and restores his people.

The second line of evidence provides a remarkably close association between language used for idols and language used by Ezekiel for the soon-to-be-restored people of Israel. As we have seen, Ezek 37:8b is an important

---

This relationship may indeed point to the original nature of v. 5a, reflecting Leviticus 26; its absence from the LXX may be explained as a simplification (in light of v. 4b), which is what occurs in v. 4a and possibly v. 6. Surely, the use of עֲרִים in v. 6 (present also in the LXX) continues the association with Lev 26:31, though Zimmerli does not resort to removing it.

In v. 6a תִּישַׁמְנָה is a difficult vocalization (if from שָׁמַם), or it may be derived from a rare root יָשַׁם (so G. A. Cooke, *A Critical and Exegetical Commentary on the Book of Ezekiel* [ICC; New York: Scribners, 1936] 74).

In v. 6b the expressions וְנִשְׁבְּתוּ וַיֶּאְשְׁמוּ, and וְנִמְחוּ מַעֲשֵׂיכֶם are also not represented in the LXX; it cannot be determined for certain whether this situation results from later interpretive glosses in the Hebrew or simplifications in the Greek.

132. As we have already discussed, Ezekiel shows many affinities with the Holiness Code, especially Leviticus 26. Ezek 6:5, in particular, exhibits a strong connection with Lev 26:30:

וְהִשְׁמַדְתִּי אֶת־בָּמֹתֵיכֶם וְהִכְרַתִּי אֶת־חַמָּנֵיכֶם וְנָתַתִּי אֶת־פִּגְרֵיכֶם עַל־פִּגְרֵי גִּלּוּלֵיכֶם
וְגָעֲלָה נַפְשִׁי אֶתְכֶם

I will destroy your high places and cut down your incense altars and lay your corpses upon the corpses of your idols. My soul will abhor you.

Here, as we saw in chap. 2, *gillûlîm* is Ezekiel's preferred term for idols.

133. John Wolf Miller (*Das Verhältnis Jeremias und Hesekiels sprachlich und theologisch untersucht* [Assen: Van Gorcum, 1955] 92) has observed a similarity between this imagery and Jer 8:1–3, suggesting that it is Jeremiah's influence on Ezekiel. The bones of Judah's kings, princes, priest, prophets, and people are exhumed and spread unburied before the heavenly bodies that they errantly worshiped. The entire context does indeed make this the terrible fate of those who worship other gods (Jer 7:16–8:3) and certainly may suggest that this was at least a shared image between the two prophets, representing punishment for this offense.

point in the movement of the text. It signals a break in the action: וְרוּחַ אֵין בָּהֶם 'And there was no breath/spirit in them'. The phrase does more than merely introduce an element of anticipation or suspense. Ezekiel appears to be developing an important analogy. This phrase, similarly expressed, can be found in contexts mocking the condition of idols. For example, Jer 10:14bβ is included in a long disputation against Israel regarding the vanity of idolatry (Jer 10:1–16; Jer 51:11–19 restates this text [note 17bβ] against Babylon). The following citation is from the conclusion of the diatribe (Jer 10:14–16):

נִבְעַר כָּל־אָדָם מִדַּעַת הֹבִישׁ כָּל־צוֹרֵף מִפָּסֶל כִּי שֶׁקֶר נִסְכּוֹ וְלֹא־רוּחַ בָּם:
הֶבֶל הֵמָּה מַעֲשֵׂה תַּעְתֻּעִים בְּעֵת פְּקֻדָּתָם יֹאבֵדוּ: לֹא־כְאֵלֶּה חֵלֶק יַעֲקֹב
כִּי־יוֹצֵר הַכֹּל הוּא וְיִשְׂרָאֵל שֵׁבֶט נַחֲלָתוֹ יְהוָה צְבָאוֹת שְׁמוֹ:[134]

(14) Every human is stupid, despite knowledge. Every metalsmith is put to shame, despite his idols; for his molten images are false, *and there is no breath/spirit in them.* (15) They are nothing, a work of derision(?). At their appointed time they will perish. (16) Not like these is the one who is the portion of Jacob, for he forms all things; Israel is the tribe of his inheritance, *Yahweh Ṣĕbā᾿ôt* is his name.

The passage is complex. Verse 14 clearly refers to the vanity of idolmakers and v. 15 to idols themselves. Verse 16, however, is less clear. On the one hand, כְאֵלֶּה may be contrasting false gods with Yahweh. On the other hand, it may be contrasting the idolmakers who form הֶבֶל with Yahweh who forms all things.[135] Clearly, though, what is remarkable for our present discussion is that Jeremiah, in the context of describing the human creation of idols, characterizes these objects as having in them no רוּחַ (v. 14bβ).[136] The deuterocanonical *Letter of Jeremiah* includes this same statement in its description of idols (v. 25), reflecting nearly exactly the Greek version of Jer 10:14: ἐν οἷς οὐκ ἔστιν πνεῦμα. In still another passage, roughly contemporary with both Jeremiah and Ezekiel, Habakkuk (2:19) mocks the enemies of Israel, using language very similar to Jeremiah and, what is more, closes with the comparable expression: a workman makes and trust his own creation, and וְכָל־רוּחַ אֵין בְּקִרְבּוֹ 'there is no breath/spirit at all in it'.[137]

134. In v. 15 תעתעים is difficult (only here and Jer 51:18).

135. This observation was also made by Richard Clifford for idol polemics in Deutero-Isaiah ("The Function of Idol Passages in Second Isaiah," *CBQ* 42 [1980] 450–64); see a similar conclusion in Knut Holter's study, *Second Isaiah's Idol-Fabrication Passages* (BBET 28; Frankfurt am Main: Lang, 1995).

136. Greek of 14b: οὐκ ἔστιν πνεῦμα ἐν αὐτοῖς.

137. Greek: καὶ πᾶν πνεῦμα οὐκ ἔστιν ἐν αὐτῷ. (Perhaps this characterization may also be found in Ps 135:17b, though there it more likely refers simply to the muteness of idols [cf. Ps 115:5–7].) A similar characterization of idols as lifeless is expressed even more bluntly in Wis 13:18: περὶ δὲ ζωῆς τὸ νεκρὸν ἀξιοῖ ('for life he honors the dead').

It appears that the vision in Ezekiel 37 halts (in v. 8) at a point that leaves Israel equal to its idols—and no better. Neither they nor the intermediate formation of bodies has רוּחַ. Thus the re-creation process must continue, as it did at creation, with God's breathing life into them. It seems certain, then, that Ezekiel 37 is consciously drawing this analogy with idols and thereby sharply signaling the distinction in the creation of the people of Israel.[138] Indeed, the description of the creation of people in Ezek 37:1–11, similar to that of idols, can be characterized as one of craftsmanship: the scattered raw material of bones is refashioned, reconstructed, and reconnected (קרב, 37:7; cf. 37:17); the physical frame then receives its covering (sinew, flesh, skin) and finally its revivification.[139]

Thus we have confirmation that Ezekiel explicitly employs creation traditions and invokes an analogy with the construction of idols. This can be established from original Ezekiel material, from other Israelite traditions, and from the Mesopotamian pattern reviewed in §2. The imagery used in Ezekiel appears to be well known to its audience.

In the same vein, G. K. Beale has argued carefully and persuasively that Isa 6:9–13 may include a polemic against idolatry in Israel.[140] The especially pertinent text is Isa 6:9–10, which Beale considers in the context of the explicit idol polemic in Ps 115:5–8 (and Ps 135:15–18).

Ps 115:5–8:

פֶּה־לָהֶם וְלֹא יְדַבֵּרוּ עֵינַיִם לָהֶם וְלֹא יִרְאוּ: אָזְנַיִם לָהֶם וְלֹא יִשְׁמָעוּ אַף
לָהֶם וְלֹא יְרִיחוּן: יְדֵיהֶם וְלֹא יְמִישׁוּן רַגְלֵיהֶם וְלֹא יְהַלֵּכוּ לֹא־יֶהְגּוּ בִּגְרוֹנָם:
כְּמוֹהֶם יִהְיוּ עֹשֵׂיהֶם כֹּל אֲשֶׁר־בֹּטֵחַ בָּהֶם:

(5) They have mouths but do not speak; they have eyes but do not see;
(6) they have ears but do not hear; they have noses but do not smell;
(7) they have hands but do not feel; they have feet but do not walk;

138. At this point, a connection with the consecration of divine statues in the *mīs pî / pīt pî* rituals would seem to recommend itself. The *rûaḥ*-step in Ezekiel appears to recollect the Mesopotamian ritual, though more research must be done to establish this connection. The ritual induction process includes many elements (e.g., washing the statue's mouth with holy water, reciting incantations, setting the statue up, rotating the statue toward different compass points, opening the statue's eyes, and taking the hand of the divine statue in procession back to the temple), but an element comparable to the inbreathing in Ezekiel cannot be indentified (see the Babylonian text BM 45749 published by Sidney Smith, "The Babylonian Ritual for the Consecration and Induction of a Divine Statue," *JRAS* [1925] 37–60 [pls. 2–4]). Still, the ritual qua ritual, representing the final stage in the making of a statue, is analogous to the final stage in the re-creation of humans in Ezek 37:1–14.

139. The imagery of "building" seems also apparent in the creation of man (Gen 2:7) and of woman from man's side (Gen 2:21–23).

140. G. K. Beale, "Isaiah VI 9–13: A Retributive Taunt against Idolatry," *VT* 41 (1991) 257–78.

and they cannot (even) make a sound in their throat. (8) Just like them are those who make them, all those who trust in them.

Isa 6:9–10a:

וַיֹּאמֶר לֵךְ וְאָמַרְתָּ לָעָם הַזֶּה שִׁמְעוּ שָׁמוֹעַ וְאַל־תָּבִינוּ וּרְאוּ רָאוֹ וְאַל־תֵּדָעוּ׃
הַשְׁמֵן לֵב־הָעָם הַזֶּה וְאָזְנָיו הַכְבֵּד וְעֵינָיו הָשַׁע

(9) And he said, "Go and say to this people: 'Keep on hearing, but do not understand; keep on seeing, but do not perceive.' (10) Make fat the heart of this people, and their ears make dull, and their eyes shut."

Here too would be a case where imagery associated with idolatry was applied to the people as both a description of their condition and a polemic against the practice in Israel.[141] In other words, the punishment quite literally fits the crime.[142] The association here, it should be noted, did not have to be made explicit. Isaiah does not state directly that Israel has become like idols; rather, the imagery of idolatry was shared knowledge to the extent that Isaiah could develop an effective metaphor. It is with this same shared knowledge of experience and expression that Ezekiel can combine and refashion these concepts in his message of rehabilitation.[143]

---

141. Indeed, elsewhere Isaiah directly condemns the practice of idolatry: the images of Babylon's gods will be smashed (21:9b); and Isaiah 36–37 sets up an underlying theological contest between Yahweh's power and the ineffectiveness of the gods of the nations (e.g., 36:18–20; 37:12, 19).

Incidentally, to see that the analogy between idolaters and their idols was apparent to early interpreters, one need only consult Philo (*De Decalogo* 15 §74), who explicitly describes the worshiper of idols in terms of the idols themselves (and in language notably close to Psalm 115 and Deut 4:28).

142. A possible wordplay in Deutero-Isaiah may produce this same effect. The prophet consistently uses *ḥrš* to describe the act of crafting idols (40:19, 20; 41:7; 44:11, 12, 13; 45:16); and in the same contexts he describes the rebellious people as being deaf (*ḥrš*; e.g., 42:18).

143. This analysis contradicts, for example, the thesis of M. Fox, "The Rhetoric of Ezekiel's Vision of the Valley of the Bones," *HUCA* 51 (1980) 1–15. He described the imagery of Ezek 37:1–14 as shocking and unexpected, and this was required for the prophet to execute his rhetorical strategy and achieve "category shifts" in his hearers. In other words, Ezekiel needed to employ a form of rhetoric that would persuasively exhort, sustain, and modify the attitudes and behavior of those whose despair threatened their continued existence and identity (as expressed, e.g., in 37:11). One of these techniques, he proposes in this rhetorical analysis of this text, was to assert the absurd. The dramatic imagery of a resurrection of bones challenges the people's "framework of expectations." Ezekiel's goal after 587 was to arouse the belief in a future national restoration, a well-nigh hopeless idea. "He (Ezekiel) sought to create *irrational* expectations in his audience by making them believe in the reality of the irrational, by getting them to expect the unexpected, to accept the

Re-creation and Repatriation of the Nation Israel

The second section of Ezekiel 37 (vv. 15–28) expands the image of human re-creation into the restoration of the kingdom of Israel. Ezekiel's concern focuses on the people as a nation. The exilic community represents an entity that can be both exiled and repatriated. Here too the prophet uses metaphors of reconstruction but now of physically joining together the two halves of the once-united kingdom.

Ezek 37:15–28 accents the image in vv. 1–14 in various ways.[144] The subject in the first section is the house of Israel (v. 11), and the people will be returned to the land of Israel (v. 12). Section two addresses the constitution of Israel. As section one promises re-creation, section two promises reunification. Both are restorations of a previous reality. As such, the two sections are connected, so to speak, by קרב (vv. 7 and 17): just as bones were joined together, so the two עֵצִים, representing the two kingdoms, will be joined.[145] The prophet literally represents this by reuniting the separate items in vv. 15–22.

---

plausibility of the absurd" (p. 7). Fox uses such expressions as "strange," "shocking," and "bizarre" to describe the imagery that Ezekiel employed in order to create new frameworks of perception in his auditors. According to Fox, the vision is radical, without precedent. But such concepts, the thesis goes, were necessary for the rhetorical strategy the prophet employed.

I have tried to demonstrate, to the contrary, that the imagery of both chaps. 36 and 37 is drawn from known categories of creation in Genesis 1 and 2. However new this creation might be, it is expressed in the terminology of the old. Indeed, the very nature of rhetoric presumes this. A message intended to persuade cannot work on what is absolutely new, without previous conceptual reference that the audience shares. It may, however, build on expectations, which it plays with perhaps in unexpected ways.

144. Unlike vv. 1–14, this section is framed in the action/interpretation form used elsewhere in the book (e.g., Ezekiel 4–5), and the action does not appear to take place in the same visionary state as the previous section. Similar to vv. 1–14, however, vv. 15–28 do incorporate the question/answer format. Here also there are various positions on the literary and redactional history of the text. Zimmerli (*Ezekiel 2*, 271–72) sees vv. 15–19 as the original base text, with vv. 20–24a being a later addition either by Ezekiel or by his school, and vv. 24b–28 being still a later redaction by his school. I would emphasize with Allen (*Ezekiel 20–48*, 191) and others the structural flow of vv. 16–24a. Repetition in the text achieves a close integration between subunits; e.g., קרב in vv. 7 and 17, אחד from v. 16 to v. 24a. The text also presents a consistent, though clearly escalating image—from the joining of the two kingdoms to one king as shepherd-prince over the united land. While a basic text may have been supplemented at a shortly later date, the redaction suggests an amplification, nowhere compromising the integrity of the original.

145. Interestingly, *The Testament of Zebulon* 9, a pseudepigraphical work, interprets the worship of idols as a direct result of the division of Israel into two kingdoms, which in turn leads to exile among the nations (see translation by H. C. Kee, "Testaments of the Twelve Patriarchs," *OTP*, 1.807).

The term עֵץ (vv. 16, 17, 19, and 20), the principal object of the oracular demonstration, is difficult to interpret exactly and may in fact be multivalent. The LXX renders it ῥάβδος 'rod, staff, stick' (compare Zech 11:7ff., מַקְלוֹת, ῥάβδους; Num 17:16ff., מַטּוֹת, ῥάβδοι). The targum understood it as a wooden tablet (לוּחַ). W. E. Barnes argues that "tree" is meant, since elsewhere Ezekiel uses עֵץ for representing Judah as a vine tree (12:6ff; 19:10) and עֲצֵי־עֵדֶן for the enemies of Egypt (31:9).[146] It is not impossible that here, too, Ezekiel may be associating Israel with idols. Consider, for example, Hos 4:12, עַמִּי בְּעֵצוֹ יִשְׁאָל 'my people consult wood', clearly a reference to idols (see also עֵצָה in Hos 10:6 and Jer 6:6).[147] This association is not certain. But the action, that of joining, reconnecting, or grafting, is clear enough. What was once whole will become one again.

Two further points contribute to the thesis at hand and suggest an important direction to Ezekiel's message. First, the chapter associates creation traditions with nationalism. A similar juxtaposition occurs in Deutero-Isaiah (for example, Isa 42:5–7; 43:1; 44:24–28). Yahweh's power is witnessed in creation, and this recollection serves as a reassurance that Yahweh can save his people.[148] The universal scope of the creation narratives has been particularized in Israel. As order is brought out of chaos in creating the world, Israel will be returned from chaos in its restoration from exile. Gerhard von Rad's observations are particularly appropriate.

> Jahweh created the world. But he created Israel too. In Is. li.9f., the two creative works are almost made to coincide. The prophet apostrophises the creation of the world, but at the same time he speaks of Israel's redemption from Egypt. For hardly has he spoken about the driving back of the waters, in the language of the mythical struggle with the dragon of Chaos, than he jumps to the miracle at the Red Sea where Jahweh again held the waters back "for the redeemed to pass through." Here creation and redemption almost coincide, and can almost be looked on as one act of dramatic divine saving action in the picture of the struggle with the dragon of Chaos. . . . Creation is part of the aetiology of Israel![149]

146. W. E. Barnes, "Two Trees Become One: Ezek. xxxvii 16–17," *JTS* 39 (1938) 391–93.

147. For a discussion of these passages, see Francis I. Andersen and David Noel Freedman, *Hosea* (AB 24; New York: Doubleday, 1980) 558.

148. See a similar theme expressed in terms of covenant, election, and deliverance language in Deut 10:12–11:5.

149. G. von Rad, *Old Testament Theology* (trans. D. M. G. Stalker; New York: Harper & Row, 1962) 1.137. On this, see also Richard J. Clifford, "Isaiah, Book of; Second Isaiah," *ABD* 3.499. And consider the comments of Samuel E. Loewenstamm, who identifies a relation between humans as the image of God (see above, chap. 2) and Israel as God's elect: "Both the idea that man is created in the image of God and that the people of Israel

Second, people and nation are the objects of God's power and activity. The Davidic leader who will be installed (מֶלֶךְ in Ezek 37:22 and 24; נָשִׂיא in v. 25[150]) is also a recipient of God's restoration. Indeed, the emphasis at the end of the chapter is the eternal covenant (בְּרִית עוֹלָם, v. 26a; compare 16:60–62) and the eternal sanctuary (מִקְדָּשִׁי בְּתוֹכָם לְעוֹלָם, vv. 26b–28; anticipating the return of his presence in 43:4), both of which Yahweh establishes.

Yahweh will restore his people to renewed life and repatriate them to a renewed land (36:8–10, 24, 28–31, 33–36, 37–38; 37:25–26; 39:25–29).[151] Yahweh will reestablish the sanctuary and city (promised in 37:26–28, described in chaps. 40–48) to which he will return of his own will and power. Neither Israel, people or leader, nor its conquering foes contribute to these events. This is made explicit in Ezek 36:22, "It is not for your sake, O house of Israel, that I am about to act, but for the sake of my holy name, which you have profaned among the nations to which you came." Ezekiel 36–37 functions as a significant hinge in this movement, highlighting the instructive nature of work: Yahweh is the sole power on the international level, carrying out the new creation of his people.

The Mesopotamian pattern discussed in §2 identified common features of Assyro-Babylonian imperial policy. In the process of coercing an enemy, a monarch might typically despoil the divine statues of the conquered people. In due course, these gods might be repaired and restored to their lands. Section 3 has shown how Ezekiel parodies this pattern. The prophet delivers a message of restoration of Israel following its spoliation. He enlists Israelite

---

are the sons of their God have their common origin in court language which attributes to the king a special relationship with the godhead. These terms developed in the Pentateuch in a similar, but nevertheless somewhat different direction. The first idea was transferred to encompass all humanity, the second to the people of Israel" ("'Beloved Is Man in That He Was Created in the Image,'" in *Comparative Studies in Biblical and Ancient Oriental Literatures* [AOAT 204; Kevelaer: Butzon & Bercker / Neukirchen-Vluyn: Neukirchener Verlag, 1980] 49).

150. This is the characteristic term used in Ezekiel 40–48 for the royal ruler. See E. A. Speiser, "Background and Function of the Biblical nāsîʾ," *CBQ* 25 (1963) 111–17. See also Jon D. Levenson, *Theology of the Program of Restoration of Ezekiel 40–48* (HSM 10; Missoula, Mont.: Scholars Press, 1976) 57–107; and Iain M. Duguid, *Ezekiel and the Leaders of Israel* (Leiden: Brill, 1994) 10–57.

151. Bodi is correct when he states, "Ezekiel fixes his hope for the future . . . on the faithful among the exiles out of whom the new Israel will be created (Ezekiel 33–37). For Ezekiel and Jeremiah alike, the true remnant is represented by the company of exile, i.e., by those who have survived the catastrophe through deportation" (Bodi, *Ezekiel*, 288). Carl S. Ehrlich has recently argued the same ("Anti-Juda[h]ism in the Hebrew Bible: The Case of Ezekiel," AAR/SBL Annual Meeting, Chicago, 1994). Moreover, it appears that Ezekiel legitimates this through his portrayal of the community as cleansed, restored, and returned by Yahweh.

creation traditions to portray the re-creation of the people. Furthermore, Israel's cleansing and rehabilitation from the sin of idolatry is expressed in language that directly associates the people with the idols they worshiped. In the final analysis, though, it is Yahweh who (re)creates and returns Israel, not an earthly king; and it is the people who are restored, not the so-called gods the people created.

Using this imagery of creation and idolatry, Ezekiel formulates two elaborate arguments for the exiles. The first combines an attack on idolatry with a message of exhortation. Ezekiel describes Yahweh cleansing Israel from idolatry prior to its restoration, and he uses terminology that substitutes people for idols. Thus the rehabilitation of Israel both reveals the vanity of idols and reinforces the message that I reasoned was elemental to Ezekiel's theology, namely, that humans are the image of God, not the idols that humans create.[152] Second, by substituting Yahweh as the actor in the pattern of exile, restoration, and return, Ezekiel affirms that Yahweh is sole king and creator who controls even the affairs of nations. Exiled Israel can therefore have hope in Yahweh, for neither king nor god can stand in the way.

Yahweh's Power and Presence at Creation

Before turning to a summary of conclusions in this chapter, I will identify additional ways in which Israelite traditions—and especially exilic traditions—typically connect the power of creation with polemics against idolatry.

Outside Ezekiel, polemics against idols are directly and contextually connected with the power of creation. The act of creating idols is explicitly mocked as naïve and feeble-minded (Jer 10:1–10, 14–15 [= 51:17–18]; Isa 44:9–20; Hab 2:18–19), using a rhetorical argument associating agency with potency: if humans create idols, then that action suggests human superiority to the god formed.[153] The logic is notably direct in the rhetorical question of Jer 16:20: הֲיַעֲשֶׂה־לּוֹ אָדָם אֱלֹהִים וְהֵמָּה לֹא אֱלֹהִים 'Can man make for himself gods? (Of course not! If he could,) They would not be gods'. Similarly, the Song of Moses describes Israel's following after "new gods" in terms that metaphorically recollect the nonrepeatable, nontransferable scene of birth (Deut 32:18): צוּר יְלָדְךָ תֶּשִׁי וַתִּשְׁכַּח אֵל מְחֹלְלֶךָ 'The Rock who bore you, you

---

152. See above, chap. 2.

153. Commentators have long noted the similar sentiment (especially close to Isa 44:9–20) expressed by Horace in *Satires* 1.8.1ff.: "Once I was a fig-wood stem, a worthless log, when the carpenter, doubtful whether to make a stool or a Priapus (the garden-god, used as a scarecrow), chose that I be a god" (translation from H. Rushton Fairclough, *Horace: Satires, Epistles and Arts Poetica* [LCL; Cambridge: Harvard University Press, 1973] pp. 96–97). See also Clifford's comments on Isaiah 44 ("Function of Idol Passages in Second Isaiah," esp. p. 463).

ignored; you forgot the God who labored in childbirth for you'. No stepgod can claim this relationship. Deutero-Isaiah voices the same sentiment in 44:2. Jeremiah (2:27) mocks the leaders of Israel, אֹמְרִים לָעֵץ אָבִי אַתָּה וְלָאֶבֶן אַתְּ יְלִדְתָּנִי 'who say to a tree, "You are my father," and to a stone, "You gave birth to me"'. When the leaders approach these inanimate objects for deliverance in time of trouble, Jeremiah sharply marks the irony; humans who created the idols, claim to have been created by them: וְאַיֵּה אֱלֹהֶיךָ אֲשֶׁר עָשִׂיתָ לָּךְ 'Where are your gods you made for yourself?'[154] Widespread is the scornful remark that idols are the product of human hands.[155]

Additionally, the general creation of the cosmos furnishes an indirect claim against impotent idols.[156] In Jer 10:11–16 (= 51:15–19, recontextualized as an oracle against Babylon), Isaiah 40–41, Isaiah 42:5–17, Isaiah 44–45, and Psalm 115, the polemics against idols are located in the same context as Yahweh's claim to be sole creator of the heavens and the earth.[157] Indeed, in Jer 10:16 (= Jer 51:19) the comparison between the all-powerful Yahweh and worthless idols is made explicit.[158] Such an argument may be the basis for

154. The sentiment that God (alone) kills and makes alive is expressed in the Deuteronomistic historical work (Deut 32:39; 1 Sam 2:6; 2 Kgs 5:7; the only other passage in the Hebrew Bible in which the *Hiphil* of מות is expressed absolutely without an object is Job 9:23).

155. Deut 4:28; 27:15; 2 Kgs 19:18 = Isa 37:19; Hos 8:4–6; 13:2; 14:4; Mic 5:12; Isa 2:8; Ps 115:4; 135:15; Jer 1:16; 10:3; 25:5–6; 40:8; 2 Chr 32:19.

156. See also C. J. Labuschagne, *The Incomparability of Yahweh in the Old Testament* (Leiden: Brill, 1966) 108–12). It seems, however, that Labuschagne's overestimation of Yahweh's unique role in history—his mighty deeds in history—prevents a full appreciation of this theme, as the following statement indicates: "What is relevant and of importance to us now is the fact that Yahweh's activity as Creator does not figure prominently in the conception of His incomparability. . . . It is completely subordinate to and dominated by the conception of Yahweh as the redeeming God, active in history" (p. 109). To lay the claim of incomparability upon a universal footing (as Labuschagne, pp. 146–47) is not only effective, but required; the ascription of creation to Yahweh furnishes the most ready proof.

157. For two contrasting views on the origin of idol polemics in Deutero-Isaiah, compare Wolfgang M. W. Roth, "For Life, He Appeals to Death (Wis 13:18): A Study of Old Testament Idol Parodies," *CBQ* 37 (1975) 21–47; and Clifford, "Function of Idol Passages in Second Isaiah," 450–64.

158. In pseudepigraphical and deuterocanonical literature from the Second Temple period, we find this same contextual association. For examples, see Wisdom of Solomon 13; *Sib. Or.* 3:9–45; 8:359–425; and especially *2 Enoch* 66, in which the focus of the book is on God as sole creator (so F. I. Andersen, "2 Enoch," *OTP*, 1.91). See also (Pseudo-) "Sophocles" quoted by Hecataeus, preserved in Clement of Alexandria *Stromateis* 5.113: "One, truly one is God who made both heaven and the wide earth. . . . We throngs of men go astray in our hearts when . . . we set up as statues of gods figures worked from wood, or images of copper, gold or ivory" (translation by R. Doran, "Pseudo-Hecataeus," *OTP*, 2.912). The NT book of Acts describes Paul and Barnabas using this argument among

closely associating sabbath violation and idolatry in Ezekiel (20:7–8, 12–13, 16, 18–21, 24; 22:8–9; 23:36–39; note also Lev 19:3–4; 26:1–2, 27–35). According to Priestly theology, Sabbath observance commemorates the creation of the world by Yahweh (Gen 2:2–3; Exod 20:11). Profaning the Sabbath offends God's creative act. Worshiping idols affronts God as the creator.[159]

Besides this proof that only the creator can be God, the prophets contemporary with Ezekiel develop an argument close in sensibility to Ezekiel's use of the pattern described above; that is, Yahweh creates and carries Israel, not vice versa. Consider the imagery portrayed in the following texts: Jer 10:5; Isa 40:20, 41:7, and 46:7 describe the immobility of an idol on its pedestal, implying this condition reflects its puissance. Furthermore, if the idol has movement it is only because a human carries it (Jer 10:5; Isa 45:20). Isa 46:1–4, a complex text, develops this imagery with particular skill.

כָּרַע בֵּל קֹרֵס נְבוֹ הָיוּ עֲצַבֵּיהֶם לַחַיָּה וְלַבְּהֵמָה נְשֻׂאֹתֵיכֶם עֲמוּסוֹת מַשָּׂא
לַעֲיֵפָה: קָרְסוּ כָרְעוּ יַחְדָּו לֹא יָכְלוּ מַלֵּט מַשָּׂא וְנַפְשָׁם בַּשְּׁבִי הָלָכָה: שִׁמְעוּ

Gentiles in Lystra (14:15; also 1 Thess 1:9). *Jubilees* contrasts idols with the creator, living God (95:3).

Incidentally, the book of Hosea ends with a related contrast: It is Yahweh who is the creator and sustainer of Israel (14:6–8); therefore, God can ask, אֶפְרַיִם מַה־לִּי עוֹד לָעֲצַבִּים (v. 9). (Note, too, the wordplay in v. 6 using אֶהְיֶה, which occurs at the outset in 1:9 and which certainly is a play on the expression in Exod 3:14 [the recommendation in BHS to read אלהיכם for לכם אהיה in Hos 1:9 is unnecessary].) Furthermore, the unique expression in Hos 2:1, בְּנֵי אֵל־חָי, may function very concisely to indicate both the contrast between Yahweh and other lifeless gods, and the affirmation that Yahweh is the creator of his people.

159. As an aside, we might consider the association among the Sabbath, the creation of the world, and the building of the Temple/sanctuary—the Temple as a microcosm and token of the world (see Jon Levenson, "The Temple and the World," *JR* 64 [1984], esp. pp. 282–98; and idem, *Creation and the Persistence of Evil* (San Francisco: Harper & Row, 1988) 78–99; also M. Weinfeld, "Sabbath, Temple and the Enthronement of the Lord: The Problem of the Sitz im Leben of Genesis 1:1–2:3," in *Mélanges bibliques et orientaux en l'honneur de M. Henri Cazelles* [ed. A. Caquot and M. Delcor; Neukirchen-Vluyn: Neukirchener Verlag, 1981] 501–12). On the association between the creation account and the Sinai sanctuary, see J. Blenkinsopp, "The Structure of P," *CBQ* 38 (1976) 275–92; P. J. Kearney, "Creation and Liturgy: The P Redaction of Exod 25–40," *ZAW* 89 (1977) 375–87; and Gordon J. Wenham, "Sanctuary Symbolism in the Garden of Eden Story," in *Proceedings of the Ninth World Congress of Jewish Studies* (Jerusalem: World Union of Jewish Studies, 1986) 19–25. This discussion is intriguing in relation to the theme of a renewed Temple in Ezekiel 40–48 (note the repetition of Sabbath commands in chaps. 44–46). support from the versions (see C. F. Whitley, "Textual Notes on Deutero-Isaiah," *VT* 11 [1961] 457–61). Clifford emends the text ("Function of Idol Passages in Second Isaiah," 455 n. 19). BHS proposes emending עשיתי 'I have made' to עמשׂתי 'I have carried (a load)', though here, too, with no support from the versions. For a roughly similar oracle, see Jer 50:2–3 (note the use of *gillûlîm*).

אֵלַי בֵּית יַעֲקֹב וְכָל־שְׁאֵרִית בֵּית יִשְׂרָאֵל הַעֲמֻסִים מִנִּי־בֶטֶן הַנְּשֻׂאִים
מִנִּי־רָחַם: וְעַד־זִקְנָה אֲנִי הוּא וְעַד־שֵׂיבָה אֲנִי אֶסְבֹּל אֲנִי עָשִׂיתִי וַאֲנִי אֶשָּׂא
וַאֲנִי אֶסְבֹּל וַאֲמַלֵּט: ¹⁶⁰

(1) Marduk has *bent down*, Nabu *cringes*.¹⁶¹ Their images are on
beasts and cattle. These things that you *carry* are *borne* as a burden
upon exhausted beasts. (2) They have *cringed*, they have *bent down* together, they are not able to *save* the burden; they go into captivity.
(3) Hear me, O house of Jacob, all the remnant of the house of Israel,
who have been *borne* (by me) from birth, who have been *carried* (by
me) from the womb. (4) Until (your) old age I am the one, until gray-
headedness I will *support* (you). I make, I *carry*, I *support*, and I *save*.

The passage is pregnant with double entendre. Parallel predicates dominate
and provide structure (chiastically in vv. 1/2 and 1/3). The subjects of the
verbs in v. 2a are unspecified: יַחְדָּו may refer back to Marduk and Nabu or to
the beasts or to both sets of pairs. Certainly, the idols are themselves the burden. They must be carried. But under the load, the beasts of burden stumble
and fall, spilling their cargo. All go into exile.¹⁶² Conversely, Yahweh carries
his people in every sense of the word: he bore (gave birth to) them, bears
(supports) them, and delivers (saves) them from captivity.¹⁶³

The Mesopotamian pattern of removal, repair, and return of deities provides the framework with which Ezekiel builds a new structure based on his
own ideological convictions. Fundamentally, the assertion is that God creates
humans, humans do not create God. Imagery that reverses this order becomes a paradigm for controverting the potency of divine statues.

Humans not only create divine statues, they are then responsible for their
care and protection. As we noted above, the practice of ingathering—that is,
collecting the local gods into a central stronghold when attack was loom-
ing—could backfire. Both Sargon II and Cyrus would claim that these gods
were taken against their will. To Ezekiel and his contemporaries this might

160. Isa 46:1b–c is certainly difficult. BHS proposes reordering the words, and Whitley
considers משׂא לעיפה a gloss and suggests omitting it, though neither solution commands
161. The translation 'to cringe' or 'to cower' fits well here: BDB 902A, 'to bend down,
stoop, crouch'; Jastrow, p. 1423, 'to contract, shrink' (also see קרס III, 'to contract, harden,
shrink', in E. Klein, *A Comprehensive Etymological Dictionary of the Hebrew Language* [Jeru-
salem: Carta, 1987]). The context presents the gods in a state of humiliation following national defeat.
162. The subject (נַפְשָׁם) in v. 2b is difficult. Note also Amos 5:26–27, where Israel is
described going into exile, carrying its own gods.
163. In Deut 32:11–12, Yahweh is described in zoomorphic terms, carrying his
people like a mother bird in the wilderness. There the writer explicitly emphasizes that no
foreign god (ʾēl nēkār) helped Yahweh accomplish this.

indicate as much about the ineffectiveness of a god whose statue was carted about, albeit willingly.[164] Perhaps even a note of satire functions in the annals of Tiglath-pileser I, who portrays the defeated residents of Urratinash fleeing with their gods in their arms: "The terror, fear, (and) splendor of the god Aš-šur, my lord, overwhelmed them. To save their lives, they took their gods (and) possessions and flew like birds to ledges on high mountains."[165]

Literature from the Second Temple period continues these same arguments, often in great detail. Two deuterocanonical texts set their warnings against idolatry in the context of the Babylonian *golah*. The *Letter of Jeremiah* poses as correspondence from the prophet to the exiles who might be attracted to these "gods made of silver and gold and wood, which are carried on men's shoulders and inspire fear in the heathen" (v. 4). The author offers ten proofs of their worthlessness, ending each with a refrain such as, "Since you know by these things that they are not gods, do not fear them" (vv. 16, 23, 29, 40, 44, 52, 56, 65, 69, and 73). Bel and the Dragon, whose setting is the time of sagacious Daniel and Cyrus the Great, offers a satirical demonstration to this effect (vv. 3–22). The representation of Abraham as a literal iconoclast receives much attention in pseudepigraphical works (for example, *Jubilees* 12; Pseudo-Philo's *Biblical Antiquities* 6;[166] and *Apocalypse Abraham* 1–8). In the *Apoc. Abraham* 4:3, we find the patriarch giving unsolicited (and financially unwelcome) advice to his idolmaking father, Terah, using the proof demonstrated above from the exilic prophets: "The gods are blessed in you, because you are a god for them, because you made them."[167]

This is part of the very argument that Ezekiel constructs in Ezekiel 36–37: promise of re-creation is coupled with his ongoing combat against idolatry. The Wisdom of Solomon contrasts the true God with lifeless images cre-

164. One might note the danger of this caricatured view inherent in the ark-sanctuary and consequently the need for stories that credit independent (divine) power to the ark, despite its otherwise passive depiction (for example, 1 Samuel 4–6 and 2 Samuel 6). (On the ark narratives as theological interpretation of history demonstrating Yahweh's superiority, see Patrick D. Miller Jr. and J. J. M. Roberts, *The Hand of the Lord: A Reassessment of the "Ark Narrative" in I Samuel* [Baltimore: Johns Hopkins University Press, 1977], esp. pp. 69–75.) The Kohath/Korah-element also successfully produces this same effect (see Num 4:15; 16:1–17:5; and 17:14).

165. *RIMA* 2 15, ii 36ff.

166. Furthermore, such a stance is foreshadowed in Pseudo-Philo by Serug and his sons, ancestors of Abraham, who alone of all peoples reject idolatry (*Bib. Ant.* 4:16; the opposite is apparently interpreted by *Jub.* 11:6, for the sake of etiology). For Pseudo-Philo, idolatry essentially separates Israel from the nations, and contact with non-Israelites leads to idolatry (e.g., 12:2).

167. Trans. R. Rubinkiewicz, rev. H. G. Lunt, "The Apocalypse of Abraham," *OTP*, 1.690. In the *Testament of Job*, Job's troubles with Satan result from his destruction of an idol shrine (chaps. 2–5).

ated by Israel's enemies (chaps. 13–15). It closes with a contrast between idols and humans (15:16–17), which is apparent also in Ezekiel 37.

> (16) For a man made them, and one whose spirit is borrowed formed them; for no man can form a god which is like himself. (17) He is mortal, and what he makes with lawless hands is dead, for he is better than the objects he worships, since he has life, but they never have.[168]

For Ezekiel, the images of God are humans, whom God has made. In contrast, idols, which humans make, are merely the 'images of men' (צַלְמֵי זָכָר, Ezek 16:17).

§4. Conclusion

The creation terminology analyzed in Ezekiel 36–37 serves more than stylistic and literary purposes; it also reflects language associated with cult statues. Ezekiel's imagery of re-creation and restoration draws on imagery of creation known from the Israelite tradition, simultaneously extending his polemic against idolatry into his portrayal of the repatriation of the exiled people. This is a hard-working oracle/vision, functioning on two complementary levels.

Ezekiel's theological subtlety is especially manifest in his method of employing the categories of exile and return of *cult statues*, adopted from his exilic hosts, as a framework for his oracle of restoration of the *people of Israel*. In doing so he has also switched actor and object. No human monarch took Yahweh as spoil; Yahweh exiled himself. Nor is Yahweh restored and returned by an earthly monarch, but he restores his people. By appropriating standard Mesopotamian language of re-creation and repatriation of cult statues, inverting the whole system by applying it to his description of the revivification and restoration of Israel, he delivers his message and subverts the original meaning. The prophet has combined an attack on idolatry with instruction and exhortation: the Mesopotamians conceive that man creates and restores gods, but Israel now knows that Yahweh creates and restores man. Israel is cleansed of idols and re-created in a fashion that belies their efficacy.[169]

---

168. Similar characterizations can be found in early Christian literature, as well; see, e.g., *2 Clem.* 1:6–7 and 3:1.

169. One is reminded of an interesting aspect of *Joseph and Aseneth*, a text from the Second Temple period. The dilemma of the marriage is that Aseneth is a non-Jewish worshiper of idols, the daughter of a pagan priest. Her inevitable conversion from idolatry is described as re-creation and revivification when Joseph prays that God might bless her "and renew her by your spirit, and form her anew by your hidden hand, and make her alive again by your life" (8:11ff. [trans. C. Burchard, "Joseph and Aseneth," *OTP*, 2.213]; also see

Consequently, in spite of the exile, or because of it, the power of Yahweh is demonstrated vis-à-vis nations and gods. On one level, Yahweh is present in his absence—that is, without sanctuary or material form—while the physical existence of idols proves that these gods are absent in their presence. In fact, as we saw in chap. 2, Ezekiel withholds even the status "gods" for these objects. On another level, Ezekiel instructs Israel that Yahweh is never absent because he is never present, at least in the conventional, "pagan" way. Thus while he can abandon his sanctuary, he remains himself a *miqdāš mĕ'aṭ* (11:16).

Chapter 1 reviewed the evidence from previous studies that suggest that Ezekiel was a literatus. This suggestion gains additional force from the results of this chapter. Not only does Ezekiel interact with Israelite tradition, which may have reached him in some written form, but he clearly knows and manipulates Mesopotamian religiopolitical concepts. The battle is joined on a literary plane.

Chapters 1 and 3 advanced elements of the structural unity of the Ezekiel book, particularly the themes of theophany (both God's absence and presence) and Temple. It now becomes apparent that the structure as well as the combination of oracles of judgment and of restoration are intrinsic to the text's meaning. Ezekiel incorporates a larger pattern, especially appropriate in the exilic context, which the prophet exploits for an extended polemic against idolatry and as a demonstration of Yahweh's activity on behalf of Israel. In relation to both the Mesopotamian pattern and the structure of the book, the restoration of the Temple and its environs (chaps. 40–48) is an obvious and essential denouement.[170]

This interpretation of Ezekiel 36–37, therefore, has several advantages, summarized as follows: (1) the material fits well into the form of the book, which closely follows a movement from divine abandonment to exile and

---

15:5; compare 18:9). Of course, conversion and new life is taken up as a prominent metaphor in early Christian literature.

170. I have not analyzed in detail this last division in the structure of Ezekiel (chaps. 40–48) and its connection with the final element in the Mesopotamian pattern—that is, the restoration of destroyed temples. Rather, I have concentrated in this chapter on Ezekiel 36–37, demonstrating its connection to the Mesopotamian pattern outlined in §2. Establishing the relationship in chaps. 36–37 required detailed exegesis and discussion. Certainly, such a detailed analysis of Ezekiel 40–48 is not necessary; the themes in these chapters and their relationship to the final renovation of destroyed sanctuaries is far more transparent than the relationship of chaps. 36–37 to the renovation of divine statues. For a discussion of the restoration of previously destroyed sanctuaries by Assyro-Babylonian monarchs, the reader should consult especially the following works: Porter, *Images*, chap. 4, on royal public works projects; and Holloway, *The Case for Assyrian Religious Influence in Israel and Judah*, 563–67, table 9, on Assyrian reconstruction of foreign cult centers.

then to restoration, and which closely resembles Mesopotamian patterns; (2) chap. 37, despite its apparent change of imagery, is quite unified in presenting corporeal restoration of both people and nation; and (3) the polemic against idolatry, a constant theme in the book, is a focus of these chapters, as are (4) the variations on the theme of God's presence and absence. In other words, through both structure and content, Ezekiel 36–37 continues and develops themes of a message that pervade the book as a whole.

Chapter 5
Summary and Conclusion

And the Spirit lifted me up between earth and heaven.
Ezekiel 8:3

§1. Depth of the Theme:
God's Presence and Absence

In this study I have addressed the complexity of the paradox of God's presence and absence in the book of Ezekiel. The theme of divine presence and absence is a chord that weaves its way through the composition—exploring and expressing the theological dilemmas that the exilic community faced in Babylonia. It is a paradox that provides the concepts for many of the questions and answers, both provoking and informing Ezekiel's responses. In this study, I have specified how the prophet develops this theme and its variations, and I have suggested why the prophet develops this paradox in the context of Israelite and, more broadly, Near Eastern theology.

The paradox of divine absence and presence in Ezekiel is not the same as the classical question of *deus absconditus* and *deus revelatus*. On the one hand, Ezekiel's concern is far more basic: Could God be present in the face of the destruction of the Jerusalem Temple and the relocation of a community to Babylonia? On the other hand, it is a subtle question, particularly for an aniconic tradition: How is Israel's God to be perceived and worshiped in his apparent absence, when other so-called gods, represented by divine images, support the victorious enemy of Israel? Together these concerns raise a complex set of interrelations that involve the representation of Yahweh, the differentiation of Yahweh from other deities, and the relationship of Yahweh to Israel in exile. The following paragraphs summarize my analysis and conclusions.

Chapter 2 identified Ezekiel's ubiquitous polemic against idolatry and his charge that for such infidelity the community was exiled. Idolatry—the misrepresentation of God's image, the illegitimate expression of his presence—resulted in the removal of God's presence and the destruction of his symbolic dwelling place. Such terms as *gillûlîm* characterize Ezekiel's scorching contempt for idols. Furthermore, Ezekiel provides the exiles with an extended argument that Yahweh alone is God, contrary to all appearances. In spite of the idol's physical presence, no divine power dwells within it. For Ezekiel an idol is not a symbol of a god's presence but the indication of its absence. Thus, exile cannot mean that Yahweh was defeated by the so-called gods that are portrayed in wood and stone.

It has generally been during the period of the exile, particularly Deutero-Isaiah, that biblical scholars have attributed Israel's explicit denial of gods other than Yahweh. I have demonstrated that Ezekiel intentionally avoids the term ʾĕlōhîm with reference to idols, and this is evidence that Ezekiel was clearly monotheistic, consciously carrying through this conviction to a radical extreme in his language and in his silence. Ezekiel is thus an important voice in the development of monotheism in the religion of Israel. This also is another component of the paradox of God's absence and presence. Demonstrating that idols were mere material objects wholly lacking any divine potential, Ezekiel opened the door to recognizing God's presence in his absence.

Ezekiel also develops rhetoric that is particularly appropriate in the context of Israelite experience in Babylonia. For example, chap. 2 suggested that Ezekiel and his audience were aware of Mesopotamian concepts associated with the construction of idols and that, while the prophet never directly uses the phrase "image of God," he knew of a usage similar to what is found in the Priestly tradition. Indeed, both P and Ezekiel contrast the Mesopotamian concept of an idol as the image of a god (ṣalam ili/ilāni) with an understanding that humans were made in the image of God (ṣelem ʾĕlōhîm). In so doing, both traditions achieve a measure of victory by blunting the effectiveness of Babylonian theology. For the exiles, Ezekiel's polemic goes to the heart of the issue: if idols are not the image of God, then their worship is in vain. Furthermore, the principle that humans, not idols, are the image of God informs Ezekiel's moral theology (as it does P's in Gen 9:6) and forms the background to the indictment that the people shed much blood. Thus here again the messages of judgment and of hope are inextricably united: that the people have misunderstood God's image accounts for their exile but permits the hope that as the ṣelem ʾĕlōhîm they might have confidence in an ongoing divine-human encounter.

In chap. 3 I discussed the ways Ezekiel communicates God's presence among the exiles and the way the paradox of God's presence and absence again contributes to the prophet's message. The prophet faced two problems: his emphasis on theodicy stressed the removal of God's presence from the Temple because of the people's profane behavior, but the exile itself necessitated an idiom that could communicate the reality of God's presence beyond the control of border and imperial might. How could Ezekiel provide a metaphor of God's presence without jeopardizing the vigor of his theodicy? The *kābôd*-theology furnished the means to bridge the gap between the Temple and the exilic experience. For Ezekiel, the exile was the wilderness revisited, and he enrolled the tradition of the mobile *kĕbôd-yhwh* to depict the complementary aspects of God's absence and presence.

Ezekiel's attempt to mediate between God's boundlessness and God's real presence is the theological dilemma that motivates the striking nature of the *kābôd*-visions. The struggle for an effective medium produces vividly graphic portrayals of the otherwise abstract theology of the *kĕbôd-yhwh*. An effective exilic theology must (1) account for the exilic experience; (2) maintain God's transcendence in order to provide the vehicle for God to trespass borders; and (3) employ an image of God's proximity whose sentient quality the prophet can communicate to those who have no vision. Thus Ezekiel's description of the divine *kābôd* stresses the reality of God's absence from the Temple and his presence in the people's midst.

The concept of God's absence from the Temple and presence in exile is accentuated by the *kābôd*-theology's adoption of Israel's traditions of its past, namely, the wilderness experience. This function of the *kābôd* is manifest through the image of the wheels. While the Temple is the initial site of God's presence, the emphasis is on the mobility of the *kābôd* as a means of expressing judgment (God's absence) and emphasizing God's availability (presence) in exile. This emphasis on the association between the wilderness experience and the exile occurs in three areas. First, it is clear that the *kĕbôd-yhwh* that rises from the Temple and departs Jerusalem is the divine presence that Ezekiel sees in exile during the sixth year (8:1–4; compare 1:2). Second, Ezekiel 20 directly connects the tradition of the wilderness with the present experience in exile. Third, as the sanctuary was a mobile presence in the wilderness, so Yahweh will be for Israel a *miqdāš mĕʿaṭ*, a small sanctuary, which departs the Temple and heads toward the east, toward the exiles in Babylonia. These associations contribute to the fundamental aspect of Ezekiel's theology: exile is both a means of punishment and an opportunity for divine presence.

Chapter 4 demonstrated how Ezekiel develops an argument that adapts and subverts Mesopotamian religiopolitical concepts and is based on the centrality of the departure of the divine presence and the eventual restoration of the Temple. Specifically, elements of the structure of Ezekiel suggest an association with stereotypical features in Assyro-Babylonian imperial policy. In these accounts the defeated nation is destroyed, persons and deities (divine statues) are exiled, and following appeasement of the conqueror the exiled gods are reconstructed (cleaned and repaired) and restored to their homeland. Ezekiel adapted these common themes both as a backdrop for his message of return and as further instruction on the futility of idolatry. The imagery of re-creation in Ezekiel 36–37 parodies Assyrian and Babylonian treatment of conquered peoples and their gods, and the prophet adapted this pattern and enlisted Israelite creation traditions in order to turn the Mesopotamian ideology on its head. Instead of an earthly conqueror restoring and returning exiled deities, the deity restores and returns his own people.

Using this imagery of creation and idolatry, Ezekiel formulates two elaborate arguments for the exiles. The first combines an attack on idolatry with a message of exhortation. Ezekiel describes Yahweh cleansing Israel from idolatry prior to its restoration, and he uses terminology that substitutes people for idols. Thus the rehabilitation of Israel both reveals the vanity of idols and reinforces the message that is basic to Ezekiel's theology, namely, that humans are the images of God, not the idols that humans create. Second, by substituting Yahweh as the actor in the pattern of exile, restoration, and return, Ezekiel affirms that Yahweh is sole king and creator, who controls even the affairs of nations.

It is particularly in chaps. 36–37 that Ezekiel integrates his polemic against idolatry with imagery of the restoration of God's people and furthers his argument that Yahweh is effectively present in exile, indeed, the only divine presence. So understood, then, Ezekiel 36–37 can be placed within the structural context of the overall movement of the book of Ezekiel, within the temporal and geographical context of exile in Babylonia, and within the intellectual context of the literary-religious concepts known to Ezekiel and his audience.

While the material analyzed here is only a fraction of the entire book, these conclusions indicate a focused and effective text, one that applies traditions from both Israel and Mesopotamia to sustain an argument that runs through (indeed, relies on) all the sections of the book. This recalls Ellen Davis's evaluation that "the elegant architecture of the book grows more impressive with further study."[1]

These conclusions point to a prophetic voice in conversation with many sources and capable of subtle adaption of their meanings. One wonders to what extent the complexity of the message was understood beyond a more elite circle. The text leaves us hints, however, that Ezekiel was highly regarded by certain elders of the community who came to him apparently seeking instruction (8:1; 14:1; 20:1). If this were Ezekiel's primary audience, then it is likely that they also had the background and experience to comprehend the prophecy and convey it to the larger community. What we find, then, is that the prophet's message meets the prosecutorial criteria of opportunity, motive, and means.

---

1. Ellen Davis, "Swallowing Hard: Reflections on Ezekiel's Dumbness," in *Signs and Wonders: Biblical Texts in Literary Focus* (ed. J. C. Exum; Semeia Studies; Atlanta: Scholars Press, 1989) 235.

§2. Impact of the Exile on the Theology of Ezekiel

The book of Ezekiel is deeply rooted in the context of the exile and the concerns of the Babylonian *golah*. The exile concretely raised the problem of God's absence and the question of God's presence. The struggle in Ezekiel over the modes of God's presence is a theological problem precipitated by the exile—a problem that underlies, as we have seen, three fundamental issues: theodicy (Why is Israel in exile?), theophany (Where is God in exile?), and theonomy (What power does God have in exile?). The exile forced Ezekiel to explain defeat, destruction, and deportation and to curb the loss of national-cultic identity. The opposition of divine absence and presence provided Ezekiel the means to resolve the theological crisis. The book of Ezekiel is a theological document that enabled its audience to withstand the fall of Jerusalem, the razing of the Temple, and exile in Babylonia—with all of the religious and political consequences that these events implied. The prophet accomplished this by developing an affirmation of Yahweh's presence that would not fail in the face of foreign idols, loss of sanctuary, or invading victorious nations. Yahweh, though apparently absent, was profoundly present, above and beyond the reach of human military might.

The prophet develops complex proofs of the presence and power of God in his absence. The book as a whole reflects variations on this theme. The paradox of divine presence and absence weaves its way as a constructive theology that generates interrelated examples of this binary opposition. The book of Ezekiel provides complicated patterns for solutions to the exilic experience in terms of this paradox. Ezekiel, the prophet carried between earth and heaven (8:3), offers a reflection on the dilemma of opposition and a sustained preoccupation with opposition as a structuring and tropic device. Binary opposition in Ezekiel involves first the dichotomy between human and divine and, second, the problem of divine presence and absence.[2]

---

2. While it is outside the scope of this study, a structuralist reading of Ezekiel, along with structuralism's influence on social anthropology and the study of ritual, presents especially useful categories to describe and analyze the book of Ezekiel. In his reading of myth, for example, Claude Lévi-Strauss undertakes to view myths as systems of binary opposites that reflect the mind's tendency to understand the world through dialectical oppositions. To quote Lévi-Strauss, "The purpose of myth is to provide a logical model capable of overcoming a contradiction" ("The Structural Study of Myth," in *Myth: A Symposium* [ed. T. A. Sebeok; Philadelphia: American Folklore Society, 1955] 229). Fundamentally, myths explain problems in reality, life, and society—especially universal problems, such as life versus death, order versus chaos, inside versus outside, divine versus human. Furthermore, myths expose these tensions, and if they cannot resolve them, express how members of a culture can live with such opposing forces, if only by blurring them. Hence, Lévi-Strauss identifies the important role played by mediators—persons, objects, or phenomena in which there

Consider now Ezekiel's use of this paradox in the context of his association with the priestly lineage. Richard Nelson has provided a fresh and perceptive study of the role of priests in ancient Israel, drawing especially on concepts developed in social anthropology.[3] According to his view, the priest mediates opposing forces: the categories of clean and unclean, holy and profane. Nelson describes priests as "boundary setters" in that they defined and separated these elemental categories and through ritual mediated their function in the community. Furthermore, priests identified, maintained, and crossed the boundaries of a culture, moving back and forth between the ordinary and human sphere, on the one hand, and the sphere of the holy and divine, on the other. Especially pertinent to the present study is Nelson's comment, "Boundaries became especially important for Israel in times of cultural peril. It was no accident, then, that the priests came into their own as Israel's theological thinkers and writers precisely during the period of Babylonian exile."[4]

The prophet's representation of God produces contrasts, tensions, and paradoxes that highlight Yahweh's supremacy and power in relation to Israel and the nations. Fundamental to Ezekiel's theology is the subtlety of the aniconic tradition. The conceptualization of Yahweh in the book defines the power and position of Israel's God in distinctively universal terms. In this contribution, the book of Ezekiel plays a central and previously unappreciated role in the development of Israelite theology, and monotheism in particular.[5] The dispersion of members of the Jewish community to regions

---

exist complementarity, androgyny, or liminality, that do not fit neatly into systems of classification, that are associated with both sides of a problem needing to be resolved. While I am not suggesting a strict structuralist reading for Ezekiel, insights from a structuralist reading of myth and concepts from social anthropology involving boundaries and liminality are particularly suitable in understanding the book of Ezekiel.

3. Richard Nelson, *Raising Up a Faithful Priest: Community and Priesthood in Biblical Theology* (Louisville: Westminster/John Knox, 1993), esp. pp. 17–38.

4. Ibid., 37.

5. It lay outside the scope of this study to analyze Ezekiel's role in shaping postexilic theology directly, though many compelling connections between concepts in Ezekiel and related issues in the literature from the Second Temple period have been cited. It is salutary here at least to highlight H. H. Rowley's comment that Ezekiel is the "father of Judaism" ("The Book of Ezekiel in Modern Study," *BJRL* 36 [1953–54] 150). It has not been emphasized enough that it is the Priestly tradition—whose modern study too often still bears the Wellhausenian characterization as "moribund"—that provides such creative and flexible theology in exile (see, e.g., p. 425 of *Prolegomena to the History of Israel* [Edinburgh: Adam & Black, 1985]; also Lou Silberman's essay, "Wellhausen and Judaism," in *Julius Wellhausen and His Prolegomena to the History of Israel* [ed. D. A. Knight; Semeia 25; Chico, Calif.: Scholars Press, 1983] 75–82). Though P perhaps most personally felt the effects of the loss of the Temple and the tools of the cultic trade, this material features the sanctuary

outside the parameters of Judah required Israel's God to become limited by neither Temple nor land. Ezekiel presented a vision of a God who could make his revelations known and his power felt beyond the previous borders—both physical and ideological. It was only if the presence of God could be perceived in exile that they could have hope. The paradox of the presence and absence of God provided categories that offered promise in the wilderness of exile.

---

tradition, which offered a vision of God as a peripatetic presence. The same can be said for Ezekiel: this most priestly of prophets can be credited with a resilience that helped bind together a community in spite of the loss of the priestly accoutrements.

Appendix

Removal, Repair, and Return
of Divine Images

Context	Removal	Repair	Return	Evidence
Agum-kakrime (ca. 1590)	The Haneans had previously taken the statues of Marduk and Sarpanitum as spoil.	Craftsmen repair and redecorate the statues.	The statues are led back to the Esagila.	Agum II inscription i 44–ii 17 (P. Jensen, "Inschrift Agum-Kakrimís," in *Keilinschriftliche Bibliothek* 3/1 [ed. E. Schrader; Berlin: Reuther, 1892] 138–41).
Tukulti-Ninurta I (1243–1207): Against Babylon.	"He took out the property of Esagil and Babylon amid the booty. He removed the great lord Marduk . . . and sent (him) to Assyria."			Chronicle P iv 5–6 (*ABC* 22, p. 176)

For further references on the general motif of divine abandonment, see Bertil Albrektson, *History and the Gods* (Lund: Gleerup, 1967) 16–41, 98–114; M. Cogan, *Imperialism and Religion: Assyria, Judah, and Israel in the Eighth and Seventh Centuries B.C.E.* (Missoula, Mont.: Scholars Press, 1974) 9–21; and Daniel Bodi, *The Book of Ezekiel and the Poem of Erra* (OBO 104; Freiburg: Universitätsverlag / Göttingen: Vandenhoeck & Ruprecht, 1991) 183–218. For additional examples of the spoliation of divine images, see Cogan, *Imperialism*, 119–21, table 1; and Steven W. Holloway, *The Case for Assyrian Religious Influence in Israel and Judah* (Ph.D. diss., The University of Chicago, 1992) 547–57, table 7.

Context	Removal	Repair	Return	Evidence
Ninurta-tukulti-Ashur (ca. 1130): Against Babylon.	Narrates Bel's (Marduk's) stay in Assyria.		Bel (Marduk) returned to Babylon.	Chronicle P iv 12–13 (*ABC* 22, p. 176). Also R. Borger, "Gott Marduk und Gott-König Šulgi als Propheten: Zwei prophetische Texte," *BiOr* 28 (1971), esp. pp. 5–13, 16–17, 21.
Nebuchad-nezzar I (1125–1104): Against Elam.	(Removed to Elam during fall of the Kassite dynasty during the reign of Kudur-Naḫḫunte, ca. 1160).		Marduk returned to Babylon.	"Marduk the Wanderer" (Borger, "Gott Marduk," 5–13, 16–17).
Tiglath-pileser I (1114–1076): Against the land of Katmuḫu.	Carries off their gods.			Ashur Cylinder ii 31–32 (RIMA 2 15).
Against the lands of Sarauš and Ammauš.	Takes their gods.			Ashur Cylinder iii 81 (RIMA 2 19).
Against enemies in the Lower Zab.	"I brought out their gods."			Ashur Cylinder iii 102–iv 3 (RIMA 2 19).
Against the land of Sugu, in Mt. Ḫiriḫu.	"I brought out 25 of their gods." These gods, called booty, are then donated to his patron gods in Ashur.			Ashur Cylinder iv 23–39 (RIMA 2 20).

Context	Removal	Repair	Return	Evidence
Against the city of Ḫunusu in the Land of Muṣri.	Gods taken.			Ashur Cylinder vi 8–9 (RIMA 2 24).
Against the land of Lullumu.	"I gave 25 of their gods [to the . . .], gods of my city Aššur and the goddesses of my land."			Nineveh inscriptions line 23 (RIMA 2 34).
Against the land of Suḫu.	"I . . . carried off their numerous gods and their property, (and) brought (them) to my city Aššur."			Ashur inscription line 43 (RIMA 2 43).
Adad-nirari II (911–891): Against the land of Qumanu.	"I gave their gods as gifts to Aššur my lord."			Ashur inscription obv. lines 10–17 (RIMA 2 143–44).
Uncertain context.	Gods carried off to Assyria.			Ashur inscription rev. lines 4–5 (RIMA 2 144).
Against the land of Ḫanigalbat.	Carries off gods.			Ashur inscription lines 69–72 (RIMA 2 151).
Tukulti-Ninurta II (890–884): Against the lands of Nairi.	Carries off gods to Nineveh.			Ashur inscription obv. lines 7–8 (RIMA 2 171).
Ashur-nasir-apli II (883–859): Against the city of Suru, which belongs to Bit-Ḫalupe.	Carries off their gods and their property.			From Ninurta Temple at Kalah i 85–86 (RIMA 2 199).
Tiglath-pileser III (744–727): Accession year; against Shapazza.	Captures gods.			Babylonian Chronicle 1 i 5 (*ABC* 1, p. 71).

Context	Removal	Repair	Return	Evidence
Sargon II (721–705): Against Israel.	Gods of Israel deported.			C. J. Gadd, "Inscribed Prisms of Sargon II from Nimrud," *Iraq* 16 (1954) 179 (iv 32).
Against Media.			Returned gods to Harhar.	L. D. Levine, *Two Neo-Assyrian Stelae from Iran* (Occasional Papers 23; Toronto: Royal Ontario Museum, 1972) 40 (ii 44).
Against Merodach-Baladan II.	Sargon reports that Merodach-Baladan gathered the local gods (i.e., against their will) into Dur-Yakin.			*ARAB* 2 34, §66. See below.
Against Merodach-Baladan II.			Sargon destroys Dur-Yakin and returns the gods, "captured" by Merodach-Baladan, to their shrines, including Ur, Uruk, Eridu, Larsa, Kullab, Kisik.	*ARAB* 2 35 §69. Compare the similar exchange of claims between Nabonidus and Cyrus. See also Babylonian Chronicle.
Against Merodach-Baladan II.	Gods pillaged from Dur-Yakin.		Gods returned to Dur-Yakin.	Gadd, "Inscribed Prisms," 186 (vi 61–62).
15th year of Merodach-Baladan II.			Gods of the Sealand returned to their shrines.	Babylonian Chronicle 1 ii 4'–5' (*ABC* 1, p. 76).
Sennacherib (704–681): 6th year; against Uruk.	Assyrian army captures gods of Uruk.			Babylonian Chronicle 1 iii 1 (*ABC* 1, p. 79).

Context	Removal	Repair	Return	Evidence
6th year; against Uruk.	Elamites capture gods of Uruk.			Babylonian Chronicle 1 iii 1–3 (*ABC* 1, p. 79). See their return below in 1 iii 29.
8th year.			Gods of Uruk returned from Elam to Uruk.	Babylonian Chronicle 1 iii 29 (*ABC* 1, p. 1). See their removal in 1 iii 2–3.
2d campaign; against Babylon.	The gods dwelling in Babylon are smashed.			Bavian inscription line 49 (OIP 2, p. 83; *ARAB*, 2.152, §340). See also Bīt-Akīti Inscription lines 36–37 (OIP 2, p. 137; *ARAB*, 2.185, §438).
Against Babylon.	Marduk and the gods of Babylon are angered and fly off.	(See below under Esarhaddon and Ashurbanipal.)	(See below under Esarhaddon and Ashurbanipal.)	*Bab* recs. B and G, ep. 3 (R. Borger, *Inschriften Asarhaddons* [AfO Beiheft 9; Graz: Weidner, 1956] 12; *ARAB*, 2.245, §649). Also *Bab* rec. E (Borger, *Inschriften*, 14; *ARAB*, 2.255, §662). See return under Esarhaddon.
Against Arabs.	Carries off gods of the king of Arabia and brings them to Assyria.	(See below under Esarhaddon and Ashurbanipal.)	(See below under Esarhaddon and Ashurbanipal.)	*Nin* rec. A, ep. 14 (Borger, *Inschriften*, 53, §27; *ARAB*, 2.214, §536; Prism A [also Prism S on p. 207, §518a]). Also K3405 lines 1–8 (*ARAB*, 2.365–66, §943).

Context	Removal	Repair	Return	Evidence
Esarhaddon (680–669): 1st year.	(Gods of Dêr carried off by Sennacherib.)	(See below.)	Sataran (Ištaran) and other gods returned to Dêr. Also mentioned is Dur-Sharukkin (Khorsabad) as destination.	Babylonian Chronicle 1 iii 44–46 (*ABC* 1, p. 82). See also *AsBb* rec. A, lines 40–44 (Borger, *Inschriften*, 84; *ARAB*, 2.262, §674).
1st year (see above).			Anu-rabu and the gods of Dêr returned to Dêr. Also mention of Humhumya and Shimalya.	Esarhaddon Chronicle, lines 3–4 (*ABC* 14, p. 125; *ANET*, 303).
1st year (see above).		Detailed account of the repair and renovation in Ashur of gods taken from Esagila (see esp. rev. lines 35–40, Borger, *Inschriften*, 83–84; *ARAB*, 2.261–62, §§673–74) and other cities (Nineveh, Dêr, Uruk, Larsa, Sippar-Aruru), "all that Aššur and Marduk commanded" (see rev. lines 41–44, Borger, *Inschriften*, 84; *ARAB*, 2.262, §674).	Reports the return of these statues to their restored sanctuaries.	*AsBb* rec. A (see Borger, *Inschriften*, 78–95, §53; *ARAB*, 2.256–63, §§667–77). Also on the creation process of the gods in Ashur, concluding with a reference to *mīs pî / pīt pî* ceremony, see rec. E (Borger, esp. pp. 88–89, §57; *ARAB*, 2.275–76, §712).
Regarding Babylon and Dêr; and other unnamed places.	Reference to the gods who had previously fled to Assyria (presumably referring to Sennacherib's reign).		Marduk returned to Babylon, Anu returned to Dêr; mention of general return of deities who had fled to Assyria.	*Uruk* rec. A (Borger, *Inschriften*, 74, §47; *ARAB*, 2.280, §731).

Context	Removal	Repair	Return	Evidence
General amnesty.			Return of plundered gods from Ashur and Elam to their places.	*Bab* rec. C, ep. 36 (Borger, *Inschriften*, 25, §11).
Regarding Uruk.		Letter mentioning the repairs in progress on the statue Nanâ, as well as the soon-to-be-completed work on Uṣur-amātsa.		*LAS* 277 (p. 223); also on Nanâ, see above; and on Uṣur-amātsa, see above *AsBb* rec. A, line 43.
Regarding Nanâ.			Returns her to her restored chapel Eḫilianna.	*Uruk* rec. B (Borger, *Inschriften*, 76, §48; but see claims by Ashurbanipal; this matter is discussed in *LAS*, part 2, p. 266; also Cogan, *Imperialism*, 14 n. 34).
10th year; against Egypt.	Captures gods.			Babylonian Chronicle 1 iv 25 (var.) (*ABC* 1, p. 85; see also Borger, 121–25; *ANET*, 301–3).
Regarding Babylon and Esagila.		Defaced and disfigured images of gods and goddesses renovated and repaired.	Statues of gods and goddesses returned to Esagila.	*Bab* rec. A, esp. ep. 32 (Borger, *Inschriften*, 23; also *ARAB*, 2.247, §653). Also *Bab* rec. D (ṣa-lam ilâni^meš), ep. 32; "Black Stone" in *ARAB*, 2.244, §646. Other recensions in Borger C (*ARAB*, 2.252–53, §§659D–E).
Regarding Esagila and Babylon.		Restores gods and their temples.	Returns gods to their places.	*Nin* rec. A, ep. 3 (Borger, *Inschriften*, 45, §27; *ARAB*, 2.203, §507).

Context	Removal	Repair	Return	Evidence
Against Sandu-arri, king of Kundi and Sizzû.	Gods desert Sandu-arri and flee to the mountains.			*Nin* rec. A, ep. 6 (Borger, *Inschriften*, 49, §27; Prism S in *ARAB*, 2.206, §513).
Regarding Hazael, king of the Arabs.	(Gods captured by Sennacherib.)	Esarhaddon repairs gods.	Returns gods.	*Nin* rec. A, ep. 14, lines 6–16 (Borger, *Inschriften*, 53, §27; Prism A in *ARAB*, 2.214, §536 [also in Prism S in *ARAB*, 2.207, §518a]). See also *ARAB*, 2.364–65, §§940–41 (K3087); and *ARAB*, 2.365–66, §943 (K3405), see Cogan, *Imperialism*, 16–19 for transliteration and translation.
Against Uaite', son of Hazael, king of the Arabs.	Carries off his gods.			VAT 5600 (*ARAB*, 2.367, §946).
Against the land of Bâzu; Lailê, king of the city of Iadi' in land of Bâzu.	Carries off their gods.		Returns their gods after Lailê appealed to Esarhaddon.	*Nin* rec. A, ep. 17 (Borger, *Inschriften*, 56, §27; Prisms B and A in *ARAB*, 2.209, §520, and p. 214, §537, respectively).
Regarding Elam.			Ishtar of Akkad and other gods of Akkad returned to Akkad from Elam.	Babylonian Chronicle 1 iv 17–18 (*ABC* 1, p. 84) and Esarhaddon Chronicle lines 21–22 (*ABC* 14, p. 126).

Context	Removal	Repair	Return	Evidence
Against Tirhakah, king of Kush.	Takes gods and goddesses as booty.			*Mnm* C (Borger, *Inschriften*, 101, §67; Dog River Stele in *ARAB*, 2.228, §584).
Ashurbanipal (668–627): Accession of Shamash-shuma-ukin.	(Captured by Sennacherib.)		"Bel and the gods of Akkad went out from Libbi-ali (Ashur) and . . . entered Babylon." For further, see immediately below.	Babylonian Chronicle 1 iv 34–36 (*ABC* 1, p. 86). Ashurbanipal's claim that he completed the unfinished work on Esagila and returned Marduk to Babylon are mentioned often (*ARAB*, 2.§§883, 954, 956–57, 962, 971, 975, 979, 988–89, 1016).
Accession of Shamash-shuma-ukin.	Narration of the stay of Bel (Marduk) in Baltil (Ashur): 8 years during the reign of Sennacherib, 12 years during Esarhaddon.		Return of Bel (Marduk) from Baltil (Ashur); resumption of the *akitu* festival.	Esarhaddon Chronicle lines 31–37 (*ABC* 14, p. 127). The same series of events, including the resumption of the *akitu* festival is in Akitu Chronicle lines 1–8 (*ABC* 16, p. 131); see also *ABC* 16 lines 18–19, 20–21, 23, 27, as well as the Religious Chronicle iii 4–10 (*ABC* 17, p. 137, reign of Nabu-mukin-apli, 977–942) for the suspension of the *akitu* festival.

Context	Removal	Repair	Return	Evidence
7th campaign; against Elam.	Carries off gods from a lengthy list of cities in Elam.			*Rassam Cylinder* V 59–62 (M. Streck, *Assurbanipal und die letzten assyrischen Könige* [VB 7; Leipzig: Hinrichs, 1916] 2.46–47; *ARAB*, 2.307, §804).
8th campaign; against Elam in area of Bashimu.	Reports various treatments of statues of gods: smashed gods, carried off gods and goddesses to Assyria; scattered gods.			*Rassam Cylinder* V 118–22 (Streck, *Assurbanipal,* 50–51; *ARAB*, 2.308, §808; see also *ARAB*, 2.355, §920).
8th campaign; against Susa.	Shushinak and other Elamite gods and goddesses, "together with their paraphernalia, their property, their vessels, as well as their priests . . . I carried off to Assyria."			*Rassam Cylinder* VI 1–76 (Streck, *Assurbanipal,* 50–57; *ARAB*, 2.309–10, §810; see also *ARAB*, 2.358, §926).
8th campaign; against Elam, regarding Nanâ.			After 1,635 years of self-exile, she is returned from Elam.	*Rassam Cylinder* VI 107–24 (Streck, *Assurbanipal,* 58–59; *ARAB*, 2.311, §§812–13; see also *ARAB*, 2.365, §941 [K3101a + K2664 + 262 8]; note K1364 [*ARAB*, 2.355, §919], where a letter to Ummanaldash, king of Elam, requesting the return of Nanâ is unheeded).

Context	Removal	Repair	Return	Evidence
9th campaign; against Arabs.	Gods taken to Damascus.			*Rassam Cylinder* VIII 120–IX 8 (Streck, *Assurbanipal,* 72–73; *ARAB,* 2.317, §824).
9th campaign; return.	Gods of Ushu, on the shore of the sea, near Acco, carried off to Assyria.			*Rassam Cylinder* IX 115–21 (Streck, *Assurbanipal,* 80–81; *ARAB,* 2.319, §830).
Regarding the Arabs.	(Reference back to the policies of Sennacherib and Esarhaddon in removing gods.)		Apparently shows favor on behalf of these gods.	K3405 (*ARAB,* 2.365–66, §943; see Cogan, *Imperialism,* 17–19).
Regarding Babylon.	Because of the evil deeds of his rebel brother, Shamash-shum-ukin, gods grew angry and left for other lands.			K4457 (*ARAB,* 2.403, §1104).
Nabopolassar (625–605): Against Kish.	Captured gods taken to Babylon.			Babylonian Chronicle 2 6 (*ABC* 2, p. 88).
Accession year.			"Returned to Susa the gods of Susa whom the Assyrians had carried off and settled in Uruk."	Babylonian Chronicle 2 19 (*ABC* 2, p. 88).
1st year; hostilities between Assyria and Babylon.	Shamash and the gods of Shapazzu brought into Babylon for safekeeping.			Babylonian Chronicle 2 19 (*ABC* 2, p. 89).
1st year; hostilities between Assyria and Babylon.	The gods of Sippar brought into Babylon for safekeeping.			Babylonian Chronicle 2 21 (*ABC* 2, p. 89).

Context	Removal	Repair	Return	Evidence
10th year; Babylonian campaign against Assyria.	Captured gods of Mane, Sahiri, and Balihu.			Babylonian Chronicle 3 8 (*ABC* 3, p. 91).
10th year; same campaign.	Captured gods of Hindanu.			Babylonian Chronicle 3 9 (*ABC* 3, p. 91).
14th year; against Nineveh.	"Carried off booty from the city and the temple."			Babylonian Chronicle 3 45 (*ABC* 3, p. 94).
16th year; against Harran.	"Carried off vast booty from the city and the temple."			Babylonian Chronicle 3 45 (*ABC* 3, p. 94). See also the "Harran Inscription of Nabonidus" (Adad-Guppi), which describes the abandonment of Harran by the gods (*ANET*, 560–62).
Nabonidus (555–539): Regarding Harran.	(See above under Nabopolassar for the abandonment of the city.)		The gods return to the rebuilt temple Ehulhul.	Harran Inscription of Nabonidus (Adad-Guppi) (*ANET*, 560–62). See also "Nabonidus and His God" (*ANET*, 562–63).
Defense of Babylon.	Gods of Marad, Zababa, Kish enter Babylon for safe-keeping.			Nabonidus Chronicle iii 9–11 (*ABC* 7, p. 109).
Defense of Babylon.	Deposits a restored statue of Sin in Esagila for safe-keeping.	Restores the image of Sin, which had been damaged during the destruction of an enemy and which had been originally restored by Ashurbanipal.		Nabonidus Inscription (*ANET*, 308–11).

Context	Removal	Repair	Return	Evidence
Cyrus II (559/538–530): Cyrus's entry into Babylon.			Returns gods that Nabonidus brought into Babylon.	Nabonidus Chronicle iii 21–22 (*ABC* 7, p. 110; *ANET,* 306).
Commemoration of Cyrus's "liberation" of Babylon.	Narrates that Nabonidus had brought the gods of Sumer and Akkad into Babylon.		Restores sanctuaries and returns images to sacred cities: regions as far as Ashur and Susa, Agade, Eshnunna; towns of Zamban, Me-Turnu, Dêr; and region of the Gutians.	Cyrus Cylinder lines 30–32 (*ANET,* 316).

Index of Authors

Index of Scripture

Hebrew Bible / Old Testament

New Testament

Index of Deuterocanonical, Pseudepigraphical, and Early Jewish and Christian Literature